WOMEN AND LEADERSHIP

The Baptist Convention of South Africa

REVISED EDITION

AF077489

WOMEN AND LEADERSHIP

The Baptist Convention of South Africa

REVISED EDITION

Nelson Hayashida

Available at missionbooks.org

Women and Leadership in the Baptist Convention in South Africa
Copyright © 2005 by Nelson Hayashida

All rights reserved. No part of this publication may be reproduced, stored in a retrieval system, or transmitted in any form or by any means—electronic, mechanical, photocopying, recording, or other—without the prior written permission of the publisher.

Cover design by Mike Riester
Front cover photo by Oladimeji Odunsi, unsplash.com.

Published by William Carey Publishing
10 W Dry Creek Cir
Littleton, CO 80120
www.missionbooks.org

William Carey Publishing is a Ministry of Frontier Ventures, Pasadena, California   www.frontierventures.org
ISBN: 978-1-64508-307-8

23 22 21 20   Printed for Worldwide Distribution

CONTENTS

FOREWORD	vii
PREFACE	xi
INTRODUCTION: Purpose, Relevance and Method	1
Purpose	1
Relevance	2
Method	5
Notes on Introduction	16
CHAPTER ONE: The Views of Feminist, African-American Womanist and African Womanist Theologians in the African and Non-African Milieu	21
Introduction	21
Feminist Theology – A Definition	23
Feminist Theology – A Description	36
The Challenges to the Social and Ecclesiastical Emancipation of Women	53
Notes on Chapter One	65
CHAPTER TWO: Views and Experiences of Women and Men in the Baptist Union of South Africa	71
Introductory Remarks	73
Technique	74
Methodology	75
Sampling	76
Questionnaires, Interviews and the Respondents	77
A Descriptive Analysis	81
Concluding Remarks	114
Notes on Chapter Two	118

CHAPTER THREE: Views and Experiences of Women and Men in the Baptist Convention of South Africa	125
Introductory Remarks	127
Technique	127
Methodology	129
Sampling	130
Questionnaires, Interviews and the Respondents	131
A Descriptive Analysis	140
Concluding Remarks	187
Notes on Chapter Three	192
CHAPTER FOUR: Summation, Comparison, Evaluation and Liberating Praxis	201
Review of Previous Chapters	202
The Aims of this Chapter	204
Conclusion	243
Notes on Chapter Four	248
WORKS CONSULTED	253
ABOUT THE AUTHOR	289

FOREWORD

The content of this book can best be understood by the prevailing context at the time of writing. My wife and I met Nelson and Sandra while they were serving as missionaries to South Africa in the early 1990s. I was the General Secretary of the Baptist Convention of South Africa, their receiving agency at that time. The Hayashidas were appointed as theological educators to the Baptist Convention College in Soweto. This theological seminary was established to educate future South African Baptist church leaders to face the challenges and maximize the opportunities of the dynamic and growing African church. When they concluded their term, they were endeared and loved for their respectful approach and liberating values.

While the Hayashidas served in South Africa the country was undergoing tumultuous and seismic changes of monumental proportions. The country had just successfully begun the long transformation process from an Apartheid to a Democratic order. Nelson Mandela was elected the first democratic president and the entire social order was undergoing fundamental changes. The extent of the changes was tempered by the reality of limited financial and human resources. The society was coming to terms with the challenge of dealing with the debilitating and demonic actions perpetrated by the Apartheid State and its pervasive organs.

The church could not escape the effects of these changes. Two key questions relating to this book were discussed amongst the many issues debated. The first was understanding and redefining the missionary relationship with agencies that had resources. The second was the definition of the extent of what it meant to be liberated. More specifically, what did liberation mean for women who formed the overwhelming majority of this denomination?

The Baptist Convention of South Africa was a "mission church." This branch of indigenous Black African churches was started as a distinct and separate yet dependent entity, under girded by a very paternal relationship in 1927. In 1987, after failing to create structure that would represent a relationship of equality, the Baptist Convention declared its independence from its white self-appointed "custodians" to pursue a journey of discovery and development. This was a courageous decision based on faith in God. This church had little financial resources at that time.

The Convention's critique of this paternalistic missionary model was devastating. At one stage there was a debate within the Convention whether to use the term "missionary" because it was deemed irredeemable. This relationship was characterized by painful, oppressive and dehumanizing experiences, often motivated by political ideals of subservience. Notwithstanding this, much good work was done and many precious personal relationships were formed between missionaries and receiving partners. The Hayashidas represented such a positive experience.

The fact that African women cooperated to have a male American missionary document their stories speaks volumes of the capacity for grace, tolerance and forgiveness on their part. It also speaks to the regard that they had for the Hayashidas. While this book is invaluable in contributing to a burning issue within the Af-

FOREWORD

rican church, it can never become the substitute for African women writing and reflecting their own story, using their own idioms. Nelson Hayashida demonstrated how skilled people can facilitate the liberation process for others.

The pressing issue that faced the Convention in 1987 was institutional and individual racism. In 1990, at a conference called to examine the effects of this horrible nightmare, a new vision for holistic proclamation of good news emerged. One of the key elements of this vision was the emancipation of women to exercise their giftedness and calling at the highest level. These sentiments were later developed to reinforce this ideal. I was justifiably proud in 1999 when women were amongst the first students who graduated from the Baptist Convention College.

This book exposes the gap between carefully crafted statements affirming women and the reality of reluctant submission to women in leadership. We hear the voices of women themselves. This book is academically sound and characterized by excellence based on sound methodology. I therefore believe that the questions raised, the voices heard, and the potential corrective measures, are a vital contribution to an important conversation within the church community. While this book is mainly focused on the Baptist church in South Africa, it presents many possibilities for stimulating debates and policy and experiential changes in other faith communities.

I receive this book first as an African. The African church is the fastest growing sector of the Christian church. There are exciting examples of churches that are rediscovering what it means to be an African Christian. This exercise does not mean the uncritical

WOMEN AND LEADERSHIP

baptism of everything African with the Christian message. The gospel has a critical component to all cultures. Sexism manifested in silencing and subjugating the voices of women cannot be tolerated no matter the sources of justification. Physical, sexual and emotional abuse that undermines the intrinsic value of women should not be tolerated in the African church.

I receive this book as a man. I was raised in a society that reinforced the superiority of men systemically. I am therefore a "recovering sexist." This does not mean that I should inflict such guilt that I deny my manhood. On the contrary, it means that I should redefine my manhood in the light of the advantages that I had in society. It also means that I need to listen and work to design policies that would relate to liberating practices.

I am presently directing the Global Prophetic Network. The aim of the center is to intentionally mentor the next generation of prophetic leaders. The challenge is to shine a light on the many prophets who are addressing those issues that cause us to critically examine the inconsistencies. One of the major prophetic issues facing the global church is the inclusivity of all God's children without regard to race, age, nationality, ability, sexual orientation or gender.

Desmond Hoffmeister
Executive Director
Global Prophetic Network
American Baptist Seminary of the West
Berkeley, California, USA

PREFACE

The book describes the emergence of the Baptist Convention of South Africa (BCSA) as a distinct denomination since 1987 and its developing sense of self-identity. The aims of this study are to establish the *nature and extent* to which South African Baptists have suppressed the abilities and roles of women in church leadership; secondly, to uncover through the stories and experiences of women and men in the Baptist Union of South Africa (BUSA) and in the Baptist Convention of South Africa (BCSA) the attitudes and practices of local Baptist churches toward women in leadership; thirdly, to propose the *value* of women in leadership by describing the significance of the full embrace of women in church leadership for the BCSA; fourthly, to seek to propose a strategy for the BCSA to bring to reality women's liberation and church transformation.

Concern for the social, historical and theological contexts of South African Baptist experience and thought shape my methodological starting points. Research in books, journals, Baptist magazines, newspapers, handbooks, reports, commemorative documents, other Baptist publications and unpublished doctoral theses form the basis for social, historical and theological information pertinent to this work. The range of literature being studied requires analysis and interpretation.

In addition to the literary, socio-historical methodology and theological analysis described above, oral and written narratives form a substantial part of this study. These testimonies or stories are presented through questionnaires and oral interviews. Both the quantitative and qualitative approaches to social research are used. While large sample size and statistical significance can in some measure be gained from the quantitative approach, the qualitative approach provides an in-depth research method, seeking to get underneath raw data, to find reasons and meanings, hopes and feelings, perceptions and aspirations of individuals and groups.

The methodology of women's research being proposed should lead to action plans, praxis and change. The narrative, in the intimate sharing of women's stories, proves to be the essential foundation in discovering pragmatic approaches to emancipate women and the church (women and men), in South Africa as well as the ecclesia diaspora, for wholeness, healing and service.

I must acknowledge my debt to two colleagues who both inspired me and provided keen observations and evaluations along the way. Willem Saayman and Christina Landman, both professors at the University of South Africa, Pretoria, South Africa, offered careful, incisive and constructive comments. Their broad awareness of women's issues in the culturally diverse churches of South Africa proved to be invaluable.

Likewise, I am indebted to UNISA (University of South Africa) for providing the framework for my research.

PREFACE

I want to acknowledge Dr. Moriyoshi Hiratani and the First Baptist Church of Pearl City, Hawaii, for their loving support over the years of my ministry. The depth of their belief in me and acceptance of my endeavors, notwithstanding huge geographical and time separations, are testimonies to the faithfulness of God.

Most affectionate acknowledgement goes to Sandra, my wife, who became my able assistant, on yet another occasion, and enduring conversant thinker at all points down the lengthy road.

INTRODUCTION

PURPOSE, RELEVANCE AND METHOD

PURPOSE

Greg Cuthbertson, in a paper under the subheading "Women without history; history without women: history with a mission," claims that history in South Africa remains predominantly androcentric. This is inclusive, he claims, of ecclesiastical history. Books on South African mission Christianity and church history omit 'gender' and 'women' from their indexes but list page references for 'sorcerers' and 'witches.' Scant space and attention is given to gender and women issues and their historical, social and religious significance. This historiographical condition has led feminist theologians and historians to become actively engaged in regular critique and dialogue with established scholarship, which ignores women and female oppression (Cuthbertson 1997:11-12).

What Cuthbertson describes as the state of affairs for South African historiography in general is true in the particular case of South African Baptist historical books, handbooks, and other reports and publications of the South African Baptist Historical Society. That is, as obvious as is the androcentric orientation of the Baptist mindset, equally obvious then is the lack of prominence of Baptist women in the trail of Baptist history in South Africa.[1]

WOMEN AND LEADERSHIP

This study is concerned with the emergence of the Baptist Convention of South Africa (BCSA) as a distinct denomination since 1987 and its developing sense of self-identity[2], with particular focus on the role of women in church leadership as a distinguishing mark of self-identity. The aims of this study are to establish the *nature and extent* to which South African Baptists have suppressed the abilities and roles of women in church leadership; secondly, to uncover through the stories and experiences of women[3] and men in the Baptist Union of South Africa (BUSA) and in the Baptist Convention of South Africa (BCSA) the attitudes and practices of local Baptist churches toward women in leadership; thirdly, to propose the *value* of women in leadership by describing the significance of the full embrace of women in church leadership for the BCSA; fourthly, this study will seek to propose a strategy for the BCSA to bring to reality women's liberation and church transformation.

RELEVANCE

James Ian Harris, in his 1996 doctoral study submitted to the University of Cape Town entitled Baptist Identity in Ecumenical Perspective: A Critical Exposition of the 1987 Statement on Baptist Principles of the Baptist Union of South Africa, claims that in spite of the Baptist Union of South Africa's (BUSA) 19th century origins it has yet to articulate and establish "its particular vision of Baptist identity to date" (1996:7). The Baptist Convention of South Africa (BCSA), though birthed in 1987 as a separate denomination after long years under the white controlled BUSA, is actively engaged in discovering its sense of purpose and identity. After twelve years of existence, the BCSA is undergoing an evolutionary process, shaping its dreams and aspirations as an Afro-centric denomination.

INTRODUCTION

It was in 1994 at the BCSA Assembly in George that the idea of a Winter School of Theology was enthusiastically received. Its purpose is to theologically educate ministers and their spouses, laypersons within and without the Convention who are involved in various forms of Christian ministry, ministerial students studying at other (non-Convention) theological colleges, and ministerial students as well as prospective ministerial students within the Convention (a BCSA theological college opened in Johannesburg in late 1995, transferring to Orlando East in January 1996) "as to the present aims and mission statement of the Convention." In 1995, the first Winter School commenced, with 65 persons participating, women and men. The consensus of the participants was that the Theological Education Committee (TEC) of the BCSA should make this week-long effort an annual Winter School of Theology (Kretzschmar 1995:1).

It is my contention that while the struggles to discover the fledgling denomination's purpose and identity necessarily is hammered out in part at the grassroots among rural and urban churches, the Winter School has evolved to be a strategic center-point at which denominational leaders, experienced pastors, laypersons and ministerial candidates are learning to theologically articulate its growing sense of self-identity as a denomination.

The annual BCSA Assemblies are business oriented. The annual Winter Schools are theologically oriented. While one should not minimize the role the annual Assemblies play in conscientizing the BCSA churches to their mission and identity in the discussions and decisions made, it is in the Winter Schools that doctrinal and theological papers are presented, workshops and seminars are provided, and intellectual dialogue instigated that give rational expression to

WOMEN AND LEADERSHIP

the role and destiny of the new Convention.

The theme of the 1995 Winter School was: "How can we achieve the creation of a Holistic, Afro-centric and Participatory form of Christianity for the Baptist Convention of South Africa?" This theme was inspired by the Convention's Mission Statement adopted at the 1994 BCSA Assembly. The full statement follows:

> The Baptist Convention of South Africa is a Fellowship of member churches whose mission is to develop and proclaim a holistic, Afro-centric, and participatory understanding of the Gospel of Jesus Christ and thereby equip its constituencies to facilitate the dynamic transformation of societies. (Kretzschmar 1995:1)

This study seeks to demonstrate that within this Mission Statement lies the theological roots and justification for the upliftment of women in leadership roles in the churches of the Baptist Convention of South Africa. Additionally, it *assumes* that as this statement is debated and defined in the Winter Schools, local churches, national Assemblies, regional conferences, and at the Baptist Convention College, the acceptance of women in the Christian ministry and in leadership roles in the churches and denominational offices, in national and regional committees, is gaining in approval and contributes to the self-identity of the denomination.[4]

It is the contention of this study that Baptist Convention views on women and women in church leadership must be informed by the wider Christian community. Ecumenical dialogue and awareness broadens the scope of biblical hermeneutics on the issue of women, and this broadening gives shape and form to a view of women in ecclesiastical leadership.

INTRODUCTION

METHOD

Terminology

In this study the phrase the "South African Baptists" refers to the Baptist Union of South Africa. Formerly established as a denomination in 1877, the South African Baptists' early heritage stems from the 1820 British settlers and their followers. Over the course of time, the phrase incorporated the Indian, African and Afrikaans Baptists who were "in association" with the Baptist Union. The phrase also can mean those Baptists who separated themselves from the Union in 1986, forming in 1987 the independent Baptist Convention of South Africa. In this study, particular stress will be given to the African (Baptist Convention) and the largely white (Baptist Union) components of the South "African Baptists," ignoring the other components for reasons of space and focus.

The title of the study is "Women and Leadership in the Bap-tist Convention of South Africa."

The term "women" in the title of the study means African (black) women. The Baptist Convention is currently overwhelmingly black. African women, who have been systematically victimized by the political, economic and social institutions of South African society, have also been, to add insult to injury, victimized by the church as well. Male dominance in leadership, especially at pastoral and deaconship levels, has subjugated a powerful resource in Christ's church. These are the "women" I mean.

WOMEN AND LEADERSHIP

The term "leadership" in this study is taken to mean church leadership. In his own study, Harris seems to almost equate the term "leadership" with the term "discipleship," for he argues that church leadership from top to bottom must be undergirded by discipleship. Discipleship is defined as the self-giving of one's life in other lives in order to witness Christ being obeyed in life's total reality, physical and spiritual. Following the example of Jesus, authentic Christian leadership is courageous, sacrificial, and loving (1996:223). If this is the kernel of "leadership" (discipleship/leadership, discipled leadership, disciplined leadership) in Christ's church, then women and men are potential candidates for leadership as they are both candidates for discipleship. The argument I make then, is that neither one ought to be in any way marginalized or uprooted from their privilege and responsibility to be equal and full participants in Christ's church and the leadership thereof. Tantamount to being a follower of Christ, for women and men, is to be "disciplined and discipled leaders."[5]

Methodological Starting Points and Parameters

Concern for the social, historical and theological contexts of South African Baptist experience and thought shape my methodological starting points.[6] Research in books, journals, Baptist magazines, newspapers, handbooks, reports, commemorative documents, other Baptist publications and unpublished doctoral theses form the basis for social, historical and theological information pertinent to this study. The range of literature to be studied requires analysis and interpretation.

In addition to the literary, socio-historical methodology and theological analysis described above, oral and written narratives form

INTRODUCTION

a substantial part of this study. These testimonies or stories will be gathered by both questionnaires and oral interviews. I will therefore use both the quantitative and qualitative approaches to social research. The disadvantage of the quantitative research approach (questionnaire) is that it tends to reduce human beings to scores on socio-economic charts. To counter that, I will incorporate open-ended questions throughout the questionnaire so that comments can be made to explain or qualify objective responses to questions. The advantage to the qualitative research approach (sometimes understood as "Participatory Research Approach") is that it tends to study human beings multi-dimensionally. Thus, while large sample size and statistical significance can in some measure be gained from the quantitative approach, the qualitative approach gives us in-depth research method, seeking to get underneath raw data, to find reasons and meanings, hopes and feelings, perceptions and aspirations of individuals and groups.[7]

I will use the questionnaire, in many cases, as a springboard for depth interviews/oral histories of women[8] and men in the church. In other situations I will utilize the interview only. Both urban (township) and rural Baptist church members will be given questionnaires and some of these will be subjects for interviews.[9]

The method of "participant observation" will be used as I circulate among the Baptist churches of the BCSA in particular, with less involvement in BUSA churches. "Participant observation" is a qualitative social research technique in that it provides checks on collected data as well as providing the occasional novel data not otherwise collectable. This approach, then, allows for verifiable processes to take place.

WOMEN AND LEADERSHIP

Interpretation of the questionnaires and oral interviews is critical. In the questionnaires, each question offers an opportunity for the respondent to write a comment if an explanation or qualification is necessary. These blank spaces were used frequently. This helped me immensely in interpreting the meaning behind the "yes" or "no" response. In the oral interviews, I consistently asked questions to validate my understanding of what was said. Because the interviews were dialogical in nature, this was easy to do. It is not to say that misinterpretation did not occur. But I feel they were limited in extent by the questions I frequently posed for clarification. In Joyce M. Nielson's Feminist Research Methods (1990), a chapter is devoted to feminist methodological concerns in oral history that have implications for interpretation of women's experiences. The affirmation of womanhood appears to be a fundamental precondition for oral feminist methodology. Another fundamental insight seems to revolve around women's cognition, i.e., what women think may not necessarily match their behavior, or vice-versa. They are often captives to their psychosocial arena. This too has implications for how data is interpreted. I have sought to keep these factors in mind in my data collection and interpretation.

In Christina Landman's The Piety of South African Women (1999a), she has a section entitled "How To Tell a Sacred Story" (1-6). Here she explores how an ordinary story can be transformed into a sacred story of liberation. By using Lady Duff Gordon's story of a slave woman named "Rosina," Landman demonstrates how method itself can become a story, i.e., take on the form of a sacred story. It becomes sacred when, in retelling Rosina's story, the theme of freedom from oppression becomes the key point of her life. It is a move away from Lady Gordon's interpretation of Rosina's story to hearing Rosina's voice by reconstructing for Rosina her story with the knowledge we have of the social plight of slave women and their dreams of

INTRODUCTION

a better existence in the Cape Colony. In this case, when a white woman of privilege tells the story for another woman of underprivilege, the methodological approach is to retell the story in a more compassionate, subjective, and meaningful way.[10] We do not let Lady Gordon's interpretation "speak" for Rosina. The muted voice of Rosina needs to be heard through compassionate reconstruction. In the context of oral interviews with South African Baptist women of BUSA and BCSA, we will *allow* these women to "speak for themselves" as they should. No one is speaking for them. I have sought to give *evaluation* to the data, however. That is, I have taken what was said or communicated and placed it in its particular cultural, socio-economic, and ecclesiastical context. Sometimes women spoke, not with their heart, but with the baggage of the church's indoctrination, preconceptions and expectations. They told their stories, sometimes with the heavy burden and backdrop of oppressive "church law" and "social law" that confines them to stereotype and subservience. Church and social laws have fostered confusion and anxiety in women. It is here that interpretation of the data must move beyond itself to evaluation of the data. By taking women's stories and spirituality seriously, their desire to be near to God and serve him, their stories become sacred stories. This I have sought to do in this study.[11] Landman I think is correct: God's true voice must be retrieved from women's sacred stories. The historical church did not represent God's voice and God's will in terms of women's oppression.

The outcome of the research will be used to construct a strategy for a way forward for women in the BCSA as well as the denomination as a whole. How can the data from the questionnaires and oral interviews be used to liberate women and the church to serve Christ in a more participatory and holistic manner? What have we

WOMEN AND LEADERSHIP

learned through analysis and interpretation that can assist in drawing firm conclusions on steps to be taken to bring about women's liberation and church transformation? In summary, the methodology of women's research I am proposing should lead to action plans, praxis and change. The narrative, in the intimate sharing of women's stories, will prove to be the essential foundation in discovering pragmatic approaches to emancipate women and the church (women and men) for wholeness, healing and service.[12]

The Limitations and Scope of the Research

Arguably, African women see their lives as holistic -- mind, body, spirit -- in a much more profound sense than white women. This intrinsic, holistic orientation carries over into their "social consciousness." They are, in mind, body and spirit, wedded to their social framework -- family, church and community -- again, in a deeper sense than white women.[13] Their need for greater affirmation of themselves as equal partners in the Lord's church and his Kingdom (in all the earthly institutions and projections of this Kingdom) is to be seen in this light. This study primarily focuses upon African women in the Baptist Convention of South Africa and their increasing consciousness and desire for access to church leadership at all levels. Implications, then, beyond the BCSA is a secondary focus and interest.

In addition, this study is focused on *church feminism.* Its aim is to address women's concerns from within the framework of the church and not from outside of it (e.g. *religion feminism*). Secondly, while the study seeks the contributions of white feminist and African-American womanist theologians to the overall debate on women's

INTRODUCTION

oppression within the church, it gives particular stress and value to what African womanist theologians are saying in the context of their own history and experiences. Finally, this study centers on the women of the BCSA. "Women's theology" is pertinent only so far as it finds its contextual relevancy among South African Baptists.

Structure

Chapter One concerns itself with the views of women theologians in Africa and the Western world. What are they saying about the biblical and theological justifications for women in leadership in the church, women and dignity, women and the Christian ministry? What are their cries and hopes? What do they perceive to be the challenges and obstacles to the ecclesiastical emancipation of women?

Chapter Two focuses upon the women of the Baptist Union. The task is to discover in what ways women experienced their faith and their struggles for self-realization and fulfillment in leadership. Do we detect gender oppression, subversion and unequal discipleship? Do we detect a suppressed female spirituality? Some women's stories and experiences from the dominant white cultural group will be investigated.

Chapter Three focuses upon the black women (and to a lesser degree the men) of the Baptist Convention. It seeks to discover their stories and experiences as women in general and women in leadership roles in the church in particular. Is there an emerging "theology of women" within the new denomination? Do these grassroots

WOMEN AND LEADERSHIP

"women theologians" from South Africa's "third world" possess something to contribute to the larger effort of women's empowerment in the Church of Jesus Christ in Africa? Along with patriarchal resistance, are there voices of resistance from black women themselves to black women's growing desire for leadership?

Chapter Four serves as the summation of the study and proposes a prescription for the future of the BCSA. A summary and comparative analysis of the attitudes and experiences of BUSA and BCSA women and men, a comparison of BCSA women with women of South Africa from non-BUSA, non-BCSA churches, a comparison of BCSA women and their attitudes and experiences with a woman of Zambia, with a woman of Hong Kong, and with women of the United States will be made. An evaluation of the findings through the use of theological analysis and a prescription for the future will be given. The aim is to bring the study to a pragmatic conclusion.

The Value of this Study

There are reasons and assumptions for this study. These reasons indicate the value of this analysis of women in leadership among the Baptists of the BCSA.

Firstly, men must join women in the fight for justice in the church. My involvement as a male writer of this study is a single contribution to a much broader, strategic goal -- the full emancipation of women in church leadership. The church is to be seen in need of reconciliation with women, without whom the church would be devastated. Men must uphold women, with their attitudes and their actions.

INTRODUCTION

A *second* reason for this study is to make another contribution to the biblical and theological justification for the full rights of women in the ministries of the church. This writer supports the view that the Scriptures do not negate women in their uniqueness or in their equality with men in spiritual gifts, dedication or versatility. The emergence of a "theology of women" within the Baptist Convention is of immense significance.

Thirdly, the South African Baptists face several critical issues to their survival and vitality in the new South Africa. The issue of women is one of them. One of the distinguishing marks of the Baptist Convention is its increasing affirmation of women in the ranks of church and denominational leadership. The BCSA can be seen as the flagship or model by which other Baptist groups can find inspiration, for the organization that liberates women liberates itself.

A *fourth* reason for writing this study is to record the voices of Baptist women in urban and rural settings. It is important for women to give their voices for a change, to speak out, analyze, critique and allow their feelings and attitudes to be heard. Traditionally, women have been the "silent-researched." Others spoke for them and about them, shaping perceptions about them and establishing their destiny. Here they are given the opportunity to speak for themselves, about matters they care about deeply, for church women are concerned about their faith and expressions of their full feminine humanity in that faith.

A *fifth* reason for this study is the need for church renewal. The BCSA and other South African denominations must be en route to transformation through re-evangelization. This study seeks to present the notion that as women are liberated to full partnership with

WOMEN AND LEADERSHIP

men in the church, men and women will be re-evangelized and renewed in their commitment and service.

A Personal Note

There are glaring and obvious handicaps in being a male, a non-African, and non-South African male at that. I could be accused, as men have been, of writing androcentrically about women and their affairs. However, I would like to bring reasons to justify myself as the researcher and author of this study.

My maleness. Personally, to attempt to see the struggles in being obedient to God and his church from the female point of view by seeking understanding, if not empathy, with feminine advocates of the faith is an exercise in spiritual growth and enrichment. As a man, it is somehow "constructive" to my humanity to feel connected to the challenges of women in being liberated to serve God both inside and outside the structures of the church. It is constructive and wholesome to feel unthreatened by the ambitions of women who seek to find freedom to exercise their call and talent in the Kingdom of God. This is what I have discovered. In addition, my maleness can provide opportunities for "emotional distance" when highly charge sentiments are being dealt with. One hesitates to say "objectivity," for to be human is to be subjective. Yet there may be, at times, the lean toward "objectivity" that emotional distance may bring.

My non-African maleness. Could it be that, in the course of interviews and discussions, the knowledge that I am *not* an African may cause some African women to share more freely and frankly about themselves or their hurts, fears and disappointments than they

INTRODUCTION

would to an African male?

My non-South African maleness. Could the fact that I am not only non-African, but a non-South African as well, contribute to more openness in dialogue with some women? Could some women, black or white, feel more free or comfortable in sharing about the disappointments felt in their local church or about their denomination if the sharing was to someone outside their church and outside the history of their struggles? Is the psychological and cultural distance of the investigator an advantage in some ways?

Perhaps the drawbacks and disabilities in being a male, a non-African male, and a non-South African male are more numerous and substantial than being an African male, or a South African male who is black or white. Perhaps the advantages to being a female African researcher are the most suitable of all possibilities. The case I am making, though, is that, at times and in some circumstances, and with some women, the reality of my own gender and non-African, non-South African identity *may* provide opportunities equal to or greater than what may be possible otherwise.

I rest my case on one other point. As an "ethnic minority" in my own country, the United States of America, and having a racial heritage that experienced its own sufferings in discrimination and marginalization in political, economic, and social spheres and in ecclesiastical institutions, I can, perhaps more than many, understand and empathize a little easier with the plight of those in an upward struggle. I do know that my own intrinsic experience of being a part of a "psychic heritage of victimization due to racial prejudice" has played no small part in my interest and selection of the topic of this research.

WOMEN AND LEADERSHIP

NOTES ON THE INTRODUCTION

1. The Western church's paternal, patriarchal and imperial extension around the world clearly portray what Russell (1984:77) calls a "paradigm of domination." The history and expansion of the Baptist faith in South Africa is no exception, as we shall see in succeeding chapters. Landman (1992:134) cites C.J.M. Halkes' anthropological insights that the men of the Dutch Reformed Church have historically viewed women as equal to men in principle but different from men in practice. This aberrant attitude constitutes a dual anthropology. It is evident Russell's "paradigm of domination" can take various shapes.

2. The term "self-identity" in the study means a sense of self-awareness primarily. But it incorporates the ideas of self-acceptance and self-practice as well -- self-acceptance as a matter of conviction and self-practice as a matter of consequence. Therefore, the way I am using the term "self-identity" is stronger than the way it is normally used. It is used in the sense that the denomination's self-identity is not only an "ideological identity" but a *developing* "practised identity" as well.

3. Schussler-Fiorenza (1982:xix) has noted that in the mainstream of theological research which tended to be traditionally male-dominated (note the date in which Schussler-Fiorenza writes), women as research objects are not taken seriously. Significant changes have taken place since 1982 in the theological research circles, and women's issues and experiences are taken much more seriously today. Yet Meyer-Wilmes (1995:152-164) indicates the need still is to take women's stories and their struggles from the marginal or peripheral to the centre of research. I tried to make this research on BCSA women do just that. See Annalet van Schalkwyk's (1997:607-632) article "Women's Research from the Periphery." She interacts with Schussler-Fiorenza, Meyer-Wilmes, Elizabetha Donini, Musimbi Kanyoro, Essy Letsoalo and others in a search for an appropriate feminist research methodology for contemporary South African women.

4. Kretzschmar (1990:25) contends that thousands of white women within BUSA are systematically ignored. The yearly Union Handbook only refers in passing to women, their numerous contributions to the church either taken for granted or ig-

INTRODUCTION

nored. In addition, no African women have been trained in the two Union colleges at the Western Cape and at Parktown (now Randburg). African women trained at the Baptist Bible Institute (BBI) in Fort White in the former Ciskei were given a much more limited course of studies than their husbands. "It remains to be seen whether, under black leadership, this suppression of the views and abilities of women will continue in the newly independent Baptist Convention of Southern Africa." We shall see in succeeding chapters that women's concerns and experiences related to their marginalization are not prioritised in the local churches of the BCSA.

5. This study will demonstrate through the stories of Baptist women that while they are allowed restricted leadership in the formal "offices" of the church, they exert much leadership in terms of influence in "ministry."

6. Holland and Henriot (1991:14, 16, 98) explain that social analysis of any particular issue necessitates exploring the social situation's structural and historical relationships. They caution that in the very process of analysing any social situation, the researcher may need to contend with inherent biases of consciousness. This may mean critiquing one's deepest assumptions and being open to new vistas of awareness. I have sought to be unbiased and open to truth or new understandings in my investigations. I have not sought to promote anyone's, including my own, preconceived notions.

7. The Participatory Research Approach (PRA) seeks to counteract the weakness of the "objective" social science in that it goes beyond the limits of mere data collection. Firstly, it is essential to establish the subjective commitment of the researcher to the people being studied. This means "value-neutrality" and the view of the researcher as a technician or tool is rejected. Instead the researcher garners an identification and sensitivity with the people. Secondly, a close involvement of the researched community with the researcher is vital. Dialogue between the researcher and the people under study is strategic, for interaction positions the researcher as a committed, participatory social being. This is a reaction to the often alienating and oppressive character of the more objective methodologies. Thirdly, the PRA is problem-centred. The goal of research is "to understand the conditions underlying a problem in order to resolve the problem by transforming those conditions."

Fourthly, the PRA is understood as an education process for the people as well as the researcher. Through discussion and dialogue, actions to resolve social contradictions or problems can be implemented. Fifthly, the approach fosters respect and dignity, for it encourages the people's own potential and capability to comprehend social dilemmas and analyse them (Bryceson, Manicom and Kassam 1982:26). To greater or lesser degrees, I believe I achieved these five objectives in the process of data collection.

8. Van Schalkwyk (1997:607) describes life histories, participant observation and unstructured interviews as appropriate methods to record women's stories.

9. But oral history, or oral account of women's stories, necessarily involves more than simply the accumulation of data from informants, for these raw fragments of evidence collected contain challenges of interpretation. Oral historians therefore face the great task of drawing theoretical conclusions from these oral expressions. These theoretical conclusions must engage not only facts and activities of women but their values, attitudes, feelings and meaning as well. "As historians, we are trained to interpret meaning from facts. But oral history gives us the unique opportunity to ask people directly, "How did it feel? What did it mean?" (Anderson, et al 1990:97-98). In this study I have made a conscious effort to be sensitive to women's feelings and perceptions of meaning related to their experiences.

10. Luera-Whitmore (1980:130) advocates the need for Christians to actively dialogue with God, to learn to encounter God *imaginatively* and *intentionally*. In doing so, we find support for Landman's call for narrative reconstruction. In a sense, it is a call to allow God to join us in giving new birth to narrative.

11. I found Bal's (1991:148) comments insightful and helpful: "To listen is, among many other things, to examine the propositions and the selection that they represent -- the attitude adopted, the form chosen; it is *also* to react . . . .To examine oneself as interlocutor. This is precisely what critical scholarship must be -- self-criticism." I could not help, as a male interlocutor, but be self-critical as I researched and interviewed and became aware of African women's voices. To what degree have I too been responsible for upholding, perhaps unconsciously, but upholding nevertheless, a skewed view of the church and of Christianity that held women down?

INTRODUCTION

12. Luera-Whitmore (1980:vi) states assuredly: "My study is that story and storytelling are excellent media for accomplishing an integration of belief and action, which can be useful and meaningful for people in the local parish. Story and storytelling are utterly appropriate for integrating belief and action because they arise out of basic human experience. Human experience *is* narrative in character, and thus an adequate theology and spirituality must also be narrative in character. As we become familiar and comfortable with stories and storytelling, we become more human, more theological, more spiritual." In this research, I consider the use of women's stories as indispensable to liberating praxis in the BCSA. Their stories manifest their humanity, dignity and spirituality.

13. Kathryn Anderson, et al, further informs us that "what they [women] think may not always be reflected in what they do and how they act." Hence, what the behaviour of women is may give an incomplete assessment of their lives, and that the missing aspects may prove to be the most informative and interesting. The conclusion is that women's consciousness must be studied, for it is the "women's sphere of greatest freedom" (Anderson, et al 1990:97).

CHAPTER ONE

THE VIEWS OF FEMINIST, AFRICAN-AMERICAN WOMANIST AND AFRICAN WOMANIST THEOLOGIANS IN THE AFRICAN AND NON-AFRICAN MILIEU

INTRODUCTION

Sometimes I wish my eyes hadn't been opened
Sometimes I wish I could no longer see
All of the pain, the hurt and the longing
My sisters and I, as we try to be free

Sometimes I wish my eyes hadn't been opened
Just for an hour how sweet it would be
Not to be struggling, not to be striving
But just sleep securely in our slavery.

But now that I see with my eyes I can't close them
Because deep inside me somewhere I'd still know
The road that my sisters and I have to travel
My heart would say yes, and my feet would say go!
Sometimes I wish my eyes hadn't been opened
But now that they have I'm determined to see

WOMEN AND LEADERSHIP

> That somehow my sisters and I will be one day
> The free people we were created to be.
>
> (Goemans 1997:7)

Riane Eisler (1987:117) reminds us how ancient the oppression of women is. While 'humanism' was admired by men who ruled Greece, it was allowed only up to certain limits. The philosopher Socrates was sentenced to death, for surely he must have been a "radical" for corrupting the youth of Athens. His crime? His notions of equal education for women and justice for women that directly attacked the androcratic premise that might makes right.

Eisler continues (1987:118) that it was Aristotle who gave to Greek and later Western culture the dictum that slaves are meant to be ruled by free men, hence women are meant to be dominated by men -- thereby perpetuating the philosophical foundations of androcratic life. After all, Aristotle argued, anything else violated the "natural," observable order of reality. His influence took deep root in the other major tradition that formed Western civilization -- our Judeo-Christian heritage. Prejudices in interpreting original sin find their source here, as in the "Christian" mythology that ranks God over man and man over woman, child and nature.

Elke Kaiser relates how, in 1996, she met a woman who was regularly beaten by her husband. This went on for years, and she remained in silence and shame. She felt that perhaps she was to blame for her situation, and that if she shared her physical, mental and emotional pain with others they too would blame her. After ten years she spoke out, leaving her husband. As she feared, the pastor of her church joined her family in condemning her, urging her to admit her fault in leaving her husband and return to him. She never returned to

VIEWS OF WOMEN THEOLOGIANS

her husband (1997:9).

The thrust of this chapter will table the discussion on Christian feminist theology with a particular look at the South African situation (African womanist theology). However, Beverly Haddad (1996:199) makes a case for the "prematurity" of it. She argues that for ordinary African women in South Africa, a "theology of survival" is what they live by, and discussions of reconstruction, transformation and liberation is really putting the cart before the horse. For the majority of African women, every day is a struggle for survival in the townships and urban ghetto. They seek a God who rescues them, assists them to find "a way out of no way." This quest for survival takes risk and faith. Many have nothing else.

FEMINIST THEOLOGY -- A DEFINITION

I will define "feminist theology" with the world in view. While South African and African women theologians inform us primarily here, it is helpful to provide the South African and African participation within the spectrum of women's plight beyond even Africa itself, for it has been conclusively observed and recorded that women around the world face similar oppressions and prejudices in the Church.[1] They seek to be released from this bondage from the very institution that pronounces salvation and freedom from sin. See the testimonies of women from around the world in this report (Living Letters: A Report of Visits to the Churches During the Ecumenical Decade -- Churches in Solidarity with Women: 1997).

WOMEN AND LEADERSHIP

Sister Bernard Mncube (1991:358) believes that feminist theology begins with the declaration that in Christ a New Human Being has arisen. This New Human Being includes the female personhood just as it supports and promotes the male personhood. A new social order where mutuality and wholeness is established must be searched for. Women desire a new consciousness, a new way to perceive truth and reality, the opportunity to explore their unique experiences with renewed religious understanding. Feminist theology seeks to allow women to define themselves in their own terms, for their own reasons, without the male-controlling institutional church setting their existential and theological parameters. Women's concerns are therefore the best of liberation theology.

Denise M. Ackermann (1985:35, 41) puts it this way: the birth of feminist theology is signaled "when the private and corporate pain of sexist oppression is reflected on critically and systematically in the light of faith." She warns that if in South Africa a feminist theological expression only reflects a middle-class, white form of rational thought and experience, it is already becoming elitist and in danger of perpetuating the oppressive divisiveness and dualism it seeks to repudiate.

Ackermann distinguishes between 'feminism' and 'emancipation.' Feminism is the effort to recognize all the claims for women's rights (political, legal, etc.) equal to the rights claimed and possessed by men. The emancipation of women is the first step toward their liberation and freedom to make choices in all areas of life (politically, educationally, and professionally) without the limitations of gender. Feminism is the movement beyond emancipation. Feminism nurtures women's critical attitude in asking how so-called free (emancipated) women experience the existing patterns and structures in society. Is it right or not to accept the current societal norms and values? Feminist theology, therefore, "asks how a conscientized woman experiences male hierarchical church structures and what may be done to effect change. Feminism tends to be critical of norms and patterns established by history and tradition: religious, theological, scientific, social, political and cultural."[2] Women want to offer their contributions in questioning these patterns, from 'the inside,' on their terms (1985:34).

Virginia Mollenkott (1987:2) speaks of 'mutuality' -- mutual deference and submission, mutual servanthood, mutual concern. This mutuality is taught in the New Testament and expressed in the life of Jesus. In this light men as well as women may be feminists, for they both share a commitment to mutuality and human sexual equality.

Louise Kretzschmar (1991:108) claims that Christian feminism not only precedes the modern feminist movement but is distinctive in a number of ways, even though it can be admitted that secular feminists have influenced Christian feminist thinkers. While feminist theology is imbedded in the Christian faith, it is critical of the Christian tradition's sexism.[3] Feminist theologians claim that women's radically new and uplifted personhood and roles in family and society can be linked all the way back to the New Testament teachings of Jesus.[4] Feminist theology is plainly against discrimination against women (sexism) whether by women or men.

Fifteen years ago Landman (1984:1) prophesied that "one day feminist theology will have repaired the schism in humanity." That "one day" is not today. The struggle continues.

WOMEN AND LEADERSHIP

Feminism and South African Black Theology (African Womanist Theology)

Why feminism? Why black theology? What's the fuss?

Women contribute 1/2 of the world's people, perform 2/3 of the world's work, yet receive only 1/10 of the income, and own less than 1/100 of the world's property (Good News for the Poor in Visual Art, Reflection and Prayer 1997:90).

Roxanne Jordaan (1987:44-45) writes that Black Feminist Theology in South Africa began in 1982 with the birth of the Institute for Contextual Theology. But the concerns and expressions of Black Feminist Theology were written on the table long before 1982. Not all South African Black Feminist Theologians are highly trained and qualified pastors. She contends that black feminist theologians are preaching "in the Nyanga bush in Cape Town, in the streets of Soweto, in the shacks of Veeplas, in the forced removal tents of Kabah." At the grassroots level, black women are developing a theology from both their gut feelings as well as their mental capacities.[5]

Landman (1995a:143) claims that a conference on feminist theology organized by UNISA's Institute for Theological Research in September 1984 marked the first time academic attention was given to feminist theology in South Africa. Her article entitled "Ten Years of Feminist Theology in South Africa" provides a brief overview of what has occurred in feminist theology in South Africa from 1984-1995.[6]

Cuthbertson and Kretzschmar (1996:298) inform us that feminist theology, which historically privileged academe and white women in the church, has been challenged by African American women who write from the context of their experiences. This emerging 'womanist' theology enlarges the frontiers of Black Theology toward a much more inclusive ecclesiology.[7]

Such a one is Linda Thomas (1997:10). Thomas observes that during the early 1980s an African woman and an African American woman used the terms "womanist/womanism" separately from the other. They were both sharing compatible experiences in specific institutions, societies and cultures of which they intimately knew. Both Chikwenyu Okonjo Ogunyemi and Alice Walker embraced womanism "as a distinctive praxis for gathering and narrating spheres of knowledge about the lives of black women."

Thomas (1997:10) helps us understand how Ogunyemi argues that black women cannot mimic the sentiments and methods of white feminism. The singular reason is simple: racism and its debilitating effects upon Africans in the social construction. Hence black women must theologize out of their painful experiences in ways that distance themselves from white theological feminism. Ogunyemi asserts that much of the effects of sexism that black women encounter can be similar to what all women encounter, but sexism for the black woman is one of many tensions she must face (racism and poverty).

Elsewhere, Thomas (1996:24) supports the claim that often white feminist theology creates an unnecessary contention over against men. Womanist theology, however, acknowledges patriarchal traditions as troublesome for the whole black community -- men as well as women and children.

WOMEN AND LEADERSHIP

While black women in South Africa far outnumber men in the church and keep the church from dying by their material support, they are paradoxically the objects of a male created, monitored and dominated church in terms of power structure and theology. Women are beginning to rise against their suppression in church and theology. Their handicap is that the overwhelming majority of black women are not well versed in understanding and analyzing South African society. This hinders their liberation since, in the opinion of Mofokeng, a "relevant theology demands a rigorous analysis of society." In addition, since it was white feminist theologians that first introduced feminist theology in South Africa, black women's theology must arise to speak to the unique and grave challenges of black women in black churches and in black townships (Mofokeng 1990:42-44).

Mercy Oduyoye (1986:122) speaks to the unique challenge of black women in black townships and in black churches. She shares with us that women's experience of personhood in relation to significant others -- as wife and mother -- dominates in Africa. A woman's prestige and status in the community do not rest on personal achievements or qualities but on these relationships and their expectations. Oduyoye reports on Christiana Oppong's research that clearly demonstrates that young university women see themselves as owned by the men who support them. Their wage is perceived as supplementary. Thus the traditional norm that women are "economic attachments to men" is perpetuated. Likewise is the norm that the home and housework are the complete and exclusive responsibility of young girls and women.

Like women in other parts of the world, African women are dealing with bitterness, resentment and anger. But the expressions of experiences are different. Although African women share with women elsewhere the bondage to male domination, women in Africa face challenges that are peculiar. For instance, in addition to trying to understand more profoundly how African Traditional Religions, Islam and Christianity affect deeply the lives of African women, they frequently find that texts from both the oral and written scriptures are mixed and manipulated to marginalize women even more (Kanyoro 1996b:5).

To a degree, South African women have liberated themselves from (i.e., are not to be defined in terms of) feminist theology but not necessarily from American womanist theology. Yet Saayman infers neither of the two actually succeeds in defining the South African or African reality comprehensively enough. The (South) African situation is unique because:

(i) the need for liberation still takes priority over the need for emancipation;

(ii) the economic reality of (South) African woman is so much different (worse) than that in the First World;

(iii) an oppressive hierarchical patriarchy is much more of a present <u>cultural</u> reality in (South) Africa than anywhere in the First World;

(iv) the church and the Christian community are still, despite anything to the contrary, more of a sign of <u>hope</u> for (South) African women, whereas it is generally a sign of <u>despair</u> in the First World. (Saayman's comments made to me on 5 April 1999)

WOMEN AND LEADERSHIP

We can conclude that, while black womanist theology in South Africa and in Africa in general may have concomitant concerns with black womanist theology of African American women, we have noted how African womanist/feminist theologians have even distanced themselves from their African American sisters. The specific context proffers sociological, historical, religious and cultural variations so steeped in parochial myths, rituals and symbols that make *total homogeneity* in "black theology" or "womanist theology" impossible. This section seems to prove that point.

Feminism/Womanism and Anthropology

Anthropology is a theme that a number of feminist theologians have investigated to draw their conclusions. Properly understood, anthropology becomes an ally and not a foe.

In <u>The Chalice and the Blade</u>, the following analysis warrants review:

> Both sexes have the highly evolved brains, with the immense memory storage and extraordinary information processing capacity, that makes us as flexible, as versatile -- in short, as human -- as we are. Thus, although a rigidly hierarchical social structure like androcracy, which imprisons both halves of humanity in inflexible and circumscribed roles, is quite appropriate for species of very limited capacity like social insects, it is truly inappropriate for humans (Eisler 1987:113).

Oduyoye states the same sentiment differently. She contends there are two erroneous beliefs that have warped the spirit of biblical anthropology. One, the assumption that 'the greater includes the lesser.' Woman is included in the understanding of man, therefore maleness means humanness. Femaleness means to somehow tamper with the male norm or to be supportive of the male norm. The second assumption is the linguistic conviction that the female notion is included in the male pronoun and, in consequence, the word *man* necessarily includes woman (1986:127).

Oduyoye (1986:134-135) systematically rejects such fractured views of the human personality into emotional and rational, subjective and objective, whereby the heart is inherently inferior to the head. This brokenness is adhered to because of a fundamental "misconception of the human core of our relationships." What then is feminism's mark on anthropology? What is the meaning of our humanity in the community of men and women? To begin with, we must affirm women's experiences as legitimate dimensions of reality for theological reflection. To deny this is to persist in a state of our human brokenness. In Oduyoye's own words, "I take as my point of reference only what Christianity says God is calling women and men to become."

In addition, the objects of God's love apply equally to men as to women. The Acts description of spiritual gifts as well as the list by Paul elsewhere marshaled no gender limitations. Both women and men, equally, fit beneath the description "a little lower than the gods," just as moral decay knows no gender restrictions (Oduyoye 1986:136).

> We cannot be happy and unashamed in each other's company if we are hiding behind our gender to shirk responsibility. As baptized people, our suffering is salvific when taken on voluntarily and our

sharing of the gifts of others gives us the ability to thank God who made us male and female. Happy and responsible in my being human and female, I shall be able to live a life of doxology in the human community, glorifying God for the gifts I receive in others and for the possibility I have of giving myself freely for the well-being of the community while remaining responsible and responsive to God. It is only thus that I can say I am fully human. When we are all willing to see the humanity of the other, then we can begin the task of understanding a Christian anthropology (Oduyoye 1986:137).

Living a "life of doxology" and "glorifying God" as Oduyoye describes above is summarized by Kretzschmar (1995d:102) who states that, ultimately, a person's faith must rest in God, not in the Church. However, if women's Christian faith is filtered through male-dominated theology, culture, Church practices and structures,[8] women may agonize in discovering and pursuing spiritual growth in wholeness and healing. Female spirituality is enhanced by women's ability to critique male paradigms and shaping a new theology of creation and spiritual transformation. Women must experience a new perception of their humanity[9] and their image of God.

Mamphele Ramphele (1991:viii) asserts that culture is frequently used as "additional armor"[10] to defend patriarchal traditions and institutions, by women as well as by men. Feminists do not strive for equality with men. They strive for nothing less than "a radical redefinition of humanity itself away from exclusivity towards inclusivity." Women want to humanize the world, to make it a more caring, sensitive and open place for persons of all ages, genders, classes and races.

VIEWS OF WOMEN THEOLOGIANS

Women are fully human, encompassing the principles of mutuality and equality rooted in a hunger for justice. Hence Ackermann can say, "anthropology is both the starting point and the central category for feminist liberation theology" (1992:13). Unfortunately, Christian anthropology has affirmed woman's *imago dei* (Gen. 1:27) and equality with man whilst proving otherwise in the nearly two thousand years of Christian praxis (1992:16).

Practical theology embodies a feminist theological praxis. It affirms that all knowledge and reality is experienced through our bodies. By virtue of a person's ability to smell, touch, see, feel and hear she is able to know and grow wise -- through our bodies. The power to harm another as much as to love or forgive another begins in our bodies. Our bodies *are* us (Ackermann 1997:18).

Feminism/Womanism and Christology

In 1984 Christina Landman voiced the centrality of Jesus Christ in much of the feminist theological debate:

> I . . . know the black feminist theology can reach out a hand to 'white' feminist theology because the belief that sexist problems can and should be solved in Christ lies at the root of the experience of both (18).

Surely "the experience of both" referred to by Landman includes the experience of male exclusion of women in strategic areas of life common to both. To this L.J. Holness adds that the significance of Jesus is his *inclusion* of women in his life and ministry, an inclusion of women (lacking in the patriarchal pattern) to faith and to life (1990:158).

Jacquelyn Grant (1994:22) refers to how "trouble" is inescapable in an interconnected and pervasive atmosphere of classism, sexism, racism and other forms of subjugation black women endure. For black women Jesus has been a reliable strength in their lives, enabling them to not only survive[11] the trials they daily encounter, but to somehow, in spite of them, move beyond them.

Historically Jesus Christ has been, and still largely remains, a prisoner to socio-political interests. This fact, Grant argues, is the central Christological dilemma faced by black women. Jesus has been subverted by human powers and principalities and used as a primary tool for inflicting oppressive measures. Jesus has been imprisoned in three ways: by patriarchy, by white supremacy, and by the privileged class. Indeed, Jesus Christ's personhood has been abused by a patriarchal church to justify the subjugation of women. As Jesus has authority and power over women and men, men have construed that they have authority and power over children and women (1994:22-24), totally misconstruing Jesus' personhood by failing to understand the true nature of Jesus' power and authority over men and women. Jesus, it appears to me, never took away a person's dignity, never disempowered, never inflicted wounds or held in captivity, those over whom he had "authority" and "power." He, instead, liberated and instilled peace and joy and fulfillment in persons.

Grant (1994:24) persuades us that Christological distortion affected the issue of women's leadership/ordination in the church. Negative Christology is to be blamed for denying women their equality, personhood, humanity and leadership in the church. Negative

VIEWS OF WOMEN THEOLOGIANS

Christology means an overbearing overemphasis on the "maleness" of Jesus that has evolved into a kind of idolatry. Jesus is held prisoner to "patriarchy's obsession with the supremacy of maleness."

Furthermore, a paradigm of mutual liberation has been discovered and experienced by African American women, i.e. Jesus redeeming himself, Jesus liberating himself. The only conclusion to be reached is that the Jesus of black women has been imprisoned in three ways: Jesus has been held captive to the sin of privilege (classicism), the sin of white supremacy (racism), and the sin of patriarchy (sexism). Jesus the Prisoner has therefore been used to keep women in their place. The passion of black women is "to move beyond mere equality to freedom," for freedom is the preeminent message of the gospels and Jesus Christ (Grant 1994:30).

To Grant, "freedom experienced is . . . freedom shared." What happens when human powers and principalities encounter the power of the gospel and the authentic Christ? Grant's conclusion is that to be a Christian means to challenge evil and unjust powers in the existential situations (1994:22).

This theme of liberation appears strategic to other feminist theologians as well. Ackermann (1985:65) admits that the most helpful feminist theological perspective is the "Christ of liberation," for it stresses the significance of Jesus for social transformation. While, in the Bible, Jesus never articulated a systematic theological/missiological method for structural change, his teachings and behavior demonstrated that he envisioned "new dimensions in human relationships" rooted in the freedom to serve one another through mutual love. He in consequence undermined existing androcentric mores and structures of suppression and discrimination.

WOMEN AND LEADERSHIP

This very suppression and discrimination is what Anne Nasimiyu-Wasike (1991:73, 78) addresses in her important article "Christology and an African Woman's Experience" in the book <u>Faces of Jesus in Africa</u>. In Jesus liberation is offered to all, but especially to the disadvantaged. She claims that in Jesus Christ the original relationship between woman and man (Eve and Adam) has been restored. Jesus sees the African woman as one who should participate freely and fully in the life and struggles of the church -- as one chosen to restore humanity in the church, where holistic, mutual and inclusive relationships can be nurtured and enjoyed for the glory of God and his witness.

Perhaps the most dramatic of all Jesus' ecclesiastical and social relationships with the "weak" were those with women. In this way he accorded persons to whom society accords little value a sense of overwhelming value (Holness 1990:246-247).

In Jesus Christ, women find God's Son, a male, but more than a male, a Person, a person who, while strong, remains gentle and understanding, able to listen and sympathize, and to offer generosity with passion and compassion.

FEMINIST THEOLOGY -- A DESCRIPTION

I have defined "feminist theology" with particular emphasis to the context of Africa in general and South Africa more particularly (African Womanist Theology). Feminists from the African American context were helpful in sharing their insights and experiences. After a definition of feminist theology, I sought to further the definition by analyzing the role of feminism in (South) African black theology, the

VIEWS OF WOMEN THEOLOGIANS

place of anthropology in feminist thinking, as well as the significance of Christology in feminist theology.

Under this section, my task is twofold:

a) to describe how the Bible is used constructively by feminist theologians to address the women's issues of personhood and dignity, and

b) to describe how feminist theologians defend their struggle for justice through full participation in church leadership and the Christian ministry.

The Bible and Women, Personhood and Dignity

UBUFAZI (WOMANHOOD)

Should I hang precariously over a cliff;
Should I be the trampling ground;
Should I be the sacrifice of wickedness;
Just because they say I am weak,
I am a woman?

I do achieve success in my efforts,
I do realize some of my wishes,
But I am deprived of all the rights
Just because they say I am weak,
I am a woman.

WOMEN AND LEADERSHIP

> Not all the women are oppressed,
> Not all of us are deprived,
> Not all the womenfolk are destitute.
> I come from the world of the women.
>
> All my efforts are in vain,
> My injunctions none will fulfill,
> My struggles none will take heed of
> Just because they say I am weak,
> I am a woman.
>
> (Ndazulwana 1997:34)

Ubufazi. Womanhood. Personhood? Yes.

Mary Daly (1985:53) decries the Catholic Church for a long historical tradition of ambivalence toward women, simultaneously idealizing and humiliating her. But is this not the historical tradition of Christianity at large?

The Christian church needs women for its survival, yet its theological praxis denies women their complete humanity and personhood.[12] Jessica Nakawombe (1996:46) claims that the Jesus of the gospels sought to restore personhood to women with behaviors toward women in sharp contrast to the expectations and norms of the time. He spoke personally, without restraint, of women, with women and to women, as human beings of worth and dignity, not as sexual beings of a lower caste. His interest and caring attitude toward women comes across unmistakably in his miracles, stories, parables, discourses and encounters. He healed women and allowed women to follow him and touch him.

VIEWS OF WOMEN THEOLOGIANS

What Nakawombe has expressed, a chorus of other women agree. Mercy Oduyoye and Elizabeth Amoah (1994:43-44) describe the "counter cultural relations" instituted by Jesus as he moved among women. No wonder he is so affectionately regarded. Jesus is the one who liberates, this teacher, friend, companion of women, this "Child of Women," because in him "the fullness of all that we know of perfect womanhood is revealed." The integrity and dignity of woman as a person is recognized, promoted and ensured through a relationship with Jesus. Mary Evans (1983:45) voiced years ago how Jesus uplifted the personhood and dignity of women, a revolutionary behavior contrasting with the Roman and Jewish behavior in his day. Sister Albertus McGrath (1972:17) is explicit -- by Jesus' regard and treatment of women in word and deed, by his universality and purity of his loving ministry, he leveled the playing field of life for women and men, eliminating all markers of inferiority and superiority.

Fabella and Oduyoye, in the book With Passion and Compassion: Third World Women Doing Theology (1994), have provided a culturally diverse and panoramic view of the issues, struggles and experiences of third world women doing theology. Personhood and dignity issues are paramount. Contributors come from Africa (Edet, Ekaya, Ramodibe, Souga, Tappa, Amoah, Oduyoye and Okure), Asia (Gnanadason, Mananzan, Park, Tse, Jin and Fabella), and Latin America (Gebara, Arellano, Ritchie, Aquino, Tepedino and Tamez), representing a wide diversity of nations: Africa (Nigeria, Kenya, South Africa, Cameroon and Ghana), Asia (India, Philippines, Korea, Hong Kong and Malaysia), and Latin America (Brazil, Nicaragua, Argentina and Mexico).

Linda Thomas (1996:23) expresses the woman's hunger for the divine right to her humanity and personhood this way:

WOMEN AND LEADERSHIP

> We are mothers, partners, lovers, wives, sisters, daughters, aunts and nieces, and we comprise two-thirds of the black church in America. We are the black church. The church would be bankrupt without us and the church would shut down without us. We are from working-class as well as middle-class backgrounds. We are charcoal black to high yellow women. We love our bodies; we claim our created beauty. And we know that what our minds forget our bodies remember. The body is central to our being.[13]

Feminist theologians have scrutinized the use of the Bible by the predominant male interpreters (remember the "hermeneutics of suspicion"), for as is implied above, the issues of personhood and dignity must be solidly ingrained in the Bible if women are to possess full partnership in God's *missio Dei*.

Elisabeth Schussler-Fiorenza (1992:5) calls for the deconstructing of the male-biased paradigms of biblical hermeneutics and a reconstructing of the biblical texts, to see them as alive and dynamic, as a changing and living heritage for us all, in order that emancipation in faith-communities is birthed. The patriarchal church as the hermeneutical center must be destroyed.

Madipoane Masenya (1997:16) reiterates Schussler-Fiorenza's emphasis in her article "Reading the Bible the Bosadi (Womanhood) Way" (see her 1996 doctoral study, <u>Proverbs 31:10-31 in a South African Context: A Bosadi (Womanhood) Perspective</u>). She advises a re-reading of the Bible to free South African women marginalized by the Bible. Women should be trained to read and critique the Bible to free themselves from sexism in South African society, from classicism, from post-apartheid racism, and even from African culture. Reading the Bible the 'bosadi' way will help restore personhood, esteem and dignity. These sentiments can also be seen in

VIEWS OF WOMEN THEOLOGIANS

her earlier article entitled "African Womanist Hermeneutics: A Suppressed Voice from South Africa Speaks" (1995:149-155).

The struggle for full life and liberation continues in spite of the downfall of state apartheid in South Africa (West 1991:15), and the struggle continues elsewhere as well. Gerald West's (1990:23) main contention in his article "Can a Literary Reading Be a Liberative Reading?" is that the principal aim of biblical studies is to embrace and serve the community, primarily the oppressed community and the poor, and in doing so biblical studies maintain a transformative role in its solidarity with the victims of society and history.

This maintenance of biblical studies' transformative role is crucial for ecclesiastical androcentric pillars are still entrenched in all churches. Landman notes that black women especially are up against a brick wall: the Bible, society, and tradition. They have only their own *experience* and the conviction that God sees their pain and identifies with it (1984:17).

Itumeleng J. Mosala echoes Landman. The Bible is the product, the site, the record, and the weapon of gender, racial, cultural and class struggles. A biblical hermeneutics of emancipation that fails to deal aggressively with this fact will find efforts to liberate the exploited and poor of the world extremely futile. Mosala claims "the poor and exploited must liberate the Bible so that the Bible may liberate them" (1989:193).[14]

An example of women ("the exploited") liberating the Bible in order for the Bible to liberate them comes from Katherine Haubert (1997:21-34). Haubert takes the two creation accounts in Genesis, the I Tim. 2:11-15 and I Peter 3:7 passages, and concludes through thorough biblical exegesis that there is nothing to indicate woman's inherent inferiority to man or a secondary nature that signifies subordination. Women are fully capable and responsible to hold leadership roles and offices within the church without restrictions.

Another example is Elsa Tamez's article entitled "Hermeneutical Guidelines for Understanding Galatians 3:28 and I Corinthians 14:34" (1993:48-60). Tamez proposes that those texts which oppress and marginalize women be seen as circumstance-bound and not normative. The contrary affirmations in Gal. 3:28 and I Cor. 14:34-35 are studied. Among the principles of interpretation are the assumptions that 1) every human being should enjoy the same dignity and privileges before God and society; 2) unjust inequalities are the products of sin; and 3) God, throughout human history, is in solidarity with the oppressed. Gal. 3:28 is normative. I Cor. 14:34-35 is circumstantial.

What Caroline Tuckey (1996:167) terms "progressive revelation" and Richard N. Longenecker (1986:83) calls "developmental hermeneutic" amount to the same conclusion. Tuckey sees a trend in the Bible. She notes that few women are amply noted or discussed in the Old Testament. More women are noted and referred to in the New Testament. This trend may be understood as a progressive revelation concerning the role and position of women. Such can be said for the role and position of the Holy Spirit in the Old and New Testaments. Today, largely stemming from the prominence given to the Holy Spirit in the New Testament, the Holy Spirit is a vital member of the Trinity. Unfortunately, many interpreters today regard women according to the first century cultural conditions, or to the cultural conditions of the Old Testament, and not to the teachings of Jesus. Longenecker's developmental hermeneutic demands that we distinguish between what the scriptures in the New Testament teach about being new creatures in Christ and its description of how that teaching was actually practiced in the first century. Longenecker argues that the implementation of that teaching is to be understood in the New Testament as only having begun and "is described as being then worked out in progressive fashion." Our focus must therefore be on the principles and ideals of the gospel teachings, not just on their implementation in the first century. The ethical guidelines and gospel principles as presented in the New Testament ought to be normative for every believer today. However, the ways the gospel was experienced and implemented in the first century should be seen as signposts at the start of an interesting and challenging journey. These signposts point to the ways we must progress in order to reapply this same gospel for our contemporary times.

Feminist theologians are clearly seeking to make the Bible a friend and not a foe. Women's personhood and dignity rest upon feminist theologians' success in counteracting centuries of oppressive biblical hermeneutic. Male "feminist" theologians have made and must continue to make pertinent contributions for, as has been so well articulated, they are stakeholders too in that the emancipation of men is tied to women's. Ultimately the church of Jesus Christ will be liberated.

Women, Leadership and the Christian Ministry

To greater or lesser degrees all branches of historic Christianity, Catholic, Protestant and Eastern Orthodox, have perpetuated

WOMEN AND LEADERSHIP

restrictions and limitations on the acceptability of women in leadership and Christian ministry, especially the ordained ministry. This section will attempt to both describe that discrimination and the feminist response to it.

Thoko Mpumlwana (1991:374-376) speaks of the barriers to women in leadership in the Church:

1) Cultural stereotypes -- there are people who use culture to justify or perpetuate women's oppression,

2) Tradition -- others rebel against moving away from traditions of sexist expectations and norms,

3) Social status -- the inferiority of women in society promotes the same attitude in the church,

4) Acquiescent women -- the preservation of the status quo is preserved by other women,

5) The Bible -- some believe the Scriptures support the restrictions of the Church on women,

6) False sense of inferiority -- young girls are systematically socialized into stereotypical roles that lead eventually to low self-esteem,

7) Biological functions -- women cannot fully participate as Church leaders when one is pregnant, menstruating or having just given birth.

VIEWS OF WOMEN THEOLOGIANS

Mpumlwana's list of barriers to women's leadership in the church summarizes what so many feminists have observed or experienced personally. Diana Cormick's (1992) dissertation is a case study of the visual portrayal of Mary Magdalene. It takes a feminist ethical view, revealing that Mary Magdalene has been the victim of a prolonged patriarchal injustice in the Roman Catholic Church.[15] She has been misrepresented in that the Church has sustained a subversive interpretation of women's inherent promiscuity. Mary Magdalene has been portrayed as a penitent prostitute, and Cormick argues that this distorted image of a great woman has been perpetrated by a patriarchal Church. Indeed, Mary Magdalene has been depicted by the Catholic Church as an archetype of woman within the Church. This moral injustice against women must be revealed, so that women disciples of Christ may be rooted, energized and informed to carry on the work of Christ in the Church without shame or inferiority.

In the social context of subjugation and systemic prejudice, women discover a sense of emotional and spiritual equilibrium, maturity and stability not easy to maintain. Libuseng Ketshabile (1997:5-6) speaks of her frustrations as a woman in the Methodist churches of South Africa. She discovered that her faith was questioned when bad events occurred in her life. This fact precipitated the tendency to cover up misfortunes or to behave as if misfortunes did not in any way affect one's life and faith. These attitudes gave birth to a "face-value theology," a "pretending theology." A pretending theology is defined as "one that contradicts the inner feelings about what one believes and why one believes what one believes." As such, questions about God's viability, and doubts about his active involvement in everyday concerns and challenges were inevitably perceived to be a lack of faith.[16]

Zodwa Memela (1994:16) testifies to women's mistreatment in the church in her article "Racism and Its Impact on Black Women: A South African Perspective." A church that proclaims to be not of this world ought to give better treatment to black women. Yet the church adheres to sexism and racism. While black men strive for power to become bishops, white men carve their way to the financially lucrative administrative posts, to ensure that the control of money stays within white hands. Black women are seen to suffer the most. They are expected to ensure a present is secured for 'our father' when male bishops are out visiting circuit/parishes. Women are expected to feed the black bishops and to help keep them in power, while they had no part in putting these bishops in their positions. Women internalize such suppression in the church, resigning themselves to such roles as organizing and teaching Sunday School classes, supervising church bazaars and running soup kitchens for the poor.[17] Black men have also blended into the system is such a way that they are part and parcel to it.

Patriarchal African societies readily received Christianity's dictum that God is male with male attributes. This collusion was made easy when one understands the African patriarchal cultures. In these, women never ruled for they were never allowed to participate in strategic discussions. Women were never consulted when grave decisions had to be made. Such deliberations and decisions included the whole community, or the clan, or simply the family. A group of male elders would discuss, settle disputes and make vital decisions, even those concerning women and children (Wamue 1997a:66).

In traditional African societies women were by hierarchical expectation dependent on men, protected by men, and guided by them.[18] They were seen as objects of use, exploitation, abuse, and a source of wealth. Yet African women often held leadership as rainmakers, seers, diviners, mediums in prophesying, counselors and healers (Wamue 1997b:56).

Christianity, based on Western culture, disseminated new forms of subjugation and oppression for African women. All types of

VIEWS OF WOMEN THEOLOGIANS

African religious leadership were deemed by colonial Christianity as satanic and evil. African women converted to the Christian faith lost their spiritual and religious freedom as a result. Western Christianity refused women access to public teaching and the priesthood. African women had to yield to the discrimination of Western Christianity. This doubled their own social and cultural disabilities (Wamue 1997b:56).[19]

A significant breakthrough came with the realization that *baptism*, not circumcision, is the sign of Jesus' (God's) calling to leadership and service for both men and women. In the act and symbolic power of baptism everyone puts on Christ or is mysteriously merged to his resurrected body as the firstfruits of a new humanity (Gal. 3:27-28). Everyone receives from the one Spirit the same gifts (I Cor. 12:13; Col 3:9-11) (Russell 1993:61).

Ada Nyaga (1996:80) supports the significance of baptism for women in African Christianity. In the old covenant, when circumcision was the sign of identity, only males were truly members of the chosen people, since only males were circumcised. Women were "considered" members of God's chosen race and benefited from the covenant by virtue of their link to their husbands or fathers. With the onset of Jesus and New Testament baptism, this rite became the sign of the people of God, equally accessible to all, woman or man, uncircumcised or circumcised, for each and all were equal through Christ's blood and salvation.

Letty Russell (1993:61) informs us that in Romans 16:1-2 Phoebe is called *diakonos* (servant, missionary, minister) and *prostatis* (governor, leading officer, superintendent, president). Russell claims that the ministry of women in the early church was not limited to specific functions or roles or to ministry only with women. Yet Russell does concede that Paul compromised the higher faith in his teachings for the sake of church order. First Corinthians 11:2-16 reflects the tensions surrounding cultural expectations when Paul says women must cover their heads but allows them to prophesy. In I Corinthians 14:33-36, Paul lays out further injunctions of women's subordination as a matter of expediency.

If women in the New Testament were called as *diakonos* and *prostatis*, as Letty Russell claims, then Renate Cochrane's (1991:26) warning should be heeded: "A woman's call into discipleship even takes priority over motherhood." In Luke 11:27-28 a woman shouts, 'Blessed is the mother who gave you birth and nursed you.' Jesus replies, 'Blessed rather are those who hear the Word of God and keep it.' In a society where bearing children and motherhood were viewed as a woman's supreme purpose and fulfillment in life, one can only imagine the earthshaking sharpness of Jesus' response.

Church leadership and Christian ministry are empty shells unless they are undergirded with genuine discipleship. Jesus proclaims that women must be free to hear a higher calling than even motherhood! But *churches* must be free to hear a higher calling for women than motherhood as well. Malika Sibeko and Beverly Haddad (1996:14-15) bemoan the fact that churches are still in bondage, for few women are being ordained and functioning as priests or ministers.[20] Women are not permitted to distribute Holy Communion or to perform baptisms. Because of menstruation, there exists a menacing attitude stemming from an interplay of Levitical texts and cultural attitudes that women are 'unclean.' When women are menstruating, even lay leaders are blocked from performing certain duties.

VIEWS OF WOMEN THEOLOGIANS

To break such ecclesiastical bondages and taboos, Beauty Nomtandazo Dlamini (1995:179) confesses that she had to "step out courageously." This was the only way she became an evangelist. One has everything if one has God, she pronounces. "You won't be left alone. I was not afraid of anything."

Phumzile Zondi (1998:5) shares her own frustration in a repressive *cultural* environment:

> I struggled with the concept of an African marriage where a woman almost disappears and adopts the life of her husband and in-laws. A woman is brought up to be someone's wife one day. This is sad because women have so much potential, which they are not free to use for the betterment of their own communities. Those women who have lived above this and have shown their gifts are either not recognized for their efforts or they are rejected by society. A few years ago when I worked as a pastoral assistant, I realized that the more I wanted to be creative the more I was reminded of behavior rules for women. The restrictions became so oppressive that I had to resign . . . . I still believe that God wants me to serve as a woman in my own right and not under someone else's shadow. I believe that I am more effective now in everything I do because I have learnt to read the Bible in such a way that it makes sense to me.

Nyambura Njoroge (1996:5-7, 10, 13) shares her pain and frustrations in a repressive *church* environment:

> I realize . . . that I have been angry and hurt because I have encountered in my ministry many women in great pain and suffering. Most of the time I felt powerless and ill prepared to deal with or even to identify with their suffering. I was ill-prepared because my

WOMEN AND LEADERSHIP

initial seminary training never brought to my attention women's issues and concerns in the life and work of the Church . . . . I also discovered that although my Church [Presbyterian Church of East Africa] pioneered the ordination of women in this county, it is still far from addressing women's concerns in a concrete way. I began to realize that not only were women excluded from leadership roles[21] and dismissed as being like children, but also that the Church excluded issues that concerned women most in their lives . . . . We have to break through the lies, secrets and silences . . . . The struggle is hard because women, too, are not free from the vices that discriminate against women. We, too, become greedy for power, money and status; we, too, can exercise dominion, control and exclusion, just like our brothers.

For five years I was the only person under 40 in my parish session (council) and I was the only woman. I had to listen to language that put women down: women are like children; don't tell your wives because they are profound gossips; women are immature; poor and single women cannot make good leaders, etc. I had to watch in silence as the great potential and skills of young people and women were wasted because of the ignorance and arrogance of the leadership. I felt helpless and frustrated. I was angry and hurt because I could identify these problems but could find no way out of them. Worse still was to see how women had internalized low self-esteem and most of the stereotypes attributed to them. Fortunately, as my inner struggle intensified, this initial experience in my ministry created a yearning and awareness of women's issues and concerns.

How can women be trained in theological colleges and enter ministry only to endure insults like these? There was a time when women were systematically excluded from theological training (see Memela 1994:19), but today it is different. Nevertheless, as Anne N. Musopole (1992:199) relates the situation in Malawi, women face severe obstacles in their ministry. The Church of Central Africa, Presbyterian does not permit women ordinands. When the Christian gospel was proclaimed in Malawi, many women responded with not only faith but a commitment to theological training and Christian ministry. Very soon after graduation, however, "they saw the women's wagon on the theological train toward church ministry slow down and grind to a halt." Deprived of ordination, these women can be found in synods all over Malawi. Why no ordination? Because the C.C.A.P. follows early Christianity in Europe which disallows women's ordination. Will the C.C.A.P. in Malawi enter the twenty-first century doing the same?

In her article "The New Eve in Christ: The Use and Abuse of the Bible in the Debate about Women in the Church," Mary Hayter (1987:170) argues that the Bible is not to be necessarily an advocate for or against women's ministry. That is, the Bible does not present us with the 'last word.' Since biblical authors were not concerned or aware of issues or questions raised in the form it has been by modern scholars and ecclesiastics, such finality is not likely. For, as Hayter attributes to Dodd, if the Bible is truly God's holy Word, it comes to us not as the 'last word' on every and all religious apprehensions and questions, but as the *seminal word* from which fresh awareness of truth arises to address the needs of his people in the context of their lives.

Hayter (1987:170) states that this era is the kairos moment for a new and vibrant realization of the unique emancipating power of the gospel to direct women and men to a fresh and penetrating expression of the reality of their shared (co-equal) creation in the *imago Dei*. The *seminal word* of the Bible clearly advocates that the ultimate issue is not whether one is female or male but whether one adheres to truth and commits one's life to God the redeemer and creator of humankind. If the Holy Spirit bestows gifts to equip a man or woman for ministerial priesthood, the church ought to encourage this call and the full and free use of these spiritual gifts.[22]

In Christ, and through him, woman's personhood and theological position is no more one of submission and inferiority to male control and authority. "Eve in Christ" transforms herself into a new creation, no more confined to subordination to the dictates of church dogma or tradition, but rather liberated to enjoy the fruits of freedom as children of God (cf. Rom. 8:21; 7:6; II Cor. 5:17). Empowered with the freedom of the Spirit, women and men together are called and jointly responsible to share *Christ's ministry* -- proclaiming release to people still in bondage, setting them free from the enslavement of the fallen world to a more abundant life in Christ. This freedom of the new Eve in Christ is compassionate to the needs of others, and never demanding or self-assertive (cf. Luke 4:18f; Mark 10:43ff). It is a liberty that enables the priestly ministry (*diakonos*) of all of God's chosen people for his glory (I Peter 2:5, 9).

In the context of South Africa, women ought not to forget their history and their experiences, for they serve as a necessary springboard for societal and ecclesiastical transformation. It is not for the betterment of women only, but for the betterment of humanity.

Nokuzola Mndende (1997:23), though an African traditionalist and not a Christian, underscores this point. She states: "A map of our past is the path finder to our destiny." We misread our map to our peril. Misreading results in misdirecting our strategy for shaping the future. The rainbow women of South Africa seek to redefine and rediscover their humanity. Anna Mghwira (1994:152) concurs with the observation that "women's issues are human issues, just as church issues are societal issues." The human race includes women. All that stimulates human development, or hinders it, including both women and men, should be jointly considered.

In conclusion, we should note that the challenge for an embrace of women's upliftment is nothing less than the challenge for freedom and justice. Until justice issues acquire human voices and faces, they do not capture the hearts of the majority. In allowing women the privilege and responsibility to share their pain and function with partnership and equality in all walks of life, we will see *concretely* what has been missing when the institutions of society disallow women to utilize the Spirit's gifts to them (Wolterstorff 1986:293-294).

THE CHALLENGES TO THE SOCIAL AND ECCLESIASTICAL EMANCIPATION OF WOMEN

I have sought to *define* feminist theology and, after having done so, to erect three major flagpoles from which this definition may be scrutinized: feminism and black theology, feminism and anthropology, and feminism and Christology. Subsequently, I have found it appropriate to *describe* feminist theology. This effort is important for it provides the substance and critical issues that feminist theology seeks to address. Two flagpoles were erected here: a) the Bible and women, personhood and dignity and b) women, leadership and the Christian ministry. In both the definition and description sections, elements of challenges to the social and ecclesiastical emancipation of women were clearly evident. The final task of this chapter is to clarify in summary fashion these challenges.

WOMEN AND LEADERSHIP

The Challenge of "Educating Ourselves"

In the July 1997 issue of the <u>Bulletin for Contextual Theology in Southern Africa and Africa</u>, Christina Landman authored an article entitled "Educating Ourselves -- A Challenge for Women's Theology in South Africa" (13-14). In it she postulates that while in the past theological education sought to train only a few for the ministry there has occurred a paradigm shift in recent years. The focus today is to provide theological training in "religious skills" to a wide spectrum of people in the communities. Whereas in the past theological education was weighted on academic disciplines, the aim today is on "life-affirming education," i.e. "teaching life skills to religious people on a participatory basis." As a liberation theology, women's theology in South Africa consistently sought the tandem of social as well as mental education of women.

Landman (1997a:13) is insistent that tertiary theological institutions are strategic today. Women in South Africa do not possess the religious skills to meaningfully engage in theological discourse, writing[23] and social transformation. Tertiary theological schools need to offer courses to women to nurture religious skills in labor, social stereotyping, sexuality[24] and to take action against prejudice and discrimination. These religious skills ought to be participatory and targeted to the grassroots. These religious skills can be grouped into three compatible and interlocking areas: "Skills to assert and transform oneself, skills to transform society, and skills to become a moral leader" (which necessarily includes leadership in shaping contextual women's theologies). In Afrikaans society, women's self-hate is a problem. Like other societies, Afrikaans society is separated into a female subculture subservient to a male dominant one. Only the male dominant culture is visible, audible and public. Writing or speaking from *within* the women's subculture is tantamount to writ-

VIEWS OF WOMEN THEOLOGIANS

ing and speaking about women's *private* experiences.[25] The socio-religious-political powerlessness of Afrikaans women resulted in exercising their piety in their personal lives to empower themselves. This empowerment, however, remains valid only inside the confines of their own subculture (Landman 1994:1-2).

Ultimately this piety of submissiveness, self-hate and internalization equipped men to perpetuate their dominance. Even after three hundred years Afrikaans women are not yet free to arise above their subculture. They are suspicious of other cultural societies different from their own. They are restricted to appeasing the male God of the male dominant culture (Landman 1994:3). Teaching Afrikaans women religious skills cannot be any more timely or urgent.

Wamue (1997b:61), giving an African perspective, is adamant that women must take the initiative for change. Women should press for the liberation of the church from male dominance. Sadly, they have "internalized the very myths that disqualify them from church ministry."

This call for initiative for change is also voiced by Ackermann (1997:17-18). She is certain that women's beliefs and convictions are worthless unless they are linked to actions producing justice, healing and liberation. Appropriate actions are aimed at achieving and sustaining a new reality, which upholds the intrinsic value of women "in all spheres at all times." Activities for change calls for collaborative efforts between women of different religious traditions, social locations and cultures.

Collaboration must reach out to African rural women. Rural women are theologizing by creating poetry, dirges, proverbs as well as singing songs. They must be heard for the unique and incisive contributions they can make. African women want inclusion and participation, or to be made aware they are welcome into the dialogue and emancipation process. For feminist theology to achieve success in the local churches and communities, women's theology must take the shape of a "communal theology" (Kanyoro 1996b:16).

But do women in South Africa really want change? Ackermann wonders (1984:76). She suspects the contrary, for she believes many women (white or black or both?) are content with the status quo. There should be no question that changing the oppressive circumstances is absolutely essential. It is a "moral imperative."

Trevor Dennis (1994:3) concludes:

> I cannot read as a woman, nor write as a woman, because I am a man. I cannot cross the border into their territory. All I can do is come to the boundary fence and listen, attempt to learn, and then on my side of it attempt to apply what they have taught me. Any movement to which I belong as a result will be subservient to theirs. They will continue to pose the agenda, and show the way forward.

The Challenge of Redefining Servanthood

A challenge connotes that there exists something incomplete or incorrect or misconstrued. This something, this "obstacle," must be hurdled to get on the other side, as one hurdles a fence to get into or out of a pasture. It is my feeling that *servanthood* in the biblical sense must be revived and that feminist theologians are helping to pave the way, to "make the hurdle," to a new way of service that is gender inclusive in every respect.

A number of women were able to voice their grievances and aspirations for the church in the July 1997 issue of the <u>Bulletin for Contextual Theology in Southern Africa and Africa</u>. One of them was Gloria Kehilwe Plaatjie (8), lecturer of New Testament at the University of the North. She claims that numerous women in township churches have experienced a negative and dark socialization whereby the values they are to cling to are 'natural' and ordained by God. Women see these values as the way it naturally should be instead of as contrived social constructs. Hence they find it difficult to challenge these values. Compounding this "hurdle" are sermons heard regularly in their churches that the Bible justifies these values. Women are not being empowered by sermons and theological/pastoral statements by men in leadership.

Nomathamsanqa Tisani (1989:83) is certain that the guilt for the church's spirit of oppression of women lies both with women and men for yielding to traditions contrary to the teachings of Christ. Therefore, liberated men and women in Christ must point the way to a new community and a new understanding of mutual servanthood. I would like to interject that the tendency to "yield to traditions" is exacerbated (or explained) by the fact that so many men and women were children or youth when they encountered Christianity and therewith learned almost through osmosis the gender values of 'tradition.'

What we are realizing, I think, is that men's and women's awareness of biblical 'discipleship' is skewed, thereby skewing 'servanthood' in the process. Nancy Charton (1992:4-5) advocates that both churchmen and churchwomen are required to reflect on their own servanthood. "Is the servanthood of women mere submissiveness, or is it of the transforming re-creative nature of the servanthood of Jesus?" Jesus' servanthood was a sharp and cunning one, for it never succumbed to an outright acceptance of authoritarian ecclesiastical figures, or to 'divine' laws and regulations. In some places, women and men are already joined in a task of transforming the relationship between the sexes. This covenantal manner of relating to one another approaches that which is reflected in creation (Gen. 1:26) and in re-creation as experienced by Paul (Gal. 1:13). This shared task is not merely a selfish act of emancipation but is an act of holy love for each other, penetrating the divisions and boundaries created by tradition and culture.

I therefore fully concur with Ackermann's (1984:79) acute and gritty observations:

> Christians today need to face the fact that women are not only in the church. They, like men, are the church. To argue that women are equal in creation but subordinate in function is no more defensible than the familiar 'separate but equal' dictum for the races. The basic argument for women's rights is one of justice, an argument from which the church is not exempted. Justice does not admit of exception. If something is due, it is due now. If women have rights, they have rights in the church as they do anywhere else.

Men bring their unique attributes to the Christian fore. So do women. The church needs them all. The unique contribution that African women offer feminist theologies is the prime importance of culture. African women bring naturally the totality of their being to the inner workings of theology. They bring their strong gender,

VIEWS OF WOMEN THEOLOGIANS

sometimes misinterpreted as weak and fragile, they bring their ethnic culture and their socio-economic trappings. They want the Bible to speak to their *whole being*. Women's struggle to experience a new humanity is genuine. They want their men to change. Women who are astute desire a partnership of equals with men in church and community (Lebaka-Ketshabile 1995:48-49).

Carol Francisco's (1996:118) statement from her article "Christian Women on the Red Road" stresses the harmony of opposites as the true lifeblood of the true church:

> The yoke of Christ to which the Church is called is a double one, harnessing polar opposites in creative tension: newness with tradition, immanence with transcendence, masculine with feminine, matter with spirit, light with dark, death with life.

Genuine servanthood in the church requires this kind of harmonious duality. Landman prefers to speak of the masculine-feminine duality as an exploration toward a "duality free consciousness." While recognizing that men and women bring their respective uniqueness and *imago dei* to the church, Landman advocates for women's theologies to enhance their own death. Women must steer the totality of all their efforts toward eliminating gender inequalities, which still make their feminist endeavors necessary. Three areas of women's concerns are: investigating lay participation in the churches, utilizing biblical stories in defining contemporary women's stories, and developing creative ways to present women afresh into Africa's communities and churches as full human beings (Landman 1995b:14-15).[26]

WOMEN AND LEADERSHIP

When servants of the church of each gender can relate to and serve God with total freedom, and to each other in like manner, where love and respect are preeminent, enabling the growth of the *imago dei* in each and all, then and only then will the church be the church, for then and only then will 'servanthood' be truly understood and affirmed.

The Challenge of Transforming the Church

Catherine Albertyn (1995:12) describes women in South Africa as a severely disadvantaged group enduring inequality in all spheres of life. The problem is "pervasive but it is also often hidden, complex and insidious." The emancipation of women of all races and classes is a long-term process. Social transformation is the goal. What is needed is a radical challenge in the way society is viewed and organized.

The transformation of the church cannot be effected in complete isolation from society, for the church in the community is one of the primary institutions and church members are adherents drawn from these communities. Yet if transformation toward gender equality in worship, leadership and service in the churches of 'God' and his 'Spirit' fail, what hope is there for equality in the institutions and social structures of 'man'? Feminist theologians, however, have helped us to realize that biblical hermeneutics that shape theology and church practice that is in bondage to male prejudices could be a challenge equal to or greater than what is encountered outside the church. Religious convictions, on both sides of the argument, pose a daunting challenge when God is perceived to be on one's side.

In her article "The Relevance of Feminist Theology Within the South African Context," Kretzschmar declares that the key obstacle to women's liberation is the church itself. This is true in relation to the church's structure, doctrines and practices (1991:115). I believe what Kretzschmar is saying is that the problem with the church *is* the church. It is not as if something from the outside has entered the church and if this 'thing' is identified and expelled then all is well. The very premise and presuppositions of the church in terms of its anthropology and Christology are being questioned. Not a malignant object inside but the *nature* of the church at its core is what women theologians are calling attention to; not surgical removal but *transformation* at the foundations of church history and tradition, the foundations of biblical hermeneutics and the foundations of ecclesiastical male dominance.

Wamue (1997b:61) advocates the removal of male dominance in church affairs by: a) allowing women equal enrolment and participation in theological training at all levels,[27] b) educating the church community to affirm women as human beings formed in the image of God, c) revising church or denominational constitutions that prevent women from serving in ministerial posts, d) providing more and wider responsibilities for women on church committees and councils, e) including women in all levels of decision-making and leadership, and f) establishing a pattern of Christian education that fairly analyses historical and scriptural facts that questions the tradition of male domination in the church. Transformation calls for changing "the myths that mystify church ministry."

I will conclude with the helpful article by Dorothy Ramodibe (1994:14-21) entitled "Women and Men Building Together the Church in Africa." The following quotation, though lengthy, expresses well what feminist theologians are saying about the transformation of the church:

> The theme 'Women and Men Building Together the Church in Africa' is problematic for me as an ordinary woman from Soweto, Johannesburg -- a woman who has experienced terrible oppression

WOMEN AND LEADERSHIP

from men in our society and even in the church, where I expected my salvation to come from, the church that one would have expected to be a refuge for the weak, poor, and downtrodden. We need to ask the question: Is it possible for women and men together to build the church in Africa when there is exploitation, oppression, and domination of women by men? Is working together possible when there is no equality between men and women?[28]

To me, this sounds like the same apartheid drums that I hear at home, where people (particularly P. W. Botha) call upon whites and blacks to build together the 'nation' of South Africa while apartheid remains intact. No, there can be no cooperation between whites and blacks as long as legalized inequalities exist. It cannot happen until there is equality and justice. No, there can be no cooperation between women and men as long as the oppressive and exploitative structures of the church remain intact. There can be no cooperation as long as men retain their dominant position in the church. The problem here is that the church uses the traditional understanding of the theology, or doctrine, of reconciliation, which consciously or unconsciously assumes that you can reconcile justice with injustice, righteousness with unrighteousness, good with evil. Actually they want to reconcile the devil with God. This traditional theology of reconciliation does not insist on repentance as a prerequisite for reconciliation. Those who understand reconciliation in this way will always call for peace where there is no justice. You will hear them saying, "For the sake of peace let us be reconciled" without their lifting a finger to deal with the injustices. I am going to argue that for reconciliation to be possible we must do away with evil, injustice, and sin.

There is another question that we have to ask: Which church are we building -- the historical church of the dominant classes or the church of Jesus Christ? Is it the old, oppressive church or is it the 'new,' liberating church? Are we invited to participate at the will of the dominant group in this old church, just to be accommodated, to be co-opted into the system, to collaborate in our oppression? Are we asked to soothe the consciences of men by being seen to be working side by side with men when we have no powers at all?

Behind the questions raised here, I sense a common theme: women are being asked to join men in continuing the work long begun by men. I shall argue that it is impossible to correct, develop, or improve the church, within the same old system, to accommodate women. Women want to *change* the church and not simply 'improve' it. Women want *liberation* of the church from men.[29] The theme, on the other hand, seems to suggest development rather than liberation (14-15).

Ramodibe (1994:19-20) provides us with the still relevant text of the Final Statement of the Black Theology Conference held in Cape Town in 1984:

We . . . regard it as belonging to both the nature and task of a Black Theology of Liberation to embrace in its program the question of the liberation of women and we call upon all to:

1. Embark on definite educational programs directed to both the male-dominated Church leadership who are the victimizers and the women who are the victims.

2. Transform those social and economic structures of society, which are unjust and oppressive and not simply substitute women for men in them.

3. Encourage those cultural patterns and customs whose function promotes equally the interest [and] well being of all members of the community and to eradicate those that dehumanize women or serve the interests of men at the expense of women.

WOMEN AND LEADERSHIP

4. Encourage and facilitate the meaningful involvement of women in Church life and in community and women's organizations.

5. Challenge ecclesiastical oppression against women, e.g., the reluctance or absolute unwillingness of some Churches to accept full ordination of women to the ministry of the word and sacraments.

We also express our concern about the need for more critical analysis of the cultural and economic forces that serve to reinforce the ideology of male dominance and humbly call upon feminist theologians to inform Black Theology and forge an alliance with it.

The Black Theology Conference in Cape Town obviously centered much of the debate on the issue of *justice*. The church has been unjust and sinful and the failure to change and transform simply perpetuates the old paradigm of male domination. There was a call for black theology to include feminist issues in its ongoing theological agenda for South Africa -- thus firmly positing the link between women's liberation and justice-righteousness.

VIEWS OF WOMEN THEOLOGIANS

NOTES ON CHAPTER ONE

1. Clossy Lebona's article depicts how women are as "slaves" today, in the church as well as the home and community, just as in the Egyptian domination of the Hebrew people in the Genesis account. Women seldom receive positions of authority though they perform the majority of the church's weekly tasks (1993:24).

2. Louise Kretzschmar (1991:107) agrees completely.

3. It should be noted that to many Western feminists, the suggestion that the Christian church has the will to liberate women seems highly improbable. Elizabeth Isichei (1993:209) asserts that Mary Daly is an example of one who has concluded that the Church has gone past a Christian position and is "irredeemably patriarchal."

4. It is specifically the teachings of Jesus and the Bible that we will be focused on in this study. Christina Landman (1984:1-2) does, however, remind us that feminist theology can include not only Christian forms but Jewish, Muslim and other non-Christian feminist theologies. A case in point is the experience of women in Native American spirituality, where women participate freely in the expression of deep spiritual growth denied them by the androcentric, authoritarian church. Women feel fully affirmed as women (Francisco 1996:115).

5. Musimbi Kanyoro (1996b:16) is of the opinion that the print media will continue to marginalize the voices and struggles of ordinary African women. But African rural women are creating proverbs, poetry and dirges, and they are singing songs. These women are challenging us to do theology differently. We must take their cue and make theology a communal theology.

6. This claim seems to be verified by her in another article years before (1984:22) when Landman stated: "If there is any feminist theology done in South Africa, the media, popular or academic periodicals, and I myself are ignorant of it. Though I believe its roots do exist orally, it does not have a prominent spokesperson."

WOMEN AND LEADERSHIP

7. In 1989, Dwight N. Hopkins (173) bemoans the invisibility of black women in black theology, calling this neglect a "hypocrisy" of black male theology of liberation. Musimbi Kanyoro (1996b:5-6) also is critical at this point. She argues that "the first-hand experience of African women is still largely untold." She goes on to say: "We have only started to scrape the edges as we begin to present new realities of Gospel and culture through women's eyes." And then more tellingly and poignantly: "Our African male theologians have often packed culture into one bag and used it as a way for Africans to find their feet in the theological jungle. We women have lived both the joy and hurt of culture and do not want to simply idolise culture. We want to analyse it and put it to the test in order to know what to discard and what to keep."

8. See Linda Thomas' article: "Womanist Theology, Epistemology, and A New Anthropological Paradigm" (1996:19-32).

9. Indeed, feminism nurtures creativity, openness and dynamic human relationships (Oduyoye 1986:121).

10. Anne Nasimiye-Wasike (1991:71) is convinced that African women's primary struggles are against those forces, which destroy their control over their freedom and destiny and keep them from fulfilling their God-ordained potential.

11. Remember Beverly Haddad's "theology of survival."

12. Malawian theologian Anne Nachisale Musopole advises us to remember the words of Jesus: 'The thief comes only to steal and kill and destroy; I have come that they may have life, and have it to the full.' Men who control and oppress women are like thieves raping the humanity of women (1995/1996:5).

13. Women must be liberated from self-hatred, neurotic suspicion of others, and fear (Kretzschmar 1995d:98). This self-hatred necessarily includes their bodies. Landman's (1998a:137-140) chapter on "African Women's Theology" stresses women's theologies of mind, body, womb and sexuality.

14. Lebaka-Ketshabile (1996:179) believes the traditional biblical hermeneutics have mortally harmed women's self-esteem and self-confidence. She, too, calls for

VIEWS OF WOMEN THEOLOGIANS

women to reinterpret God's Word for themselves. Caroline Tuckey (1996:163) promotes a reading of the Bible with a "hermeneutics of remembrance." What should not be overlooked or denied, she argues, are "mistakenly sinful religious understandings" and the "terrible incidents" of the historical church in faith and practice.

15. According to Mary N. Getui (1996:36), there are "hardly any" women Roman Catholic priests in Africa in the strict sense of the word. The few who received theological training experience grave difficulty achieving ordination. The few who are ordained find restrictions in fulfilling their calling and duties because of the multitude of obstacles they face as women.

16. Oppression, more than a rational reality, is something felt. It is a deeply personal experience that should not be generalised or intellectualised. Each person should deal with the pain in her own way (Mndende 1997:25). Although Mndende is an African traditionalist and not a Christian, her sentiments have relevancy for Christian women's situations.

17. But women in Africa have demonstrated their capabilities in preaching, reading of scriptures, evangelism, ecclesiastical duties, etc. All these verify women's abilities equal to men in the ministry of the church (Wamue 1997b:59).

18. In African culture, taboos, proverbs and folklore denied women public office because they portrayed women in negative and debilitating ways. See Wamue's (1997a:68f) article: "Restrictions on Women's Participation in the Ministry of the Church."

19. Ellen Kuzwayo (1985) has a chapter called "The Church and the Black Woman" (251-257). In it she lauds the Christian churches of South Africa for helping to educate girls and women through Christian schools, and for providing spiritual guidance and nurture. At the same time, she decries the fact that women were systematically refused training and/or acceptance as ordained priests or ministers.

20. In chapter three of Isabel Apawo Phiri's Ph.D. study (1992), we learn that Christianity denied women leadership positions while liberating Chewa women

from degrading cultural practices. Can this duplicity be denied?

21. See E. N. Mashao's (1989:135f) discussion of exclusionary practices of the N.G.K.A. She urges the male officials of this Church to: "Allow us to serve as elders. Allow us to train as ministers."

22. An expression of spiritual gifts was seen in a service that took place in Lenasia, an Indian community in Gauteng, at St. Thomas Roman Catholic Church, 1995, where women's leadership in the worship was prominent, in spite of the presence of the priest at the centre spot behind the altar. The use of women and the worship pattern experienced had an important symbolic effect not only on the lives of these women but on the community as well (Hird 1997:68-70).

23. The "Women in Ministry and Theologians Conference" (Kempton Park, 3-5 November 1996) brought out the reality that religious women in South Africa need to be engaged in writing a theology of *their own* as well as having *access* to such theology (Landman 1997a:13 and Landman 1997b:13, 18).

24. The "Church Women United Conference" (Johannesburg, June 1996) addressed the threefold dimensions of controlling in society, namely, controlling women's labour, their public and private lives, and their sexuality. Landman is of the opinion that white women in South Africa have been suppressed and tamed by their faith for such a long period that they are unable to agitate for change nor to initiate processes for social transformation. Black women in the country, however, have succeeded in defining and articulating the "liberative side of religion" and utilised their awareness to contribute to political freedom and social transformation (Landman 1997b:16-17, 19).

25. Marie Du Toit (1880-1931) believed that neither nature nor the Lord Jesus Christ himself restricts women to a perpetual private life. As long as women are content in their lowly positions, men will be content to keep them from public life. For women, persons and experiences are at the core women's contribution to biblical interpretation and theology. This unique contribution must go public (Landman 1994:115-116).

26. Landman projects that "a time is dawning in which researchers will be liberated

from their gender, when a man will not write only as a man and womanness will not be foremost in a woman's writing" (1996:3).

27. Seventy-two percent of all the missionaries in the world today are women (Samuel and Sugden 1998:264). I presume these women are variously trained by their respective denominations or mission agencies. Perhaps the percentage is similar at the grassroots level whereby women constitute the majority of active workers and supporters, at least in the churches of the third world.

28. The role of women in the church is not one of slavery but one of partners with God (Ramodibe 1994:18).

29. Ultimately, the task is to resurrect a new church in order to construct a new society (Ramodibe 1994:20).

CHAPTER TWO

VIEWS AND EXPERIENCES OF WOMEN AND MEN IN THE BAPTIST UNION OF SOUTH AFRICA

RE-IMAGING GOD

Growing up
in my father's house
at the missionary's feet
I saw you as a
grey-bearded white man from far beyond
a large all-seeing
all-knowing
EYE

stern and demanding
throw away your brass and stone idols they said
He is a jealous God
serve no one but He
Burn your totems and
change your name
save your soul from
heresy.
growing up

WOMEN AND LEADERSHIP

learning to read
in letters of a foreign tongue
cogitate and debate
I spelled you out in words and syntax
struggling to grasp
you in the cacophony
of my mind
and in my understanding.

I hear you now in the common silence,
wind in the trees
you call me to walk with you
on water
homeless and in-between
to name what I do not know
tread the rainbow bridge
from this world to eternity
across time and space
over the fences of tradition
see the past and future in the present
as you restore the ancient lineage

I taste you in the breaking of the bread
the wine
kneeling, my mouth at the altar
open, hungry for the word
take and eat
memory and faith
meet in palms outstretched
You touch the suffering faces of children.

suckling mother on the street

VIEWS AND EXPERIENCES IN BUSA

your body in the pain and wounds
of the woman raped
discarded to die
you cradle all in your breast
your dark wounded side
in depths of love
dark and fathomless

growing up
a new childhood begins
I listen for your heart
hidden
questing
in the places long shadowed
meet you again in roads untrammeled
the spirit criss-crossing where it will
I enter the awesome tabernacle
and wait to perfume your aching feet

(Betty Govinden 1997:148-150)

INTRODUCTORY REMARKS

The aim of this chapter is to describe the views and experiences of women (and a few men) of the Baptist Union of South Africa in regard to church leadership. Both theological and ecclesiastical categories have been selected which deal with these views and experiences. They are:

1. Current church practices regarding women

2. Perceptions of male attitudes toward women

3. Natural abilities of women

4. Views on women as pastors

I have sought to allow the respondents to tell their stories without any blatant bias or tainting on my part. That is, I have not sought to tell their stories for them but have sought to allow the respondents freedom to articulate their attitudes and experiences.

TECHNIQUE

The techniques employed were the *half-structured questionnaire* and the *moderately structured interview*. The questionnaire necessarily includes structured questions or inquiries. Yet for each question, the respondent was given the opportunity to "comment" on the "yes," "no," or "I don't know" response. This approach allowed for elasticity in the structured question. Individuals were able to remark in any way they chose if they felt the question was too narrow, unfair, biased or misleading. Many respondents added comments to their objective responses, bringing a degree of subjectivity to the questionnaire.

Ackermann (1985:133) states that the interview allows for assessing nonverbal behavior, encourages spontaneity, and provides opportunity for greater complexity. On the other hand, disadvantages can be less anonymity, less standardized wording to questions and bias of the interviewer can cause error in the data.

The moderately structured interviews allow for both structured questions as well as unstructured spontaneous follow-up questions. Hence the interviewer becomes a participant observer in the drama of dialogue. While recognizing that asking errors or recording errors are ever present, the interviewer understands that that which is to be gained is greater than the risks, i.e., the stress on values, goals and desires, the stress on social perception, and the stress on attitude. These subjective data is often a critical advantage over the objective-based questionnaire (Ackermann 1985:134-135). In addition, the subjective approach provides avenues to discover feelings and emotion less available otherwise.

In conclusion, both the half-structured questionnaire, as well as the moderately structured interview, incorporate the theological and ecclesiastical categories outlined in the introductory remarks.

METHODOLOGY

My investigation procedures employ both quantitative and qualitative dimensions. As stated in the description of technique, the questionnaire is based on set questions with the option for respondents to add comments if desired. The interviews are structured in the sense that pre-formulated discussion topics revolve around the theological and ecclesiastical categories referred to in the introductory remarks. They are, however, moderately structured in the sense that I sought to allow for spontaneity and flow, thereby permitting extensive elaboration or tangents into other areas of interests and concerns on the part of either the respondent or the interviewer.

Hence, the methodological procedures, while both quantitative and qualitative, paid particular attention to qualitative and phenomenological tendencies that reflect the respondents' attitudes, feelings, perceptions, beliefs, experiences and stories that mirror meaning and significance in their lives. Particularly in the interviews, the narrative approach is heavily utilized. Women who had specific experiences or stories to tell were encouraged to do so. The descriptive analysis section later in this chapter reflects ample narration.

SAMPLING

This chapter uses a diverse sampling involving women predominately and men only as a way of mild comparison. Women were asked to complete questionnaires or to respond in dialogue fashion in an interview. Some women chosen for questionnaires or interviews were selected at random, while others were selected because of leadership positions held. The majority were women and men not previously known to the researcher.

Multidimensional sampling was sought, whereby respondents from various Baptist churches in South Africa and from various ethnic backgrounds were engaged. It has been seen in chapter one that the Baptist Union's history and leadership have been white dominated, reflecting a Eurocentric theology and ecclesiology. I have therefore made it a priority to investigate white women's views and experiences. However, I have made it a point to also investigate

VIEWS AND EXPERIENCES IN BUSA

African and Asian (Indian) women and men and have done so in both the questionnaires and the interviews, giving more priority to African women than to Asian simply because of their larger numbers in the BU.

The size of the sample in this chapter is confined and deemed to be sufficient for the purposes of this study.

QUESTIONNAIRES, INTERVIEWS AND THE RESPONDENTS

The majority of respondents to questionnaires and interviews were contacted in person as the researcher visited churches and traveled throughout South Africa. Only a few were contacted by telephone. The nature of the research was explained and voluntary participation was solicited. On occasion, interviews were made on the same day of contact. In the majority of cases, an appointment was made, and the venue was normally in homes or churches. The questionnaires were frequently left in the hands of those who expressed interest, occasionally mailed by post. In the case of the questionnaires, individuals were encouraged to freely make comments after the more objective portions of the five page document. A number of questionnaires were never returned.

WOMEN AND LEADERSHIP

The Interviews

The interviews averaged between forty-five minutes to one hour and forty-five minutes. A total of ten were interviewed, nine women and one man. The man was an African aged over 60 from Zwelitsha in the Eastern Cape. The women were Asian and white. Two Indian women, one from Johannesburg and one from Stanger, were interviewed. Seven were white women from Johannesburg. The women's ages ranged this way: 20s, 21, 27, 50, 50, 50s, 50s, 52, 52. The interviews took place between May 1997 and November 1998.

In some cases a tape recorder was used. The major advantages were twofold: a) more eye to eye contact and awareness of body language and other non-verbal nuances, and b) a more accurate and complete recording of what was actually stated in the interview. The major disadvantage was the time-consuming nature of transcription.

The man interviewed was the pastor at P. S. Memorial Baptist Church in Zwelitsha (Eastern Cape).

The women interviewed were:

The secretary of the Baptist Women's Department of Brackensdown Baptist Church (Johannesburg)

The pastor of Baptist Faith Center in Stanger for eleven years and former deaconess of the church and president of the Baptist Mission Women's Department (Kwa-Zulu Natal)

VIEWS AND EXPERIENCES IN BUSA

Teacher of teenage Bible study group, editor of youth newsletter, Honeyridge Baptist Church (Johannesburg)

Lay preacher, Roosevelt Park Baptist Church (Johannesburg)

"Ministry Assistant" at Grace Baptist Church (Johannesburg)

President of the BWD of the Baptist Union and member of Glenvista Baptist Church (Johannesburg)

Pastor of Berea Baptist Church and interim Missions Director of the Transvaal Baptist Association (Johannesburg)

Director of Women's Ministries, Randburg Baptist Church (Johannesburg)

Sunday School teacher at Robertsham Free Baptist Church (Johannesburg)

All except one of the women were married. The one exception is a widow.

The Questionnaires

Eleven questionnaires (out of forty-nine) were returned from nine women and two men. The two male respondents were from so-called colored churches in the Cape (Pniel and Blackheath). Of the nine women, four were black and five white. The four black women were from Empangeni, Bisho and Ladyfrere. The five white women were from Johannesburg and Port Alfred. The two men were aged 52 and 57. The nine women were aged 26, 27, 34, 36, 42, 45, 45, 50s, 54. The questionnaires were dated from May 1997 to December 1998.

Their leadership roles and church affiliation are described below:

Pastor's wife, worship team leader, BWD president, Port Alfred Baptist Church (Eastern Cape)

Director of Women's Ministries, Randburg Baptist Church (Johannesburg)

Lay preacher, Roosevelt Park Baptist Church (Johannesburg)

Teacher of teenage Bible study groups, editor of youth newsletter, Honeyridge Baptist Church (Johannesburg)

"Ministry Assistant," Grace Baptist Church (Johannesburg)

Member of Ladyfrere Baptist Church (Eastern Cape)

Deacon, youth leader, Ngwelezane Baptist Church (Empangeni, Kwa-Zulu Natal)

Member of Bisho Baptist Church (Eastern Cape)

Women's leader, Ngwelezane Baptist Church (Empangeni, Kwa-Zulu Natal)

Elder, Blackheath Baptist Church (Western Cape)

VIEWS AND EXPERIENCES IN BUSA

Pastor, Pniel Baptist Church (Western Cape)

All the respondents to the questionnaires were married.

A DESCRIPTIVE ANALYSIS

As explained earlier, the questionnaire and interviews were created to address the following theological and ecclesiastical categories: current church practices regarding women, perception of male attitudes toward women, natural abilities of women and views on women as pastors.

Some of the questionnaires were replete with comments. Others were completed with no subjective remarks at all. Some interviews were lengthy and inundated with extensive and provocative stories and information. Others were less so. These variations no doubt reflect the interests, passions, experiences, or the lack of them, of the various respondents. The uneven data should not be construed, however, to convey a shortage of authenticity or integrity of significance.

The respondents in both questionnaires and interviews were encouraged to share their *experiences* and *attitudes* freely, from the perspective of women (and men) in their respective Baptist churches and their own participation in the history and religious ethos of the Baptist Union of South Africa.

WOMEN AND LEADERSHIP

Current church practices regarding women

The questionnaires and interviews here seek to discover the impressions Baptist church women and men have regarding the leadership involvement of women in the Baptist churches. What roles do women play in the church? How significant are women in the life of the church? Are women suppressed or subjugated to marginal roles in the church?

From the questionnaires we find that six women and one man reported women serving as deacons in their churches. Two of the six women were from white churches, four from black churches. The man who reported having a woman deacon (or deacons) is from a so-called colored church. The survey did not include the number of deacons in each church or the ratio of women deacons to men. One respondent said, "But they've just started this year." Her use of the word "they've" may convey a lack of ownership (hers, women's) in the decision-making processes of the church. One white woman said, "A balance of gender in the diaconate is important because viewpoints and approaches of male and female differ." One Indian woman from a racially mixed church, though predominately white with a white pastor, said, "My pastor is very open for women to serve in anything." Another woman interviewed stated that when she was a member of Rosebank Union Church she "was given plenty of opportunities for leadership. I was included with mostly men. I felt included and I felt welcomed. I feel the senior pastor was responsible for this. I was included to serve communion, etc." But she confided that at Honeyridge she feels "pushed to the side...preaching or teaching is something I cannot do...teaching is my gift but I cannot teach."[1] Another woman confessed to hurt, anger, embarrassment at male-controlled church restrictions on women. Yet she expressed determination to struggle along for inclusion in church leadership. She con-

VIEWS AND EXPERIENCES IN BUSA

tinued, "A woman can go to the mission field and do all those things, but as soon as she comes back home to the local church, she has to sit down and be suppressed." This same woman said, "In the Assembly of God church, I was overlooked as being a deacon of the church. I think if a woman is organized, she is perceived as being a threat."

There is evidence from these comments that some women feel or have felt more freedom in churches with a more tolerant pastor or church leadership, whereas others feel severely restricted and stifled in their desire to serve in their churches. We note that a competent woman leader can be seen as a threat to men. Anger, hurt and embarrassment have been expressed. We note, however, resiliency and determination on the part of one woman to persevere and press for her divine rights.

An interview with a woman revealed male prejudices in the diaconate:

> As a woman in the pew, as just a church member, there was never a time when I was denied an opportunity to serve as a teacher, etc. I was never approached to be a deacon. In this church, it was believed a woman could not be a deacon. Everything else, but not a deacon.
>
> Once we went into full-time ministry in a Durban church, my husband was all for women in leadership. I served on a management committee. We didn't have enough men to serve as deacons. Two older men deacons were absolutely against women serving as deacons. So my husband changed the name to a 'management committee.' These two men were happy with that. They felt that according to the Scriptures women could not be 'deacon.' But otherwise the 'management committee' was exactly

like the deacon committee. This attitude of these men did bother me. At the end of the day when women came on the 'management committee' they were performing all the duties of the deacon and doing it well. The contradiction really bothered me. I had to respect the attitudes of these elderly (70s, 80s) men but I disagreed. I quite frankly couldn't understand where they were coming from. A large percentage of members of this body were women. Yet women could not be fully liberated, even the very capable women leaders. We women on the 'management committee' were able to do our duties as well as men.

Clearly, this respondent felt great dismay ("the contradiction really bothered me") at the attitudes of the elderly deacons. When she said, "I had to respect the attitudes of these elderly men but I disagreed," what did she mean by saying she "had to"? Does it not convey powerlessness on the part of the women?

Also revealing were her further comments:

On another occasion I was called to serve, as a women's representative, on an executive committee of the Natal Baptist Association. There were only two women and twelve men on the NBA E.C. I felt very unwelcome. I didn't seem to fit in an all-male committee. I felt vibrations from one or two of intimidation. The other woman on the committee was very strong and dynamic and very quick to air her views on issues and place of woman in ministry. She came across as a 'woman's libber,' which I'm not, very abrasive, and caused a stir among the men. So I had to express where I'm coming from, that God is able to use us women in ministry if God has called us. The moment I said that, the men's attitude toward me changed. I was told later that men do not like aggressive women. Men saw me as a threat, like the other woman, but when they saw me with a different spirit than this other woman, I was given more respect. This woman came on with a 'superior than thou' attitude toward men. I want to remain a woman, not a man, but free to serve the Lord. I had a wonderful rapport with the men on this committee. They respected me for the three years on this committee. I felt good about my participation as an equal. Only two had a problem with me. The majority had no problem with me as a person.[2]

Diplomacy as a tactic was used to gain the support of the male majority. While behaving not as "aggressively" as the other woman on the committee, the respondent nevertheless had to diplomatically and firmly state that God "uses" women in ministry and God likewise "calls" women to ministry. The men seemed to respond to her pronouncement and she gained respect. She appeared not to cower to male dominance, which would have been the other extreme.

In another interview, a woman expressed her utter joy as a teacher of a women's bible study, "this is my gift, this keeps me alive!" Yet she demonstrates ambivalence toward her place in the ministry of the church:

I think what opportunities I as a woman can do or is given is according to what my husband permits. I have perfect freedom because of an understanding husband. This is very important to me. In other churches, I've never felt put down. I've always taught Sunday School since I was sixteen. I've been involved in worship committees, choir, etc.[3] I have been approached to be an elder, but I battle with this issue of women in that position. My husband is an elder. I am not sure that it is appropriate for me as a woman, as well as my spouse being an elder. I have found such acceptance by the church these four years in my role that, if I were asked again, I may just accept the offer to serve as an elder. I am looked upon as a person that cannot be easily marginalized.

WOMEN AND LEADERSHIP

She is obviously a highly motivated woman who "cannot be easily marginalized." However, the fact that she is "not sure that it is appropriate for me as a woman" to serve as an elder portrays a theological uncertainty that is extremely disconcerting to her. She has been approached to serve as one, we are told, but her theological conscience creates in her guilt and doubt. I wonder if the respondent will ever fulfill her leadership desires? We are reminded by Landman (1998b:368) that the Boer missionary Erasmus Smit's wife, Susanna Smit (1799-1863), once remarked that some Afrikaner women were ambitious to fill roles in politics and society, but because women in Afrikaner society were marginalized by both men and women they never fulfilled their leadership desires. It would appear that to varying degrees in contemporary South Africa the legacy of marginalization persists.

The respondent continued:

> We have two women on our diaconate. The elders are two males. Three years ago a woman preached in the morning and evening services. It was the only time in nine years I've seen a woman preach. I do believe that women should do whatever God has gifted them for. I feel that this church is changing.

One wonders how much *she* is changing from her position of theological ambivalence!

Another young woman believes that women are subservient in the church because of an entrenched mindset:

> Scripture is misrepresented to serve male dominance point of view. I feel the pastor should bring this problem to the attention of the church. It must be discussed. As a body of believers we are uni-

fied. We are weaker if parts of the body are kept from full freedom to serve God.

The charge of Scriptural misrepresentation is a serious one, serious enough to bring this problem before the church for discussion!

One man who stated his church has no women deacons said, though, that, "at the moment, we are talking about it with the deaconship." We see here once again, to what degree men carry the role of decision-makers in the church. He believes the church would not die if all the women members left. His church has fifty men and about two hundred and seventy-five women.

If it is true that women outnumber men in the Baptist churches, as in the above statement where women outnumber the men by two hundred and seventy-five to fifty, if it is true that many churches do not permit women deacons or elders, if it is true that if a few women are permitted to high offices their numbers are more symbolic than they are representative of their gifts, abilities, calling, and desire, and if it is true that their numbers are far fewer than men leadership in high church offices, then there is definitely a longer struggle ahead for a liberating praxis for women in the Baptist Union churches, white, black, Asian or colored.

Perceptions of male attitudes toward women

The questionnaires and interviews here seek to discover the perceptions Baptist church women and men have regarding male attitudes toward women in church leadership. Are men changing their

WOMEN AND LEADERSHIP

views on women and their potential for leadership in the church? Is it mostly men's attitude and image of women that must be changed in order to liberate women into church leadership at all levels?

The questionnaires showed that by two to one, more white women than black women seem to perceive young men today changing their attitudes toward women by thinking more highly of them and their potential for church leadership. The two male respondents were split on this issue. A few questionnaire comments were: "Both young and old seem to recognize gifts of leadership in women," "Men don't trust women's faith," "Men are not quite confident of women doing everything in the church," and "It all depends on society, especially now in our country in the last couple of years."

Without specifying age (young men or old), the respondents seem to convey a lack of confidence in women's abilities and the ability of the male-dominated church to change unless society at large changes first. This is a dim view of the church.

On the issue of old or older men viewing women more highly and capable of church leadership, the questionnaires revealed that both white and black women held the older men in suspect more than they affirmed their positive views on women's leadership. The two male respondents were again split on this one. Some comments were: while younger men view women more highly in terms of abilities in leadership, "today there seems to be more willingness of older men to allow women greater privileges than twenty years ago," "Especially the older men involved in church matters" are regarding women more highly and "those on the sidelines are the most resistant," "Older men will say, 'a woman knows her place,'"[4] older men are "more conservative," "It is not clear, but we want the youth to follow what we women are doing," and "Old men are realizing now

VIEWS AND EXPERIENCES IN BUSA

the importance of the women."

All the women and all the men respondents in the questionnaires and interviews perceived youth today as being more willing to give women a higher regard for their abilities in church leadership. Their further comments were: "Youth today accept equality but this too is not always a good thing as for some of them the respect of our differences has been lost," "A generation ago women were not as encouraged to leadership as they are today," "Youth plan now and do," "Young men and females appreciate women doing work as compared to men," "Youth have a higher view," "but in my church youth keep back from influence and assertiveness."

On the issue of whether it is mostly men's attitude and image of women that must be changed in order to liberate women for church leadership, the questionnaires revealed that, three black women and the two men (from colored churches) said, "yes." Those who answered "no" were four white women. One white and one black woman said, "I don't know." Those who said "no" remarked: "I still believe that according to biblical principles the man is the head of the woman. If this principle is dealt with in the correct manner, with love and respect, there is no problem," "I think it is both men's and women's attitudes toward women that needs changing," "no, it is women as well; the older women are as much a problem as men," and "women are often the most resistant when another woman breaks a traditional role." Those who said "I don't know" remarked: "This is not clear to me," and "I almost think that women's attitude is a ma-jor detriment."[5]

More research and data are needed to determine if, in the black churches, the general perception is that males are the primary

WOMEN AND LEADERSHIP

agents of black women's suppression of roles,[6] and in the white churches the general perception is that women are the primary perpetrators of the suppression of women in leadership roles in the church.

The interviews revealed hurt and anger. I made a concerted effort in the interviews to decipher how women were feeling about their stories of marginalization in the church. One said:

> Scripture is biased. It's biased by its culture. I felt very hurt, angry, when it comes to the role of the women in the church. If she is denied teaching or certain authority roles, this angers me. At the BU theological college, the guys are seeing that I can preach. We must have a fresh understanding of what Paul was actually saying.

The wife of a pastor expressed frustration at the unresolved tension and confusion over women's place in church ministry both at the local church level and the denomination at large:

> As far as my husband is concerned, he supports me and all other women in church leadership -- deacons, etc. The rest of our leadership is not quite as supportive. They are a bit wary of women coming in as leaders, especially women as deacons. This is a historic problem because of past problems. People in the congregation are divided. Some men and women would not have problems. Some men and women would have major problems with women in leadership, mainly in the deaconship. As president of the Baptist Women's Department of the BU, in my travels to our churches around the country, I can easily sense animosity from some men who are obviously anti-women in prominent leadership positions.

VIEWS AND EXPERIENCES IN BUSA

Another woman confessed:

> Our church has not given attention to women serving in any leadership position in the church. Elders in our church are males only. In our missions department, there are two women. Men are supportive of women in missions. The issue of women to be free in leadership in the church has never been raised to consciousness.

While we have noticed that some churches are at least wrestling with the role of women in church leadership, this church seems to carry on either unaware or unconcerned with spiritual trauma in women's lives.

Hurt and sadness at male attitudes toward women is revealed in this testimony:

> I cannot teach at Honeyridge. One of our male theological students who is a member is given opportunities to preach. As a member, and as a theological student as well, I am not allowed by the male leadership to preach. I would feel a lot more angry than I do if I was not affirmed at home. My husband and parents affirm my abilities and my personhood. This is a great encouragement. I feel frustration and sadness at the shortsightedness of the people regarding the issue.

The above respondent, whose husband is a theological student, shared the following story, which again reflects male negative attitudes toward women's leadership potential or role in the church:

> When a male friend and I both applied to come to college, the amount of money given to him was a lot more than what was of-

fered me. I don't know if it was because my husband was already given a bursary by the church. I felt hurt that I was treated as a wife of a student and not a student in my own right. I think when I am asked by the college to preach in a local church, my church Honeyridge will victimize me again.

The interviews help us to see how resistant churches seem to be to allow women equality in exercising their gifts in the body of Christ. In addition, we have seen that the perception of many women is that younger men regard women's abilities and role in the church to be more positive and that old or older men are perceived to be less positive and more resistant to the empowerment of women. We have also seen that, especially among white women in white churches, the perception is that women's negative attitude and image of other women impede a liberating praxis of women's leadership in the church as much as or more than men's negative attitudes. Anger, hurt and deep dismay have been uncovered as women have shared their experiences of subjugation and marginalization, yet the strength of women's resolve is clear, a resolve to continue to press toward full realization of their personhood in the community of faith, the church.

Natural abilities of women

The questionnaires and interviews seek to discover how Baptist church women and men view the natural abilities of women and how these abilities or lack of them may affect women's leadership capacities in the church. A few of the areas investigated are: women's abilities in preaching and teaching, women's hermeneutical uniqueness, women's courage, intelligence, commitment and other personal qualities, spiritual strength and leadership abilities, and perceived female strengths and weaknesses as they may relate to leadership in the church.

In all of these areas of inquiry mentioned above, from both the questionnaires and the interviews, I found overwhelming similarity in responses from the white, black, and Asian women, from the two colored men and the one black man.

Three white women reported that their church allowed women to preach only to women and children. No non-white respondent claimed this restriction. A comment was: "Women would be allowed to give a talk or testimony to the whole church body, but if it were to preach there would be opposition." An Indian woman testified, "I have seen women subjugated in other churches, but not in the two churches I've been members of." There clearly exists a range of behaviors and "policies," a confusing cloud of theologies.

Another comment from a woman ministerial candidate reflects the marginal and prescribed role for women in her church:

> Preaching, communion, worship leading -- my pastor would not allow me to lead in, but other pastoral roles he would allow me to do, but not with recognition as a 'pastoral candidate.' A woman cannot be an elder. Elders can be elected. Our 'called elders' are our pastoral staff. Elders fill spiritual roles. Deacons fill practical roles.

Women were overwhelmingly found to be able to teach both men and women in the congregation. Only one white woman and one black woman said this was not allowed in their church. Some comments were: "Because both men and women are children of God," "They look down upon the integrity of women and they feel embarrassed to be taught by women; they regard women as minors and culturally that is not done," "Women teach Sunday School only to younger ones, i.e. boys and girls, not adults," and "Teaching is not a problem but when it comes to preaching, the church looks to a man; Biblically I believe this is correct" (so said a woman). Teaching men in the audience is problematical with two churches as seen above. Preaching a sermon appears to be an even more severe obstacle, especially if women too have their own doubts about its theological validity as expressed by one woman.

A white woman and ministerial candidate offered this observation on the natural abilities of women:

> Women are still in a more subservient way with regards to preaching, eldership, otherwise there is a partial equality because women may go on visitation, may be a worship leader, teach Sunday School, be a superintendent of the Sunday School. When it comes to ministry, especially my pastor, he doesn't see women as equal. He may tell stories in front of groups, but women are not on equal ground as men in the ministry. Women can give spiritual songs, give prophecy or give encouragement, but that is as far as it goes. Members in my church are very open to women in ministry. They are very interested in me in ministry. This interest is primarily from women. In representing the church in conferences, women and men are equally offered opportunities for participation.

It is obvious that a woman's personhood and image of God is being questioned by the pastor who relegates women to subservient roles only. The respondent above is descriptive of women's natural and God-given talents. She describes all the skills a pastor, deacon or elder must possess as spiritual leaders of the church. She states that women especially in her church are very supportive of her ability to function "in ministry."

Inquiry into the importance of the woman's point of view in interpreting the Scriptures revealed interesting results. All respondents affirmed the importance of women's hermeneutical uniqueness. What was revealed was not that all women interpret Scripture identically, but that women bring certain perspectives and qualities addressing women's concerns and sensitivities. A comment was: "Women often see things differently to men[7] and are more compassionate." A black woman remarked, "But some women undermine themselves and become afraid and fear criticisms." One man responded with, "God reveals to anyone when he wants, who he wants." This latter statement seems to imply that women too can receive inspiration from God to interpret and proclaim the Bible with the freedom of their unique humanity. The "compassionate" aspect is stressed by one respondent as generally more effusive with women.

The respondent who observed that some women "undermine themselves" and "fear criticisms" should be heard. What did she mean or imply? Is she alluding to some women who enter formerly male leadership domains with insecurity, thereby attempting to emulate male leadership styles for "fear" of being perceived as *unfit* for the job? Hence, in denying female attributes and strengths do women "undermine themselves"?

A white theological student, an older woman with adult children, espoused the unlimited breadth of the Holy Spirit in inspiring and transforming women as well as men:

One has to decipher who the Holy Spirit will convict, male or female. Who can restrict the Holy Spirit? What makes a woman drawn to spiritual things with such integrity? It's possible that if you're a mother, you give birth, you're involved with life from the very beginning. My husband is very supportive of me and my ministry. If I preach, he will give me a male perspective and critique. He allows me to fulfill my call. It feels good to have such an understanding husband who is secure in himself and in his relationship to the Lord.

WOMEN AND LEADERSHIP

What is striking in the above testimony is the acknowledgement that, when this woman preaches, she receives, perhaps even cherishes, her husband's evaluation ("If I preach, he will give me a male perspective and critique"), indicating her assumption that as a woman she will come across, potentially, differently from a male preacher both in theological/hermeneutical content and in gender characteristics, qualities, insights, experiences and sensitivities.

A white woman theological graduate, serving as a "Ministry Assistant" in a Baptist church (she cannot be called a *pastoral* assistant), offers this extended comment on the woman's point of view, which contains definite implications for the way women may engage in biblical hermeneutics:

> I think male and female is distinctive and created differently. And so in the ideal situation we can correct or supplement each other's perspective or weaknesses. I often like to think that if companies had both feminine and male input into decisions they would have healthier working relationships within the company right down to grass roots. Women often see or have the human side at heart. Maybe it's the mothering aspect. By being women you would see women's issues, so in a work situation a woman would logically think about things like children and you would have things like a create at work and thereby make healthy family relationships. Men making decisions on the structure of the company would never think of it. In the church, a woman's perspective on the world is different from a man's and she would complement, supplement, enhance -- she doesn't have a superior perspective but she doesn't have an inferior position either. It will make for a healthier religious community. Women would raise questions men would not think of. This can avoid silly mistakes that are made, and sometimes arrogant mistakes that are made. Spiritually speaking, minis-

try into people's lives is an area that women can play a role. I see that in my pastor's life. He allows himself input from his wife and from other women. This affected his preaching, the way he spoke about things because he suddenly understood the woman's perspective and was therefore able to speak to his whole congregation. A man who never takes the time to do that will never touch aspects of half his congregation, which is the same if the church becomes racially inclusive. The pastor will then realize he needs to start listening to those people belonging to these groups coming in so that he can start meeting their unique needs as people.

From the above discourse we can surmise that, apart from women's unique perspectives in interpreting Scripture, they bring their ways of applying the Scripture to their context and world view, for they are products of their context and experiences, their female lenses, their *imago Dei*, their humanity, their intuitions and unique sense of relational awareness.

A mature white woman pastor of a predominately black church in Berea (members are from other African nations) speaks about how she copes as a pastor providing spiritual counseling to men that of course necessitates personal spiritual insights and hermeneutical skills:

I offer men friendship. I'm good at keeping confidences. They can say things to me that they can't say to their male counterparts. I feel very relaxed and at home amongst men. I grew up with men in the home. That gives me the edge now. Women see things differently from men, and present things differently. Men perceive this as weak, but it's not, it's just a different but legitimate way of viewing things or explaining things. Men are often perplexed at my explanations. But once they understand they are accepting of it.

WOMEN AND LEADERSHIP

While the remarks above were not given in the context of preaching or hermeneutics, their relevancy to preaching or hermeneutical exercises are unmistakable. She says, "I offer my friendship to men," can only be taken to mean that, as a woman in her 50s, she offers her womanly/motherly advice and friendship. When she says, "Women see things differently from men," she is not in denial of her humanness as a woman but affirms her womanhood and in so doing makes her unique contribution as a servant of God. She acknowledges that her views are "legitimate ways of viewing things or explaining things," confirming that she can and will think as a woman and express herself as a woman, and that her message has pertinence to women and men. To deny her divine right and divine talent in spiritual/hermeneutical perceptions and expressions of divine truth is tantamount to a denial of her credibility as a human being.

An Indian woman testified about the loving and joyful nurture she received in a Christian home. I bring this to light here to demonstrate how the humanity and warmth of this woman can be potentially and easily transferable to the Christian ministry and the gospel proclamation:

> I was born and grew up in a Christian home. There was lots of love. I had lots of joy as a Christian. I needed to accept Jesus in my heart. I did that at twelve years of age. And since then I've walked with the Lord.[8] I've taught Sunday School on the North Coast of Durban. I learned that a Godly woman had to be respected in the Lord.

Notice the words *love* and *joy* and the stress on *relationships* to Christ and others. More will be said in a later chapter about women's unique qualities and the need for these qualities to find expression in the leadership of today's churches. Suffice it to say here that in my view the above qualities are urgently and desperately needed in today's churches, whether they are promulgated by women or men.

On the issue of women's courage, intelligence, public speaking, commitment, spiritual strength, motivation, compassion, energy and other natural abilities, the overwhelming majority responded that women are not inferior to men in these ways. Even the men thought so! Only one black woman felt that women were inferior to men in the above-mentioned ways.

A black woman said, "The culture of white women is such that women inherited to be inferior and eventually they lost their integrity and accepted fear for man in the place of respect."[9] Another black woman stated, "Women are strong in times of hardship." White women contributed the following: "God gifts according to his wisdom," "The only difference is physical strength," "Women are most decidedly as courageous as men in times of trial, stress or danger," "Courage is a personality strength," "Women are possibly more courageous than men," "Women are definitely not inferior to men in intelligence and in every other way; a lot of women have allowed it -- stereotypes have never been questioned," and "Faith in God plays a major role in courage. Women who have faith in God are just as courageous as men who have faith in God. God has given each of us abilities, not according to our sex." One man said that only some women are as courageous as men. Another man said women are "more courageous" than men. Another man observed, "Women are brave to water the fire when there is a dispute; they just don't go." As to intelligence, public speaking, commitment, spiritual strength, motivation, compassion, energy and other natural abilities this same man simply stated, "In most of these, women are superior."

WOMEN AND LEADERSHIP

In summary, as for natural abilities of women the men and women respondents are of one mind -- women are as gifted and able, if not more so, than men.

Finally, on the issue of whether women bring strengths or weaknesses to the life and ministry of the church as they exercise leadership in the church the vast majority of women and men were in harmony, stating that women do bring female strengths into church leadership. Here are a few remarks: "The women who serve at the church I work at often serve with greater humility and endurance to the men," "Women are more emotional. I see this as a strength because our walk with Christ involves the emotions triggered by love. Men are more analytical." By these remarks we see that women and men view women as possessing more "humility," more "endurance," more "emotion" (seen as a strength) and rooted in (more?) "love."

On the topic of weaknesses, three white women believed that women brought weaknesses to church leadership. Two of them explained: "My weakness would be in my emotions, not in my thinking," and "But anybody who is in leadership brings weaknesses." All the other women and men, except for one man who checked "I don't know," stated women brought no weaknesses to church leadership not also inherent in men. One man responded, "You must see the strengths of a person, man or woman; it would help not to stress weaknesses." Another added, "If God has called somebody, he will equip her," implying that God equips women equally as men to the leadership tasks of the church. Women, therefore, do not bring an inferior vessel to church leadership.

My investigation did not go deep enough to understand why three white women from white churches believed that women brought inherent weaknesses to the life and ministry of the church and no black women from black churches felt so inclined to say so. One woman perceived showing "emotions" as a weakness, perhaps revealing the worldview of the white culture. Do white women feel more insecurity and inferiority in the white churches of South Africa?

We can conclude this section by stating categorically that the natural abilities of women, the abilities they bring to the church, are viewed by the clear majority of respondents as not in any way falling short of the natural abilities that men bring to the affairs and leadership of the church.

Views on women as pastors

The questionnaires and interviews in this final section seek to discover views on women as pastors. Since preaching the sermon on Sunday is a major responsibility for pastors, are women being given opportunities to preach in worship services in Baptist churches? Are women capable to be pastors? Are women capable of providing spiritual counseling to men? Are women in the churches against women becoming pastors?

I have found that while women are given opportunities to preach in church on Sunday, these opportunities are few. Two white women and three black women stated that women do on occasion preach, but only on special occasions, and therefore very infrequently. The two men who completed the questionnaire said that women do preach in their churches, again only in special services. Three white women and two black women said that women are never allowed to preach in church on Sunday morning. One white woman who marked "no" to women given opportunity to preach in her church remarked, "We have never been faced with this issue, but I do think we would have opposition." A male respondent who marked "yes" commented, "At women's rally or special event." Others observed that it is very infrequent that women are given opportunities to preach. It is obvious that the complete negation of women to preach in some churches and the infrequency in other churches reflect negative attitudes towards women's abilities and/or theological justification for such practices.

In an interview, one outspoken woman respondent voiced her experiences with preaching this way:

> I see a growing possibility in the BU. There are actually some people who are very excited by that. Pastors have expressed that to me. Even in my own church, I'm not a deacon, I can't be a deacon because of the constitution, but I'm allowed to preach. That's the wonderful irony where I'm involved. Officially I have no kind of standing at all but practically they have denied me nothing, nothing where my gifts are concerned, where my education is concerned. It is primarily because of the motivation of my own pastor and his commitment to me in my ministry. I see that opening up quite a bit. As there are more and more women in Baptist ministry, acceptance of women's leadership should come. My church, which is extremely conservative, was stuck with a female theological student and had to do something with her. And they rose beautifully to the challenge and they allowed me to do so much even though officially so much was blocked towards me. Even for six months for my education I was allowed to be an observant in deacons meetings. The deacons warmly embraced me and allowed me to participate in the meetings and to be involved fully in those meetings. It meant much for my practical education. So I do think if women are there and stick at it without fighting all the little battles about

when the preacher says 'man' all the time and 'gentleman' all the time, but allowing the attitudes to slowly change. Then it won't be such a big jump for that ordination or that counselor.

Pastoral leadership in this church, as in all churches, appears to be critical in order for women to begin to exercise spiritual gifts within the church. It is not that the authority of the pastor cannot be questioned or opposed by the elders, deacons or church at large. But it does mean that as one who has been given primary leadership responsibility due to his theological and ecclesiastical training, the pastor plays a major role in shaping and even transforming attitudes toward women in leadership. It is noteworthy to observe, additionally, that the respondent above is optimistic about the future of women in leadership, even the pastoral ministry, if women are patient, resilient and diplomatic.

On the question of women's capability equal to men in pastoral leadership, five white women, three black women and the two male respondents said "yes." One black woman said "no." Her only remark was a vague, "Sometimes the way of thinking." Attitudes towards women as being as capable as men to be a pastor of a Baptist church is strikingly more optimistic than the actual practice in the churches where women pastors are largely non-existent and their opportunities to preach extremely limited. Comments were: "But the snag is when they become pregnant they fail to prepare themselves for pastoral work," "They can prepare sermons and do the work, but will the congregation see them as being capable?" "Remembering that a woman by nature will be a different kind of pastor, and for this there is as yet no allowance in the BU," and "I believe they are as capable but I don't think that God intended women to be the head of his church." These responses generally reveal positive views yet caution

WOMEN AND LEADERSHIP

and reservation due to practical concerns infringing upon the areas of sexuality (pregnancy), history and tradition, and theological stereotype.

An African male interview respondent (a pastor) observed:

> To me women in the church are a great help. More than the men. In their work, when they say 'we will do this,' they do it with wholeheartedness. Women, if they say 'we are doing this in the church,' they don't stop. They want to go through with it and finish it. If they say 'we are going to do evangelism in this village,' they do it. And I believe they should be given a wide range where they can play their role in the church. If the Baptists can allow a woman to be placed in a ministerial position, to oversee a circuit, and be given full power as a man as a minister, to control everything, I'm sure the churches will grow. I have seen this happen in the case of a woman who was given these powers.

This pastor's observation and assessment of spiritually gifted women, after years of theological education and pastoral experience in a male controlled religious sphere, must be taken very seriously. While other's assessment may be affected by traditional thinking, he was able to rise above historical and ecclesiastical prejudices and discrimination and underscore his view on the basis of his *observation*.

One woman respondent testified to her passion for pastoral work:

> I burn to preach the word of God. I always have since I came to Christ. I would preach to anyone who would listen as a 'Youth for Christ' member. I was allowed to preach for ten minutes each week to our group. Feelings for women as Christians are important. To believe that 'this is God's will' that we cannot do this or

that is not acceptable to me. Women are not only here for procreation. For a long time I was hurt, bitter and angry. I know that a lot of women 'in ministry' are feeling this way.[10] As women growing up in the church the only role we had to play was to baby-sit and make tea. I have always been accused of being a rebel. I had two brothers. I had a grandfather who said I could be or do anything I wanted. I grew up seeing I can do what they could do. I am unlike my mother and my dad. They are both quiet.

The hurt and pain of this respondent, an aspiring pastoral candidate, fifty-four years old at the time of the interview and having been a Christian for forty-two years, should not be trivialized. Who listens to the hurt of godly women? Did her grandfather really mean it when he said to the respondent many years ago, "you can be or do anything you want?" Whether he really meant it or believed it or not, the respondent took it to heart. Her grandfather's admonition still haunts her today as her story testifies.

The frustration of another woman church leader of a prominent Johannesburg church expresses her deepest sentiment this way:

It's so right for me to feel *so good* about serving God. I am thrilled about it, but the Bible says so many things about the subservience of women to men and to the church. This bothers me so much! I am so confused. I would love to be a pastor, except for what the Bible says.

To see her facial expression and tone of voice in hearing the above remarks have left a lasting impression upon me. The anguish is unmistakable, the dilemma persistent for her and for others.

WOMEN AND LEADERSHIP

Are women as capable as men to be pastors? This woman puts it this way:

> I don't think our pastor has given much thought to women as being equal in abilities and opportunities for ministry. I feel the inequalities say that women are in an inferior role than men....I've basically accepted the fact that men should be in ministry and women not. Since the beginning of this year I started questioning this position. Many women have abilities but do not have opportunities to serve God in the church. I am still searching in my heart for a clearer conviction on my feelings toward this matter. I feel anguish for those women who are struggling.[11] I don't see why if women can teach in cell groups, why can't they teach or preach from the pulpit?

While she does not convey with utter confidence that women can be capable pastors, as capable as men in fact, the respondent hints to that conviction. She portrays a developing consciousness of the abilities and leadership potential of women.

The only white woman Baptist Union pastor I found is ministering in a black church. She received her theological training in her twenties. She felt called to be a missionary. She felt this call when she was in Standard 1. She was finally ordained in 1997 at age forty-nine. She declared, in addition to and in spite of her call, she always felt like a "second-rater." Yet she asks:

> Why would God give us gifts and not allow us to use it? The majority of my Baptist pastor friends accept me as a pastor because they know I am not a feminist, I am not aggressive. They may not agree with me theologically, though, but they accept me because they know my heart and know that I am here to serve the Lord.[12]

VIEWS AND EXPERIENCES IN BUSA

Perhaps her non-aggressive personality and amenable disposition have provided the basis for her acceptance by fellow male pastors. But I wonder, could her role as pastor of an inner-city congregation made up of Africans from fifteen nations be construed as a "missionary" assignment and therefore her pastoral function deemed *acceptable*?

I listened for nearly two hours to a woman doing an MA in Old Testament at Rands Afrikaans University. She is married and aged twenty-seven. As with other interviews, only a part of her attitudes and stories can be shared in this study. Here are some of her reflections on women as pastors:

> To me the prevailing biblical theology, when it comes to leadership, is two things. First of all, it is by God's gift and, secondly, it's servanthood. And those two things make me feel that women in ministry is a part of the Lord's plan for the church. Because it's about him gifting people and his choice of people. Personal integrity, personal holiness and the servanthood attitude. Those who serve are those who lead. Church leadership in this way is different from secular leadership. As to Paul's comment that women are to remain silent in the church, I have this to say. I think the important point is to stick to the biblical principle that we Baptists hold so dearly, and that's the matter of context, the matter of understanding where it's placed, understanding not only its literary context but its social context, understanding the broader context of Paul's theology. And I think if you hold these in tension, then I think it becomes impossible to use this comment by Paul as proof of banning of women in doing anything in the church.[13] It's just ludicrous, just looking at the broader understanding of Paul's body ministry, the bride of Christ, of gifting. His gifts are never gender based. His understanding of freedom in Christ -- we are a new creation! If you hold that in perspective and you hold that particular periscope of

Scripture in its social context and its broader theological context it becomes easy to see that Paul was speaking to a particular situation and he made a principle statement. So I don't personally get flustered by things like that and I often find that great men of God who hold, exegetically, principles of Scripture in perspective, everywhere else, when they get to this issue, just seem to lose it altogether and suddenly base all of theology on one verse[14]. . . . At college I got to the point where I realized I couldn't raise the subject of women's issues because then you were labeled. It was very frustrating for me because I wanted to deal with issues and I was left to deal with them on my own.

What is clearly evident is that as women are theologically trained, at any level, they begin to see themselves and the Scriptures in new light. Their esteem as a person created in the image of God is uplifted. And their deepest convictions begin to be articulated with passion and sharpness, as in the case of the respondent above. Are women as capable as men to be pastors? The respondent above seems to say: of course.

Overwhelmingly, the respondents to the questionnaire claimed that women are fully capable of providing spiritual counseling to men. They affirm that women can be gifted with the interpretation of the word of God and proclaim it with effectiveness and offer wise spiritual counsel to men and women. Only one white woman said, "I don't know." Everyone else said, "yes." Comments were: "Because she is trained for that," "But I rather prefer she take a male elder or deacon when counseling a man," "I don't know whether it's advisable in private," "I'm sure she can but it will not easily be accepted by a man," "Some rules of sexual integrity apply here as for male pastors," " I have done it, but I would say generally no, it is a dangerous situation; one must recognize the boundaries," "This is very difficult as women are not so brave to confront men openly;

there are some phrases that a woman cannot or is not supposed to say to a man culturally." Widespread caution is seen in these remarks, yet the cautions are there for men pastors and counselors as well. These cautions should not obstruct the weight of the argument that women are *capable* of providing spiritual nurture to men based on their training, gifts, abilities and wisdom. Spiritual counseling, for both women and men ministers, can be risky, but the opportunities for service, healing and wholeness are evident.

In an interview, one woman felt that women ought not to counsel men. She does not address the question of whether women can discern spiritual truth and wisdom and are able to express that truth and wisdom to men. She is against the pastoral function of women counseling both men and women:

> The Scriptures do not seem to verify women as pastors. At this stage, I could not be comfortable with it. As a woman, I appreciated the fact that I had a pastor figure I could go to. Women can administrate, women can counsel women, but I have a problem of women pastoring a church.

As in other interviews, a follow-up interview would have been very interesting, and perhaps revealing. Must a "pastor figure" she refers to necessarily be a male? I would ask. I would ask only because she affirms that women can "administrate" and "counsel." Why can't they then "pastor"?

The following story is given by a woman pastor of an Indian church in Kwa-Zulu Natal. I include much of her testimony to demonstrate the legitimacy of her claim to counsel and to pastor, to administrate and to lead the church God has called her to serve. Her story brings justification to her religious struggles and growth. Her story testifies her claim to possess spiritual qualifications in counseling and proclamation and leadership:

> My call is amazing. Almost after I was converted I felt strongly God was calling me for a special ministry. It was confirmed by various Scriptures. I felt boldness as well. I started sharing my testimony. This started my experience of boldness. This call was twenty-two years ago.
>
> Whilst I was at Bethel Baptist Church I was elected as women's leader. The Lord gave me the healing gift as well. Healing from illness and from demons. This caused me to become more aware of the presence and power of Christ. I didn't on my own feel I had a healing ministry. The pastor came to me and said I had this gift. When it came to demons, I was able to expel them and people began to know the Lord as Savior. I formed a witnessing team of five women to be on call to go and heal and preach Jesus. The pastor would often go with us. I never had any training. But the Holy Spirit gave me utterance for every need.
>
> Bethel Baptist Church had to be extended twice to accommodate the growing numbers. What spurred me on was I believed what Jesus said, 'In my name you shall cast out demons.' I prayed and expelled in his name.
>
> I have experienced tongues and prophecy, and have experienced this in Bethel and at BFC. I've had lots of dreams, visions and revelations. God gives me Scriptures to confirm things to me. The first time I spoke in another tongue, a diseased man with alcoholism and chronic ulcers was healed immediately. We always went about with the full knowledge of the presence of the Holy Spirit. We believe in tongues and prophecy but not in everything. We don't get carried away with it.

VIEWS AND EXPERIENCES IN BUSA

When I was a non-Christian, I was very sick physically in my stomach. No help from doctors. I decided there was not gods in existence. There was a time I couldn't sleep because of the illness. For two weeks I didn't sleep, day or night. I turned the radio on. Someone was speaking about healing. He said, 'There's somebody now rolling in pain.' That was *me*! As he continued to talk, he said 'I'm going to introduce you to someone who can heal you now! His name is Jesus.' That was the name I didn't want to hear. To me he was just one of the gods. He said, 'Whoever wants to be healed by Jesus, lay your hands on the part that is painful.' This man was Oral Roberts. I had my hands on my stomach. Before he finished praying, the pain was gone. When the pain went, I wanted it back to prove that Jesus was not real, that there is no god. It's been twenty-four years the pain has been gone! I remember saying, 'Jesus whoever you are, thank you!' I was in shock, I shed some tears over a broken, small transistor radio message. My pastor came to my house, and he was thrilled.

There was a split in the church because of a problem, but when the split took place, I left along with eight to ten families. On 11 November 1987, the few families met at a home of one of these families. We decided to start our own fellowship. Five people on the same day were given Isaiah chapter 60, independent of each other. That was the confirmation that the Lord was leading us.

We needed a leader. We elected myself as the pastor when my brother declined to be the pastor. I knew the Lord had called me. There was no slightest doubt in my mind. Even with no theological training, little education, and other excuses, I knew God had called me.

Who can refute this kind of testimony? Who can say women like this one cannot receive God's anointing and God's power? Who dares to claim God cannot or has not gifted her to counsel or lead or proclaim to *all* who are in need of her divine talents, women or men?

The majority of the respondents to the questionnaire admitted to the presence of women who are against a woman becoming the pastor of a church. Four white women, two black women, and one man said so. One black woman said "no," there are no women in her church against a woman becoming a pastor, and two declared "I don't know," one was black and one white. Other comments were: "We never face this problem," "Each church is autonomous. The problem is that a lot of women resent a woman pastor. Women are funny creatures. They want equality and rights but jealousy abounds among women," "I think most, young and old, believe that a man should be a pastor: God -- man -- woman," and "Most would be against a woman to become a pastor."

Clearly, the evidence above points to the need for attitudinal transformation among women (as well as men) in order for women to be liberated for church leadership.

Interviewees responded in various ways. One woman gave her opinion thusly:

> It is a theological issue[15] and the Bible is made to back up South African Baptist culture. I don't feel women will be supportive of women in leadership. Pastor and leadership will be supportive of women in missions or leadership in private or informally but in public they would not be supportive.[16] My pastor will be happy to allow me to fulfill pastoral roles as long as I am not a 'pastoral candidate.' I am seeing hypocrisy and I'm struggling to swallow that. At times this makes me feel angry.

VIEWS AND EXPERIENCES IN BUSA

This "feeling" that women would not be supportive of women in pastoral leadership, I am assuming, is rooted in experiences and evidence, i.e., comments, innuendoes, behavior, etc. Again we see the critical role a pastor plays in shaping theological attitudes toward women and church leadership. And again we see pain!

One woman affirms women and would support them in the ministry:

> I feel there is a misconception somewhere. I can see a woman give a message with such zeal and power, and I have seen some men with less zeal and gift. If God has called women they should not feel threatened to serve God. I feel a sense of dismay at the lack of use of women. Even from a female point of view, I feel an openness to listen to other women who may have a message from God.[17]

This woman's convictions are unswervingly in support of women in leadership. She conveys an even-handed assessment of both men and women in the Lord's work. What is vital for her is "zeal" and "gift," not gender. If a woman has it, she is "open" to her leadership.

The following discourse reveals how the "unliberated" white women of South Africa cannot with ease accept women as pastors:

> I don't think white woman in South Africa is free to exercise who they are as a woman. Woman in higher position would have to start acting like men in order to be there. The higher you go up, the more you have to be a man and you cannot be there as a woman.[18]
> I can see that in church ministry as well. The higher you go up into leadership, a simple aspect like crying is questioned. When I cry men think I'm falling apart. It's my own way of dealing with

things. The space to react like that is not there for woman in leadership. The space to be a feminine woman, to allow the feminine side of me to come out is not there. Also we've done that to ourselves. A woman can't support her role as woman and homemaker any more because that's looked down upon as well. So not only is the attitude of South African white society not allowing woman to be woman, but woman in that society is not allowing woman to be woman. If a woman is defining her role wholesomely as a homemaker and a wife, then she should be given the freedom to do so without feeling inferior.

Is there room for women to affirm their humanity as women *and* leaders, or must the word "leader" automatically mean maleness only -- men don't cry, men don't show fear, men refrain from excessive expressions of compassion or joy? The respondent above speaks of "the feminine side of me." Is not that "side" as valid and God-created (image of God!) as the male "side" of one's humanity?[19]

Wolterstorff (1986:287) asks, as well should we:

Do we or do we not think that women are equal partners with men in God's creation and kingdom -- and, in particular, do we think that they are equally gifted? If we do think they are equal, we had better listen carefully to a description of the ways in which, in the past and yet today, we indicate otherwise.[20]

CONCLUDING REMARKS

In evaluating the questionnaires and interviews, I have sought to make them descriptive of personal experiences and personal attitudes. I have also sought to make them revelational or exploratory

VIEWS AND EXPERIENCES IN BUSA

in that I wanted the questionnaires and interviews to reveal sentiments, emotions, events and experiences, to explore areas of feeling and attitude that perhaps were unexpressed or unprocessed to any significant degree before. In this way the emphasis of the research technique was qualitative, not quantitative, though the objective, quantitative dimension of the questionnaire cannot be minimized.

A Brief Evaluation

Some respondents to the questionnaire made scant subjective comments to the inquiries posed. Others made frequent and ample personal remarks or observations. On the interviews, several were lengthy and immensely enriching. Others were more brief, sometimes enlightening and sometimes less so.

The interviews especially provided enormous qualitative information. Frequently discussions went in directions unintended originally. I was surprised at the frankness and openness of some, while for others I was startled at the theological depth and ecclesiastical awareness. I found the women interviewed to be co-operative. While some were guarded with their feelings, others were expressly vocal. The interviews allowed me to observe tone of voice and facial expressions that aided in picking up pain or hope or other nuances.

It was revealing to me to see, through the questionnaires and the interviews, the similar kinds of experiences and views black, white and Asian women have, generally speaking, in their respective churches. The few men in the questionnaires (two) and the

WOMEN AND LEADERSHIP

interviews (one) pointed to their awareness of women's concerns in the church but also their lack of high emotional involvement and sentiment were obvious. Their responses appear to be more rationalistic and tentative than emotive and passionate.

The frustration of women in their experiences in the church, and their willingness to share them with me, a man and a non-South African, are facts both humbling and significant. As noted before, I tried to investigate women's *feelings* and to have those feelings expressed, even elaborated upon. To the degree they did I feel I was indeed privileged to get a glimpse into their inner sanctuary.

This chapter reflects a summary of the information and emotions expressed and does not reveal its entirety. But the whole or larger was necessary to adequately interpret the part or piece. I have put in concise fashion the essential parts of the body of material and their concomitant emotional baggage that must be intrinsically part and parcel to the investigation.

The next chapter (chapter three) will describe the attitudes and experiences of women and men regarding women and leadership in the Baptist Convention of South Africa. The last and concluding chapter (chapter six) will seek to summarize the attitudes and experiences of the women (and men) of the BUSA and BCSA, and then to see how they compare, generally, with Christian women in Zambia, Hong Kong, the United States and elsewhere in South Africa who are not members of BUSA and BCSA. Concluding observations will be made as well as prescriptive comments related to the future of women in leadership in the Baptist churches of South Africa. A strategy for a liberating praxis and church transformation will bring the study to a close.

VIEWS AND EXPERIENCES IN BUSA

Ebele Eko's (1997:156-157) warning is a fitting end to this chapter:

A HARVEST OF HATE

When a field of greed
Is sown with seeds of discord
And watered in strife
A harvest of hate
Is sure to come

When man
Robs woman of
Her birthright and peace
He lights a fire
That slowly leaks
To a powder keg

Generations yet unborn
Shall yet be rocked
By the dynamite
Buried each day
As women's rights
Get robbed or sold.

WOMEN AND LEADERSHIP

NOTES ON CHAPTER TWO

1. To be passionate about something, and to know one has the ability, yet to be denied participation by the community must be excruciating to swallow. Oduyoye (1998a:121) confesses: "My ambiguity on the question of autonomy grows from the fact that no human being is entirely autonomous. You may hit yourself on the chest and say, 'I am so and so,' but it is for the community to agree to treat you as the person you proclaim yourself to be. This is what hits women most." As the woman testifies, when she knows teaching is "my gift" from God yet is not allowed by her church to do so is tantamount to obstructing the work and purpose of God.

2. In this story we notice the choices two women made in dealing with their 'minority' and 'inferior' status in a male controlled committee. Women continue to encounter difficult and controversial situations in the contemporary church. Jacobs (1998:29) believes women should feel comfortable in their choices, with no fear in their choices if motivated by a sense of God's leadership. Women should seek to develop a feasible and practical theology for themselves, which includes support for the theological choices of other women who are experiencing existential living of their own.

3. Oduyoye (1998a:110) contends that men "survive on women's selflessness." I would conjecture that so does the church. If Sharon Potgieter (1996:16) is correct, women comprise seventy percent of the South African church population. I would then declare that the church in South Africa survives not only on women's selflessness but on women's very *presence* as well.

4. Landman (1999a:27-28) recalls for us the case of Catharina Allegonda van Lier (1768-1801) who suffered from chronic guilt, self-hate and depression. Her depression could not be cured through Calvinistic piety or revivalism for, according to Landman, Catharina's Christian faith, which marginalized women to inactivity, was the root cause of her low self-esteem.

5. Second Kings 11 describes how Athaliah, the illegitimate ruler of Judah, was

undermined by her niece, Jehosheba. While one can see the justice in this, it does depict the tendency even today, even in the church, of women who seek to destroy other women. Women should strive to not only develop their own skills and potential, but the skills and potential of other women as well. This leads to a "life-affirming theology" (Landman 1998c:33).

6. Chitando (1998:73-74) does not specifically state if it is male only or male and female together who perpetrate women's subordination in the Seventh Day Adventist Church situated in Masvingo South. The conclusion of his examination points to the reality that the basic tenets of co-dependence, fraternity and mutuality are negated with the continued subordination of women in the Christian churches and in the Christian life. Speaking about the Zimbabwean churches at large, Chitando claims that power remains entrenched in male control.

7. Is it from the framework of their culture that women see things differently? Or from the framework of their experiences as women? Is it intuitive or innate?

8. This "walking with the Lord" finds expression in a multitude of ways in the local church. A Methodist women's prayer bears this out: "Almighty and ever-loving Heavenly Father, we come before You today as a group of Christian women to bring our offering of worship and thanksgiving....For all who have faithfully served You and Your church, we give thanks and pray that You will so fill us with Your spirit that we too may offer the work of our hearts, minds and hands in ever-willing service to the glory of God and the extension of His Kingdom" (Women at Prayer 1971:8). The warmth of celebration in worship and service through the community of believers, the church, and through the infilling of Christ's spirit and the spirit of his church, rings loud and clear in this prayer.

9. A chain reaction of subordination and inferiority is depicted in this response. The effects appear pervasive in South African church and society. Rakoczy (1995:32-33) pleads for the church to allow the Holy Spirit to transform the church into a new creation, a "radical new life." She recalls that this kind of transformation was witnessed in the first Christian century, which, she claims, penetrated the boundaries of gender, class and religious heritage to create a new body abiding in the spirit of Christ.

WOMEN AND LEADERSHIP

10. According to Landman (1999a:27-28), black women in South Africa are liberating themselves from missionary Christianity and its baggage of oppressive piety. Dutch-Afrikaans women are further behind in liberating themselves from the oppressive piety of historic South African Christianity. They are still deeply entrenched in patriarchal moralities and self-hate. (This is not to imply that black women do not oppress other black women seeking leadership, or that all black women do not tolerate complete male domination in the church -- Hayashida). Saayman observes that in rural areas black women appear to be as much a stumbling block as men to women's liberation. In rural areas it is often men who initiate greater scope for women (his reactions to this chapter draft).

11. When one suffers or struggles, one is conscientized to others who are suffering in the same way. In various ways, feminist theology challenges the view that women's struggles are the result of the Fall, that because women were essentially responsible for the Fall they therefore must suffer the penalty for it, meekly and obediently (Keshegian 1996:279).

12. While she is content with her role as a pastor, the following advice and experiences betray the respondent's personal history of hardships and challenges as a woman and mother in church leadership: "Perhaps more difficult for me as a woman pastor is to visit in inner-city neighbourhoods and homes than it would be for a male pastor. A single woman pastor does better than a married one with children -- children bring a range of added responsibilities. A woman who's married goes home and does work at home, mothering sentiments and obligations, etc. I wouldn't recommend any woman going into the ministry. If you can stay out, stay out. Unless God calls. Many young women could be destroyed unsuspectingly." I suppose so can a man, a husband and father of children. But women cannot as easily manage the psychological baggage of gender expectations, or cultural stereotypes, and theological prejudices not in her favour.

13. In order to affect emancipatory praxis, collaboration is needed among women of diverse cultures, social stratums and religious traditions. Women who have experienced, in their respective contexts, oppression and discrimination must engage in constructive theological discourse (Ackermann 1996a:44). To foster such dialogue, The Circle of Concerned African Women Theologians was born in 1989. Its uniqueness is in defining 'theologians' on the premise that theology should be done

VIEWS AND EXPERIENCES IN BUSA

"by the people and for the people...by women for the whole community of women and men" that incorporates Africa's Muslim, Christian and Hindu faith communities. The Circle's goal is to uncover positive or negative factors that influence or affect the lives of women (Oduyoye 1997:1-2, 4). I like what Forrester (1989:17) said, "theology is too important a matter to be left to the [professional] theologian."

14. Oppressed and oppressor need liberation -- one from suffering, the other from prejudice and ignorance (Bryaruhanga-Akiiki 1994:46). Should not, then, efforts be made to conscientize *both* to the need for healing and wholeness? In this light, King (1996:15-24) advocates the need for women's solidarity in the effort to gain healing and wholeness in their personhood and as well as in the church. Women are essential for an integrated and compassionate holiness and spirituality in the church. The effort will help transform men as well. Additionally, King advocates solidarity with women of non-Christian traditions. All women from all cultures share similar oppression. Women from differing religious and socio-economic backgrounds ought to dialogue and address issues common to them. Liberation *within* and *without* particular religious heritages ought to be attempted. New birth for women in society at large as well as within the confines of ecclesiastical structures must be the aim. Though Hulley (1996:199) cautions that, at least in the case of ordinary African women, a "theology of survival" is necessary before talk of liberation or transformation becomes meaningful.

15. Newbigin (1989:235), too, sees it as a "theological issue." In his assessment, the entire Church is called to function as a royal priesthood in daily life. And this royal priesthood requires specially called ministerial priests, women and men, to guide, serve and nourish this work of the whole body of Christ (royal priesthood).

16. Is there a sense in which women must "prove" themselves in leadership? To a certain extent so does a male leader. He cannot ride the crest of his authority on maleness alone, although some seem to do so very successfully. But women do seem to me to have more of an uphill struggle to be accepted as leaders. Susan Rakoczy (1997a:9) says as much when she says that "authority simply as authority does not work" and therefore there must abide reasons for giving a leader respect and obedience. If Rakoczy is correct, then women's strategy for leadership acceptance should be rooted in the sharpening of natural abilities, skills, and mature spiri-

tuality, even though in many cases women's gifts, creativeness and intelligence are not enough to topple "sacred" church traditions such as male supremacy.

17. I like what Keteyi (1998:48) has said about the process of liberation. Subjugated women must move from "victim to subject." To me this means to move from a position of "the problem" to the position of "personhood" and "the solution," from victimised object to a person gaining control of her life and destiny. In that sense we may see what Keteyi means when he talks about moving from "promise to fulfilment."

18. Need women behave like men to perform their leadership roles in the church? Lebaka-Ketshabile (1996:178) thinks not: "What is also frustrating is that women are expected to exercise their ministry in exactly the same way as men exercise theirs; any woman who does not do so is regarded as a failure. In order to satisfy the status quo some of these women have had to behave like men. They start to walk, talk and behave differently. In this way they disassociate themselves from other women." In doing so, I will argue that women not only deny their humanity as women but the wisdom of the God who willed their humanity as *women*.

19. Saayman remarks, again and emphatically, that "this should be included in the whole debate on the authoritarian and oppressive nature ordination has required/acquired over the centuries. To put it *very* crudely: at the moment the church expects that ordained women should have 'made it' in a *man's* world, not in a *human* world . . . we should not be misled to debate only the *right* and *call* of women to be ordained. We must debate the whole *nature* of the *ordered* (rather than ordained) ministry" (further comments made to me in reaction to this section of the chapter). Saayman's advocacy for a transformation in the meaning of "ordination" is of great significance. The debate over women's *right* and *call* to ordination forces the debate to this another, in some ways more profound and fundamental, level.

20. Kretzschmar's (1998b:365) study on the status of women in the Baptist Union of South Africa revealed unhappiness with the status quo for the majority of the women. Yet the survey also demonstrated widespread disagreement on fundamental theological viewpoints regarding the nature of women's roles in the church:

VIEWS AND EXPERIENCES IN BUSA

7%   The present structures such as the BWA (Baptist Women's Association) fully meet the needs of Christian women.

59%   The present structures are not adequate. Women are also called by God to be active in Sunday Schools, women's groups and in important ministries such as catering, hospitality, counselling and visiting the sick. But women are not called to exercise authority over men or over the church as a whole.

29%   All of the above are valuable, but women are *also* called by God to preach, exercise authority over the church as a whole and to be ordained as pastors in accordance with their spiritual gifts and ministries.

CHAPTER THREE

VIEWS AND EXPERIENCES OF WOMEN AND MEN IN THE BAPTIST CONVENTION OF SOUTH AFRICA

WHO IS THIS WOMAN?

Look at that woman
Look at the expression on her face
Can you explain that expression?
Watch it.

She is but one of the African women
Seeking desperately her liberation
She needs to be liberated
From all the social vices against her
From sexual harassment
From exploitation
From oppression of all sorts

Do you want to know her name?
She is Abena
A princess from the village
She sees to the upkeep of her family

Abena wakes up very early
Cleans the house

WOMEN AND LEADERSHIP

Feeds the children and the MAN
Sends the children to school
She goes to the market to sell
In order to bring money to the house
What is her reward for all these?

She is mocked at by men
Her own sons do not honor her
She dares not decide on her own
She must be submissive to her man

Abena is part of the local church
She walks silently into the church
She organizes women to clean the chapel
They arrange flowers beautifully in the chapel
They prepare the tea or coffee during meetings
They make sure the linen is always neat
And they prepare the sacramental table.

This same Abena does not sit with the men
She sits in a pew reserved for women
She is not part of decision-making in the church
She dares not talk when men are around.
You can now explain her groaning faith
She has a faith that must be practiced
She must be empowered out of her woes
Her voice must be heard
She must be recognized and honored
For she is a daughter of God

(Dinah Abbey-Mensah 1997:158-160)

VIEWS AND EXPERIENCES IN THE BCSA

INTRODUCTORY REMARKS

As was the aim of the previous chapter with BUSA, the aim of this chapter is to describe the views and experiences of women and men of the Baptist Convention of South Africa (BCSA) in regard to church leadership. Both theological and ecclesiastical categories have been selected which deal with these views and experiences. They are:

1. Current church practices regarding women

2. Perceptions of male attitudes toward women

3. Natural abilities of women

4. Views on women as pastors

As with the BUSA women and men, I have sought to allow the BCSA women and men to tell their stories without any blatant bias or tainting on my part. That is, I have not sought to tell their stories for them but have sought to allow the respondents freedom to articulate their attitudes and experiences.

TECHNIQUE

Like chapter two with the BCSA respondents, I sought in this chapter to use a two-pronged approach to information gathering. I have found them to be useful, appropriate and complementary.

The techniques employed were the *half-structured questionnaire* and the *moderately structured interview*. The questionnaire necessarily includes structured questions or inquiries. Yet for each question, the respondent was given the opportunity to "comment" on the "yes," "no," or "I don't know" response. This approach allowed for elasticity in the structured question. Individuals were able to remark in any way they chose if they felt the question was too narrow, unfair, biased or misleading. Many respondents added comments to their objective responses, bringing a degree of subjectivity to the questionnaire.

Ackermann (1985:133) states that the interview allows for assessing nonverbal behavior, encourages spontaneity, and provides opportunity for greater complexity. On the other hand, disadvantages can be less anonymity, less standardized wording to questions and bias of the interviewer can cause error in the data.

The moderately structured interviews allow for both structured questions as well as unstructured spontaneous follow-up questions. Hence the interviewer becomes a participant observer in the drama of dialogue. While recognizing that asking errors or recording errors are ever present, the interviewer understands that that which is to be gained is greater than the risks, i.e., the stress on values, goals and desires, the stress on social perception, and the stress on attitude.

This subjective data often has a critical advantage over the objective-based questionnaire (Ackermann 1985:134-135). In addition, the subjective approach provides avenues to discover feelings and emotion less available otherwise.

In conclusion, both the half-structured questionnaire, as well as the moderately structured interview, incorporate the theological and ecclesiastical categories outlined in the introductory remarks.

METHODOLOGY

My investigation procedures again employ both quantitative and qualitative dimensions. As stated in the description of technique, the questionnaire is based on set questions with the option for respondents to add comments if desired. The interviews are structured in the sense that pre-formulated discussion topics revolve around the theological and ecclesiastical categories referred to in the introductory remarks. They are, however, moderately structured in the sense that I sought to allow for spontaneity and flow, thereby permitting extensive elaboration or tangents into other areas of interests and concerns on the part of either the respondent or the interviewer.

Hence, the methodological procedures, while both quantitative and qualitative, paid particular attention to qualitative and phenomenological tendencies that reflect the respondents' attitudes, feelings, perceptions, beliefs, experiences and stories that mirror meaning and significance in their lives. Particularly in the interviews, the narrative approach is heavily utilized. Women who had specific experiences or stories to tell were encouraged to do so. The descriptive analysis reflects ample narration.

WOMEN AND LEADERSHIP

SAMPLING

This chapter uses a diverse sampling involving women and men. Unlike the previous one, this chapter takes a much more substantial analysis of the men of the BCSA. I felt this to be important in order to discover in what ways men of the Convention are changing in their perceptions of women's leadership in the churches due to the theoretical and verbal upliftment of women at the Baptist College, the Winter Schools of Theology, national assemblies, and in a number of local churches.

Both women and men were asked to complete questionnaires or to respond in dialogue fashion in an interview. Some chosen for questionnaires or interviews were selected at random, while others were selected because of leadership positions held. Like the BUSA respondents, the majority were women and men not previously known to the researcher.

The BCSA is overwhelmingly black. The samples reflect that ethnicity. In fact, the samples are entirely of black women and men.

The size of the sample is much more extensive than the sample of the BUSA study. It is deemed to be sufficient for the purposes of this thesis.

VIEWS AND EXPERIENCES IN THE BCSA

QUESTIONNAIRES, INTERVIEWS AND THE RESPONDENTS

The use of the questionnaires and interviews and the approach taken were similar with the previous chapter. The majority of respondents to questionnaires and interviews were contacted in person as the researcher visited churches and traveled throughout South Africa. Only a few were contacted by telephone. The nature of the research was explained and voluntary participation was solicited. On occasions, interviews were made on the same day of contact. In the majority of cases, an appointment was made, and the venue was normally in homes or churches. The questionnaires were frequently left in the hands of those who expressed interest, occasionally mailed by post. In the case of the questionnaires, individuals were encouraged to freely make comments after the more objective portions of the five page document. A number of questionnaires were never returned.

The Interviews

The interviews averaged between thirty minutes and one hour and thirty minutes. A total of twenty-five were interviewed, eighteen women and seven men. All the respondents were black. The women's ages ranged this way: 19, 23, 24, 25, 28, 30, 33, 34, 34, 38, 40, 44, 44, 49, 50, 52, 56, 58. The interviews took place between April 1997 and September 1998. The men's ages ranged this way: 20, 25, 27, 28, 34, 38, 39. These interviews took place between April 1997 and September 1998.

WOMEN AND LEADERSHIP

The tape recorder was used in some cases. It was not used in most cases.

The women interviewed were:

Youth leader, Eternal Hope Baptist Church (Alice)

Vice Secretary, Orlando Baptist Church (Soweto)

Sunday School Teacher, Secretary of Baptist Women's Department (BWD), Vice Secretary, First Winterveld Baptist Church (Mabopane)

Member of Maranatha Missionary Baptist Church (King William's Town)

Youth leader, Maranatha Missionary Baptist Church (King William's Town)

Member of Maranatha Missionary Baptist Church (King William's Town)

Member, Seshego Baptist Church (Pietersburg)

Chairperson of Social Ministries Commission, Chairperson of Communications Commission, Teenagers Commission, Finance Committee, Kagiso Baptist Church (Krugersdorp)

Chairperson of Deacon's Board, Director of Youth Committee, Finance Committee, Kagiso Baptist Church (Krugersdorp)

VIEWS AND EXPERIENCES IN THE BCSA

Choir Director, Deacon, Couples Club Facilitator, Kagiso Baptist Church (Krugersdorp)

Secretary of Communications Commission, Coordinator of Teenagers Commission, Young Adult President, Pastor's secretary, Choir member, Kagiso Baptist Church (Krugersdorp)

Deacon, Treasurer for BWD, Kagiso Baptist Church (Krugersdorp)

Treasurer of BWD, Meadowlands Baptist Church (Soweto)

Spiritual section for BWD, counselor, prayer leader, Meadowlands Baptist Church (Soweto)

Member of Jabavu Baptist Church (Soweto)

Choir member, lay preacher, chairperson for youth department, Jabavu Baptist Church (Soweto)

Church secretary, Tsakane Baptist Church (near Springs)

Youth leader, Choir Director, Kroonstad Baptist Church (Orange Free State)

Most of the women were married, some were single, but there seems to be no relevancy in this distinction.

The men interviewed were:

Youth leader, Bible study teacher, usher, Jouberto Baptist Church

WOMEN AND LEADERSHIP

(North West Province)

Deacon, Mt. Hermon Baptist Church (North West Province)

Deacon, usher, Maranatha Missionary Baptist Church (King William's Town)

Pastor, Tokoza Baptist Church (Johannesburg South)

Member, Bethany Baptist Church (Berea, Johannesburg)

Youth leader, Bible study teacher, choir director, Small Farm Baptist Church (Southern Gauteng)

Member, Bethany Baptist Church (Berea, Johannesburg)

Some of the men were married, others were single, but this did not prove to be of any relevance.

The Questionnaires

Sixty questionnaires (out of one hundred and seventy) were returned from thirty-two women and twenty-eight men. The women's ages ranged this way: 17, 19, 22, 24, 24, 25, 25, 28, 29, 29, 31, 33, 33, 34, 36, 38, 40, 44, 44, 44, 45, 48, 48, 49, 50, 50, 52, 53, 56, 68, 59, 80. The men's ages ranged this way: 20, 21, 21, 22, 22, 23, 24, 24, 24, 25, 26, 27, 27, 28, 29, 29, 30, 31, 32, 32, 35, 36, 44, 48, 50, 51, 55, 58. The questionnaires were dated from March 1997 to February 1999.

VIEWS AND EXPERIENCES IN THE BCSA

The leadership roles and church affiliation are described below. The women:

Member, Maranatha Missionary Baptist Church (King William's Town)

Member, Maranatha Missionary Baptist Church (King William's Town)

Youth leader, Maranatha Missionary Baptist Church (King William's Town)

Sunday School teacher, choir director, youth leader, counselor, Maranatha Missionary Baptist Church (King William's Town)

Church secretary, Tsakane Baptist Church (near Springs)

Member, Fairly Baptist Church (Northern Province)

Deacon, Fairly Baptist Church (Northern Province)

Sunday School teacher, Orlando Baptist Church (Soweto)

Women's leader, youth leader, Orlando Baptist Church (Soweto)

Spiritual section leader for women, counselor, prayer, Meadowlands Baptist Church (Soweto)

Treasurer of BWD, Meadowlands Baptist Church (Soweto)

WOMEN AND LEADERSHIP

Member, Meadowlands Baptist Church (Soweto)

Member, Jabavu Baptist Church (Soweto)

Preaching and teaching, Seshego Baptist Church (Pietersburg)

Lay evangelist, Seshego Baptist Church (Pietersburg)

Youth leader, Mamelodi Baptist Church (Pretoria)

Prayer partner, Mamelodi Baptist Church (Pretoria)

Usher, Mamelodi Baptist Church (Pretoria)

Women's leader, choir director, pastor's wife, Mamelodi Baptist Church (Pretoria)

Deacon, treasurer of BWD, Kagiso Baptist Church (Krugersdorp)

Chairperson of deacon's board, director of youth committee, finance committee, Kagiso Baptist Church (Krugersdorp)

Chairperson of Social Ministries Commission, Chairperson of Communication Commission, Teenagers Commission, Finance Commission, Kagiso Baptist Church (Krugersdorp)

Young adult President, Secretary in Communication Commission, Coordinator in Teenagers Commission, Choir member, pastors secretary, Kagiso Baptist Church (Krugersdorp)

VIEWS AND EXPERIENCES IN THE BCSA

Choir director, Family Bible Hour President, Couples club facilitator, deacon, Kagiso Baptist Church (Krugersdorp)

Deacon, Vaaltyn Baptist Church (Potgietersrus)

Youth leader, Eternal Hope Baptist Church (Alice)

Pastor's wife, Mabopane Baptist Church (Mabopane)

Deacon, bible study teacher, preacher, Temba Baptist Church (North West Province)

Youth leader, Sunday School teacher, Ga-Rankuwa Baptist Church (North West Province)

Youth leader, choir director, Kroonstad Baptist Church (Orange Free State)

Youth leader, Wedela Baptist Church (Southern Gauteng)

Elder, Whittlesea Baptist Church (Eastern Cape)

    The men:

Church secretary, Seshego Baptist Church (Pietersburg)

Youth leader, Cornerstone Baptist Convention Church (Leondale)

Deacon, choir director, youth leader, bible study teacher, Small Farm Baptist Church (Southern Gauteng)

WOMEN AND LEADERSHIP

Youth leader, Orlando Baptist Church (Soweto)

Usher, bible study leader, youth leader, Jouberton Baptist Church (North West Province)

Deacon, usher, Maranatha Missionary Baptist Church (King William's Town)

Member, Segoma Baptist Church (Pietersburg)

Pastor, Vezubuhle Baptist Church, Kwandebele (Mpumalanga)

Choir director, bible study teacher, youth leader, Protea South Baptist Convention Church (Soweto)

Interpreter, Grace Bible Church (Soweto)

Young adult coordinator, Kagiso Baptist Church (Krugersdorp)

Leader of intercession group, Jabavu Baptist Church (Soweto)

Pastor, Sanctuary Baptist Church (Soweto)

Treasurer, Munsieville Baptist Church (Krugersdorp)

Deacon, youth leader, Madidi Baptist Church (Pretoria)

Deacon, Thengwe Baptist Church (Venda)

VIEWS AND EXPERIENCES IN THE BCSA

Pastor, Mabopane Baptist Church (Mabopane)

Pastor, Mamelodi Baptist Church (Pretoria)

Pastor, Wembezi Baptist Church (Escourt)

Youth leader, Cornfields Baptist Church (Kwa-Zulu Natal)

Deacon, Praying Commission, Kagiso Baptist Church (Krugersdorp)

Bible study teacher, Meadowlands Baptist Church (Soweto)

Chairman, Orlando Baptist Church (Soweto)

Deacon, Whittlesea Baptist Church (Eastern Cape)

Youth leader, Whittlesea Baptist Church (Eastern Cape)

Member, Mahulupye Baptist Church (Botswana)

Choir director, Vaaltyn Baptist Church (Potgietersrus)

Youth leader, P. B. Baptist Church (Port Elizabeth)

The respondents were single, married, or widowed, and the age variation ranged from seventeen to eighty.

WOMEN AND LEADERSHIP

A DESCRIPTIVE ANALYSIS

As explained earlier, the questionnaire and interviews were created to address the following theological and ecclesiastical categories: current church practices regarding women, perception of male attitudes toward women, natural abilities of women and views on women as pastors.

Some of the questionnaires were replete with comments. Others were completed with no subjective remarks at all. Some interviews were lengthy and inundated with extensive personal stories. Others were less so. These variations no doubt reflect the interests, passions, experiences, or the lack of them, of the various respondents. The uneven data should not, however, convey a shortage of authenticity or integrity of significance.

The respondents (women and men) in both questionnaires and interviews were encouraged to share their *experiences* and *attitudes* freely, from the context of their respective Baptist churches and their own participation in the history and religious ethos of the Baptist Convention of South Africa.

Current church practices regarding women

The questionnaires and interviews here seek to discover the impressions Baptist churchwomen and men have regarding the leadership involvement of women in the Baptist churches. What roles do women play in the church? How significant are women in the life of the church? Are women suppressed or subjugated to marginal roles

VIEWS AND EXPERIENCES IN THE BCSA

in the church? Because of the large selection of questionnaire data (60) and interviews (25), this section will reflect the findings in representative and summary fashion. In addition, unlike the more culturally diverse BUSA respondents, the respondents of the BCSA represent strictly black churches in rural and township settings as seen in the description of the interviews and the questionnaires.

From the questionnaires we find that twenty-three women and twenty-three men reported that their church has women as deacons. Eight women and five men reported that there are no women deacons serving in their churches. We do not know the ratio of male to female deacons in these churches. Some women's comments were: "I highlighted the role of women as deacons. Later the executive came up with an apology for not positioning women in the church. This year we have two women deacons;" "My church was started by many women;"[1] "My church realize that even woman God used them." One woman who said that her church has no deacons added: "Because they never feel that a woman is allowed to be a deacon. They always think that it is only males who can do that kind of job." Some men's comments were: "In our church women have a say in the church. They participate in everything;" "Women in our church are treated equally. Maximum participation is being preached and practiced;" "It's only two of them in a church where women are more in number than men and are more active in terms of church work than men;" "We do not have deacons yet. I believe there will be women deacons;" "In my church there are one woman and three men deacons;" "Yes, we have three of them and they are leading;" "Sometimes women are just deacons by being elected but in some issues like church split only man will be called to discuss." A person whose church has no women deacons said: "Women have been left behind for years and it's generally accepted in the North region, due

WOMEN AND LEADERSHIP

to cultural background that women cannot take certain leadership positions." This data indicates acceptance in some churches in the BCSA for women deacons, though there may be evidence that the rural churches may tend to balk at women's leadership at this level. Yet Mugabe (1995:8-9) speaks of the significant nature of women's leadership in traditional African societies:

> The medium, man or woman, was a spiritual leader. The spirit medium, Nehanda, is sung about in Zimbabwe. The first resistance in Zimbabwe was led by this woman. Why can't women be spiritual leaders? In African society women can and do become spiritual leaders. It is not against our culture!

> In the Bible women were spiritual leaders. Our culture is not static. Elements of our culture can help us. We can exercise our gifts as people of God, not just as man or woman.

How much of the restriction of women's leadership in the church is a consequence of Western ecclesiastical tradition?

The vast majority of the women (yes - 25, no - 5) and men (yes - 25, no - 2, I don't know - 1) believe that women are participating fully in business meetings of the church where important decisions are made. Some women's comments were: "They are participating but not effectively;" "Yes, but not always;" "Another contributing factor to this regard is that women in our church are more than men." One woman who said no to women's participation in her church business sessions adds this remark: "They don't because they've never been encouraged in the past. But when I'm at home I try to highlight the importance of them being in business meeting." There is some evidence here that though women are participating in decision-making at the church's business meetings, the quality or depth of that participation is questionable. Some of the male responses were: "Because of African culture some are still hesitant to speak before men. But they participate;" "As the church secretary they make good input in the church decisions;" "Munsieville is a small local church, and the congregation too is small, so women are participating because they dominating;" "In my church, the chairperson is a woman;" "Because every member of the church must be respected;" "One of the reasons why women have full participation is that they are many as compared to men;" "Women have recently been appointed to the church committee;" "Women sometimes do not participate in some issues. Even those who are in the executive. There are things that are solved by men. Sometimes only man would be called to meetings." There appears to be an interesting mixture of experiences here. While women seem to be well represented in business meetings, women can be ignored in participating in some meetings. One gets the feeling that women are "participating" simply by being present in some churches.

Overwhelmingly, there are many more women than men in BCSA churches. Both men (yes - 27, no - 1) and women (yes - 28, no - 4) testify to this fact. Women seem to be much more active participants in church activities compared to men. Women's comments were: "We have a ratio of fifty women to twenty men;" "There are more women but not participate in the religious activities more than men;" "Men usually work far from home, women left at home continue with religious activities of the church;" "Mostly the men are doing the worship leading and preaching;" "It's only few men and they are still young men;" "Men are few and they are participating more in church developments concerning raising of funds for the building of the church. Women are participating holistically." Some of the men's comments were: "Because there are many women in the

WOMEN AND LEADERSHIP

church;" "In my local church we have more woman than man;" "Men in South Africa are not easily brought to Christ. They believe in their culture and they believe if they come to Christ they will lose their culture." There were other similar statements on the dominant numbers of women participating in worship and other religious ac-tivities of the church. It appears that women are not only much larger in numbers than men but highly active as well, though apparently not in high profile roles like worship leading, preaching and raising funds for the church building. Kanyoro (1996a:151) gives a warning that the BCSA churches should heed:

> It is imperative that the Church should hear the silent screams of millions of women who fill the pews of our churches. Despite the willingness of many women to identify with the Church, there are others who distance themselves from it, and even leave the Church, either silently or in protest.

Nine women felt that women are suppressed or oppressed in their churches, either openly or unconsciously. Twenty-two felt otherwise. One said she didn't know. Two men felt women are suppressed or oppressed, twenty-four felt they were not. Two didn't know. Some women's observations were: "There is equality in my church. Women are free, though many are still sitting back;" "But some women experience this from their own families;" "Not at all. We would speak up against it for the sake of the Lord's work;" "In some of the things women are not allowed to tell male leader, rather ladies are told to do them personally. They are not given pulpit often;" "Now lately women turn to suppress other women;" several said women are oppressed "unconsciously;" "But I think also women are look down on themselves.[2] They don't see that they can play a big role." Women's own low self-esteem, women oppressing women, failure to take opportunities, and blatant oppression are all expressed

VIEWS AND EXPERIENCES IN THE BCSA

in the above comments. Also, we notice that while the objective data shows women as little oppressed, the comments seem to give us another picture. Men's remarks were: "They are equal as men;" "There is some unconscious form of oppression. This is seen in how leadership is selected (which is more of men than women) and the preaching about women being submissive to their husbands;" "The suppression I observe as pastor is culture based but never enforced;" "Maximum participation is on practice in our church. We as a church we did away with apartheid, all people are equal;" "What happens, if a man arrives in the church. Even if he is still a new convert but being a man, he gets high position and respect in the church;" "Even though they're elected into church positions, they're not influential and their powers are limited somehow." Some men see equality and no suppression, while other men see suppression clearly. It is so for the women respondents as well. The last comment is insightful, i.e., the fact of position does not necessarily mean influence and power.

In an interview, one woman said:

> When I am in the local church I feel encouraged when I am given a chance to be a leader or to share something in the church. When we have regional meetings and see how women are treated I feel angry. Maybe this is happen because I have learned from my local church that women are as capable as men.

Note the anger felt when, at the extension of the local churches, i.e., the regional conferences, women are marginalized. She gives further explanation:

> Usually in our regional meeting, the time together is shared so that men, women and youth can have a chance to lead the services and

preach. One time women were called to be responsible, therefore they elected one to share God's word. On the previous night it was men's day and everyone was there. What frustrated me is to find out that on our day as women there were only a few people in the church, even those were women and some women were cooking. Men and youth were outside making noise. I preached to a very few number of people. I observed that because a woman was preaching men could not listen. This was even done by pastors. While I was preaching I could hear them making noise as if they were showing me that they don't care....Men must stop talking about women liberation and fail to practice it. This is what I have observed in our region and the Baptist Convention as a whole. Now it is time for them to practice what they preach.

Clearly, this experience was devastating to this woman. In her testimony she said that she is not treated in such a humiliating way in her church. She finds joy in the local church where everyone is respected and treated equally. But is not a regional conference a representation of the local churches? Is it not in fact an expression of God's people in worship? Fiorenza (1992:205) is surely correct: "We must become conscious that until every woman is free, no woman is truly able to overcome patriarchal infirmity and bondage."

Another woman shared:

When we pray for the sick, the church chooses men to pray. They were chosen by the elders (all men). My pastor's wife has the gift of healing. All the women were not comfortable with this. They were all upset because they know the pastor's wife has this gift, and this is another example of women being excluded. We keep quiet.[3]

The suppression of this woman, a pastor's wife, by other women of the church is not an uncommon occurrence. Other recorded stories depict similar incidences.

The following narrative describes the practice of subjugation in a local congregation:

> Early 80's at Pearce Memorial Baptist Church in Zwelitsha I was not given the church leadership as woman. It was only men who take all opportunities. There was a time when I felt to speak about the problem I saw in the church. I was not given a chance because I am a woman. I was not given a chance to talk in the business meeting and to make decisions in the church about issues that are not pleasing us women in the church.
>
> One time with other women, we were driven out by other deacons since our husbands were not church members. They were not allowing us to testify and correct mistakes of their leadership. They claim that we cannot correct them whereby our husbands were not there. That had made me to feel oppressed and as a marginalized person in the church. That made me to think that the church is for men only but now I thank God's love to reveal about Christ freedom for all genders.[4]

There is little doubt that women who are continually oppressed harbor underlying resentment and anger toward the church or toward men. This woman finds her strength in Christ and the knowledge of his acceptance and freedom to serve him as women. But the restrictions in the male-controlled church persist. In a conference I attended at the UNISA Sunnyside Campus ("Hearing the AIC-Voice"), Archbishop N. H. Ngada declared, "Women in mainline churches are not given leadership privileges of a high nature. This is one of the reasons for rise of AICs." A provocative thought.[5]

WOMEN AND LEADERSHIP

A man speaks of the same subjugation. A few other men had similar types of views but this one example will suffice:

> In my church I feel that women have not been given equal opportunities as men. The church is led by men and only their wives are recognized as leaders and you can even see that they only get this honor because of their husbands. Even in the church program it's men leading. Women will only asked to cook when there is a special event. Even in the community of the church there is only one woman and she is only there because they have discovered that she is more capable than they are. In the church women don't even preach, they only preach when there is a special day for women in the calendar. Then the whole service will be led by women. Even in those days you'll find out that few men attend the church.

We have heard this before -- that when a woman preaches "few men attend." Actions speak as loud, if not louder, than words. This type of story, its theme of subjugation and humiliation, is a common one in the accounts I've recorded. The same man testifies further:

> Because this is a new church and is made up of families. This woman oppression is from their homes. This is how they treat their wives, as a result it affects what they are doing because they are used to it. I also feel that women are comfortable with the way they are treated.

One of the most sorrowful statements that can be heard is: "women are comfortable with the way they are treated." Is this true? If subjugation and oppression is abusive, is it possible for human beings to become *comfortable* with abuse?

VIEWS AND EXPERIENCES IN THE BCSA

All cultures, even the African one, can ponder Bate's (1994:107) view of inculturation and its impact on the local church:

> Since culture is part of what it means to be human, culture is called to die and rise with Christ to new life and become a new creation. This is the meaning and purpose of the evangelization of cultures. . . . So inculturation is the dialogue between the community of saints: the church within a context, and others of the same culture. In this way inculturation is mission. This mission is carried out by bringing good news to the culture and in this sense, inculturation is evangelization: the evangelization of culture.

In conclusion, while most women and men testify to women serving as deacons in their churches, while most women and men admit to women participating in church business meetings equally with men, while most women and men profess many more women than men are active in their churches, and while both women and men are in agreement that most churches do not suppress or subjugate women, the interviews bring out strong qualifications. While some of the interviews substantiated the data collected from the questionnaires, women and men who are given a chance to elucidate conditions in their churches portray a more somber picture of male prejudice and ecclesiastical discrimination towards women. Hence, while the BCSA advocates a 'holistic' and 'participatory' gospel, it frequently fails to translate those ideals into the realm of many *church experiences*. There is ample evidence of male exclusionary practices as well as disdain for female leadership. Is this a case of the evidence dis-proving the statistics?

WOMEN AND LEADERSHIP

Perceptions of male attitudes toward women

The questionnaires and interviews here seek to discover the perceptions Baptist Convention churchwomen and men have regarding male attitudes toward women in church leadership. Are men changing their views on women and their potential for leadership in the church? Is it mostly men's attitude and image of women that must be changed in order to liberate women into church leadership at all levels? Since I did considerable investigations into male attitudes and experiences regarding women, this section will capitalize on that information to a significant degree.

The questionnaires revealed that both women (yes - 25, no - 5, I don't know - 2) and men (yes - 21, no - 7, I don't know - 1) feel strongly that young men in the rural and township churches show more willingness to view women more highly and thereby allow for the possibility of more female leadership in the church. As always, individual interpretation to each questionnaire item may vary. Hence comments are helpful. Here are a few from the women on this issue: "They view male and female equally;" "Still struggling to understand a woman pastor in a local church and in relation to her spouse;" "Many times a woman's view is not so taken; they think as young men they have a better understanding;" "The older men seem to be more resistant than the young men to women leadership;" "But few and only those that are still young;" "In 1992 I was chosen to represent the whole body of the department of youth. Why as I asked them in my church, they viewed me more highly and finding out that I'm suiting to be recommended to go abroad;" "They say women still lack knowledge in leadership and have noise, even if it is not true. Some women are good in leadership, and have skills of it;" "Men are always want to be the leaders. If you are a female they find some difficulties to follow your instructions as the female. They take themselves as the head, always they are the best." The last respondent conveys a degree of despondency if not bitterness at male attitudes. Even young male attitudes. She was one of several who felt that young men do not show any more willingness than others to view women with respect by allowing them to serve in church leadership. Rebecca Mashiane's (1996:106-113) account of her pilgrimage in ministry as a BCSA pastor's wife should dispel any doubt to women's strength, faith and abilities.

Some of the comments by men on the above issue were: "Most young men encourage their wives to enter teacher education. Most of those women are part of the teaching staff in our Family Bible Hour;" "Views are about the same;" "Though there are some individuals who are still trapped in the old tradition -- whereby they say that they cannot be lead by a woman;" "Today young man are saying woman are the same as them. They all have to take part in what they are doing as men;" "In my church the youth committee is run by more girls;" "Most of young men are having problems because they become oppressed too. The women in leadership authorize even things beyond their position;" "Men in the church don't see that they are oppressing women but they just think things are supposed to go this way;" "The younger generation has a positive attitude towards women leadership." Those men who gave a negative vote convey strong feelings, but as with the women, the majority feel that young men do show more willingness to affirm women's leadership.

There was more hesitation by both women (yes - 16, no - 13, I don't know - 3) and men (yes - 16, no - 9, I don't know - 3) when it came to the attitudes of older men. As can be seen, there were many "no" decisions to the question of whether old or older men are seen to have more willingness to allow for women's leadership in the church.

WOMEN AND LEADERSHIP

Women tended to be more negative than the men on this one (16 to 13, compared to the men's 16 to 9). Some of the women's remarks were: "They always overlook women;" "But it is not all of them who are free with the leadership of woman;" "Older men have more problems;" "It is difficult because of the tradition that only males can be leaders." Several said, "We don't have old men of the church;" "Because of their age and culture;" "For they respect their (women's) dedication in the ministry;" "Especially in my church, women are now viewed more highly because of the old or older men of which we call them at home the pillars of the church." One woman who said "no" to the question said, "Always the same to the young and the old." Men responded this way: "Not certain -- this is half and half. Some older men are very open to female leadership and some are still conservative;" "Very few;" "Women are allowed in leadership, but during meetings when men discuss and make some decision women would be in the kitchen;" "It is not the same; older men have more doubt on women;" "They believe that some women are corrupt;"[6] "Though in many churches they are those still battling to accept this;" "Olden days of our past woman was nothing and even today they are practicing the same to their woman in our tradition; "There are old people with the old mind. We do have people that had left the church because of leadership of women;" "Because it is hard for them to accept the change of time. Everything is turning around so it is hard to understand. They are trapped in the olden times;" "Due to strong cultural background there's still some resistance on older men to accept women leadership at all levels." The above comments demonstrate significant unwillingness by both women and men to accept the view that older men are sympathetic to women's leadership in the church, even though a slight majority felt otherwise.

Women (yes - 23, no - 5, I don't know - 4) and men (yes - 24, no - 2, I don't know - 1) overwhelmingly felt that the attitudes of youth today (both male and female) are different from the attitudes of the elderly (men and women) in regard to women and their leadership capabilities. The women's comments were: "Young people realize that we are all equal and have equal potential;" "Yes, because nowadays women are allowed for the possibility of leadership in the church even is 1% out of 99%;" "Youth can tolerate or accept women speaking better than older generation. They are more comfortable;" "In the olden days, the view was that women must stay in their place, but today the youth view male/female more equally." The men's responses were: "Young people do not have a problem as to who is their leader. Because of the modern cosmology the criteria is not on gender;" "The youth from universities seem to have a better attitude towards women;" "There's still a misconception among elderly, that men are better leaders;" "It is clear that we are living in the 90s, so we view things differently (youth than the elders). So the youth's reasons differ from the old people;" "Youth have a different view, more positive;" "Youth today see women as free as they are;" "Old people still believe that man are capable than women. Even if they believe we are equal but when they are given an opportunity, they are mostly reluctant to take it." One cannot differentiate the remarks of the women from the men. One of the most hopeful signs of women's empowerment in the affairs of the future Christian church may be the liberating views that youth seem to express. We shall see how the interviews to follow will prick the bubble of optimism found in the questionnaire.

On the question of whether it is mostly men's attitude toward and image of women that must be changed in order for real progress to be made in the local churches for women's liberation, both the women (yes - 17, no - 8, I don't know - 7) and the men (yes - 19, no - 7, I don't know - 1) demonstrate mixed convictions -- the women

WOMEN AND LEADERSHIP

more so. Some of the women's observations were: "Even women must change and not undermine themselves in this regard;" "It is about equal. Both men and women's attitudes need to change;" "Both because there are women who do not know their rights in the church;" "The attitude should start to change from home[7] not only in church;" "Neither. Women are in leadership of late;" "Men feel threatened by strong women;" "Because even if women are capable but they need to be encouraged and get a chance;" "The fact is in the days we are living God is using everybody and they are aware of the fact;" "There need to be workshop in terms of gender equality;" "It is both male and female. We still have female minds that must be liberated;" "Men and women must change, especially women. They must change from their self-centered behavior, sometimes it is not due to men's attitude, is due to their fear and self-pity;" "It is equally men's and women's problems. Women do not like younger women in leadership;" "Men have good attitude toward women;" "They are slaves of their upbringing -- culture and laziness." The reactions vary. While an obvious majority (men and women) see women's oppression in the church as a male perpetration, many caution with evident conviction that women are often at least as guilty as men in lowering the expectations of women.

Comments made by men on the above issue were: "Both of them must change;" "Because some men are prejudiced, they still look down upon women;"[8] "Women also have negative attitude towards women who can be pastors, especially the elderly women;" "It is women's attitude of self-esteem which must change;" "But women too need to change their attitudes;" "Also mostly women's attitude and image must be changed for their own image;" "The men, because they feel superior they must change their attitude and also women must stop feeling inferior. They must raise their voices and concerns;" "I think women have to outgrow the past and take-up their rightful place and not wait for men to change their attitude towards them;" "If it will happen that way it will work, because men will be helped by women as they do help their husbands at their homes with ideas;" "But women must change to complete their liberation. It works both sides;" "Not always man's attitude only against women because some woman have that oppressive minds from their homes where they are from as woman to be;" "There are some women who have accepted the fact that they do not need any liberation. Things and the state of affairs should remain as they are;" "Man's attitude should be changed;" "It is women in my church who look down on other women in leadership;" "Men have dominated the leadership position in the church in the past. They still have their pride of the past. They are the ones whose image needs to be changed. Women need some little change because of their inferiority complex;" "Both men and female attitudes must be changed for the better." We must credit men for their honesty and self-criticism. They state that not only do men and women oppress women in the church, but women's own oppression of themselves (self-doubt, inferiority complex) is a major problem. While some women have expressed or implied these two oppressions, the men have stated them more vividly and emphatically.

Perceptions of male attitudes toward women, then, both by women and men, have revealed that the problem lies with female and male attitudes toward women. The following excerpts from only a few of the interviews help clarify or qualify the questionnaire data. These excerpts were carefully chosen to represent what others have said but for lack of space were not selected for inclusion in this thesis.

WOMEN AND LEADERSHIP

One woman respondent decried:

> I am not sure that they support us. There are times whereby the church is electing and the good person in that portfolio is the woman. They elect the man since all the time the portfolios are used to be taken by men, like preaching. By this the pastor and the leadership are not trying to encourage or train the women in this portfolio or other leadership role that the man are used to take.

In this case, the men of the church harbor belittling attitudes toward women. Many of the women and men respondents in the questionnaires echoed this dominance. This same respondent had this also to say regarding female inferiority and self-depreciation as poignantly revealed in the questionnaires:

> I feel that they are embarrassed in other times. Other women are ashamed to take these opportunities since they were not given the chance in the past. Others who are in they are feeling as if not doing good when they compared themselves with men.

We, of course, do not know whether these women were or were not doing as good a job as the men. One wonders how much disapproving looks or negative remarks or suspicious body language by women and men undermine the women's effort to not only perform well but to feel affirmed and to feel good about themselves.[9]

Another common complaint made by women is represented by the following, though we are not sure if the oppression is done by young or old men or both:

> There are people who are preventing women in these roles. They are making comparisons with other churches which are not giving

VIEWS AND EXPERIENCES IN THE BCSA

women opportunities. They have felt ashamed to be given women the roles that are for men, like deacon, pastoring and preaching in the Sunday service. They felt that women are to sing and take other service not leadership in the church.

Ecclesial practices sanctified by tradition make many Baptist Convention churches captive to immortalized hierarchical patterns of behavior. Perhaps a way to 'crack this hard nut' is to liberalize the minds of a roster of theological students so that they will begin to read scripture with a gender-sensitized notion that will translate into transformation of the attitudes of women and men in the churches.

Another woman addressed the problem identified in the questionnaire data, i.e., the attitude of pastors and other male leaders to support the BCSA's promotion of full gender inclusion in local church practice yet deny it in actuality:

> The Baptist Convention has its own view and vision of women in leadership, but most pastors are not utilizing this vision in the local churches. Most pastors say, 'This is my church.' Meaning everyone is subjugated to his authority. They are owning the church. It is their kingdom. Women who are more capable than pastors' wives are not allowed to be prominent in the church. This problem is still there. Many capable women are therefore discouraged. Some therefore find expression of leadership outside the church since they have been denied leadership in the church. This is still a problem.

This woman's perception of male attitudes toward women in leadership is negative, especially toward pastors who control their 'turf' and obstruct the BCSA's vision of women's freedom to serve in all spheres of church life.

WOMEN AND LEADERSHIP

A candid confession by Finca (1998:8-10) illustrates the perceptive awareness that some men have on the gravity and variable extent of discrimination against women in the church. Finca's observation is enlightening:

> Born and bred into an unashamedly patriarchal society, I was socialized from childhood into a system which just does not discriminate against women and treat women as second-class human beings; but goes further than that and appropriates to men the right to define and determine the entire social order, the right to decide what is normal and what is abnormal, the right to set up acceptable standards of behavior -- and do all this ... from a man's point of view. In such a society when you challenge the sexist stereotypes, you are deemed to be unwell, abnormal, and in need of the help of a physician. This is not only how men see and judge you, but how the entire society including women see and judge what is acceptable and what is abnormal ... I do not see a way in which I can talk about the status of women in the Church except in a spirit of humble confession. Because the Church has failed women. And I believe in failing women, the Church has failed Christ, the Christ who expects the Church to be his Body in the world, a light that shines in the darkness, a city built on the hill-top, the salt of the earth ... How do the structures of our Church governance depict the reality that the overwhelming majority of our Church membership is women and only a tiny minority men? How are women consulted when the most burning issues on the doctrine and governance of the Church are being debated and legislated on? How much of the Gospel proclamation is done in our Churches by women -- not only women to other women but I mean proclamation by women to both men and women and even by women to men ... How many of us are working seriously at discovering the alternatives and at revising the liturgy itself to be more gender-sensitive? ... I have not dealt with the problems posed to the Church by the prejudices of women against women, the fact that the most powerful force against

women leadership in the Church is that of women themselves. I have not dealt with the dynamic of racism amongst women themselves and the absence of solidarity of sisterhood between a white Christian woman and a black Christian woman. I have not dealt with the class struggle between the rich woman and the poor woman, between the woman the employer and the woman the worker (and how they relate to each other within the Church and its structures).

Finca puts fault at the feet of both men and women. His remarks convey the comprehensive nature of and need for church renewal.

The following interview excerpt reflects a male perception of male attitude toward women in the church.

In the executive of the church you may find one woman or two. The rest are men. If a woman speaks, a man must support her view or her position will not be taken by the group.

If behavior is determined by attitudes, then the attitude reflected in the above account depicts a lack of respect for the woman's gifts, abilities and depth of her spirituality. And does it not reflect man's ego, and his arrogance, or his (supposedly) divine right to superiority?

The following male respondent conveys what other men and women of the interviews convey, and what has been surfaced by comments made in the questionnaire data:

My church elect women in leadership, but women have an inferiority complex. Some women don't have the motivation. It makes me sad that women are not able to identify themselves as who they are.

WOMEN AND LEADERSHIP

That is caused by their culture and the past government that kept them down. They should be encouraged.[10]

'Motivation' cannot be generated from the soil of degradation and inferiority but from the soil of encouragement and hope. Motivation requires courage; it assumes the possibility of success. This man is 'sad' to find women so down on themselves. Can the Christ of the Bible transcend 'culture' and 'the past' in order to liberate the church from the perpetration of women's dehumanization?

The male respondent in the following account portrays the male-dominated church executive as questioning the ability of women. We are not sure if the church executive has reason to or not. It appears to be sexism:

> The pastor is supportive to empower women. The problem is other members of the executive are against it because they say since we elected women in the committee things are failing. They don't just question their capability as any human being but as women.

If we assume that a typical church executive is largely constituted by older or mature men, we can assume that this interview respondent shares a perspective similar to so many in the questionnaire data, i.e., that older or mature men tend to depreciate the value and abilities of women perhaps in most cases more than the youth of the churches. Is this not sexism? We have seen that there are exceptions, but can we surmise that they are the exception and not the rule?

I would like to end with an excerpt from this male interview respondent. It represents a number of churches, based upon the data, that do attempt to support women, even encourage them, and permit them to serve in their churches:

VIEWS AND EXPERIENCES IN THE BCSA

At my church we make a program for a month. The pastor preaches two times, and others, including women, are scheduled to preach. We don't have deacons, we just have a church executive. Nine members in executive, including three women. There are more women than men in the church. Most of the women are single. Men are very few. Four of the men are strong leaders, others not so strong. But there are many strong women. Women are very involved in teaching in the Family Bible Hour.

Most of the women are working, travelling by taxis, bus and train. A few of these women are preaching in the trains and buses. We have about one hundred members in our church.

This account shows the positive male attitudes toward women. It reveals a bold trust in the abilities of women in high profile responsibilities, both within and outside the church. The perception of this male is that the men of his church are not just tolerant of women, but see them, at best, as necessary *partners* in God's work.

Like the BUSA data, the BCSA questionnaires and interviews reveal the resistance of many churches to the equal role of women in the higher levels of ecclesiastical life. Since we have accumulated much more data from the BCSA churches, we take note of the obvious perception by both women and men that men of the younger generation regard women's role and abilities in the church to be more positive and that old or older men are perceived to be less positive and more resistant to the empowerment of women. We have also seen that the perception by both women and men of the Baptist Convention is that women's negative attitudes and image of other women as well as women's own self-depreciation and low self-esteem impede a liberating praxis for women's leadership in the church. Hence, while men's negative attitudes toward women are pervasive and crippling for women, it is not by any means the only factor in the suppression of women's abilities in the local churches. Anger, frustration, and sometimes a sense of hopelessness have been uncovered in many women, and these emotions have also been revealed in the remarks by a number of men. We have discovered that, with a (hopefully) growing awareness on the part of men to the plight of gifted churchwomen, women can find encouragement and support from them in some quarters. We have seen, too, that women are (hopefully) growing in awareness of their responsible role in the church yet appear stunted in their practical attempts at liberation.[11]

Natural abilities of women

The questionnaires and interviews seek to discover how Baptist churchwomen and men view the natural abilities of women and how these abilities or lack of them may affect women's leadership capacities in the church. A few of the areas investigated are: women's abilities in preaching and teaching, women's hermeneutical uniqueness, women's courage, intelligence, commitment and other personal qualities, spiritual strength and leadership abilities, and perceived female strengths and weaknesses as they may relate to leadership in the church.

I found overwhelming similarity in the responses of both women and men in all areas of inquiry mentioned above, from both the questionnaires and interviews.[12]

On the question of whether one's church allows women to preach to women and children only, women (yes - 7, no - 25) and men (yes - 8, no - 20) stated that in some churches this was so but in the strong majority of cases when a woman is allowed to preach men are present. The women's comments were: "They are preaching to everybody (this was said several times);" "Though you might see that they just want to judge and have some questions at the back of you;" "They only preach to women only on women's day;" one woman who said "yes" added: "This is unfair to the ministry and women for their progress and development of gifts;" "But they do it unconsciously not openly." The men's responses were: a number said some variation of the following, "Women preach to all in main services and preach very good;" "My own observation is that this habit of culture is changing -- because the present leadership encourages women to preach to the entire church;" "The church is not against women preaching but they have just been doing it this way and no one in the church has suggested to give women a chance to preach;" "The role of women in our church is very complicated. I can't determine what their role is;" "In my church women are given chance to preach. It is them who don't take this responsibility. They prefer to preach when they are alone as women." It appears that women's opportunity to preach before the whole church is infrequent, such as on women's day. As shown, a few churches outright disallow women to preach where men are present. Seemingly, all is well and quiet with churches in general when women preach to women and children only.[13]

In the area of teaching, women (yes - 28, no - 3, I don't know - 1) and men (yes - 26, no - 2) said overwhelmingly that they are allowed to *teach* both men and women. Here are the women's comments: (The following three remarks indicate that the respondents confuse or interchange 'preaching' and 'teaching.') "But not regularly, preaching is known to be a men thing;" "This is rare.

WOMEN AND LEADERSHIP

The pastor and those who are gifted in preaching do the preaching -- unfortunately only men;" "Sometimes we invite a woman preacher to speak at church;" "Women are only allowed to teach or preach in women's fellowship;" "You'll ever find that men are making more requests from women to come and bring some teaching;" "I'm not sure whether they will allow them;" "We are promoting the use of gifts." The men's comments were: "Yes they are allowed. Sometimes it is women who look down on themselves. They are used to depend on men;" "They can preach to both but not from pulpit level;" "Never seen it done in the two years being in that church;" "But sometimes other men have problem when the visitors from different churches visited. And other men left the church because their tradition doesn't allow them to be lead by a woman;" several said something like, "We do accept their teaching;" "For teachings we just see it in our conferences and regions. In my local church I never saw that happening;" "Both preaching sessions and Family Bible Hour sessions;" "Because some are called by God to teach -- real teachers, anointed to teach;" "To children and youth as well." Again we see that while women are allowed to teach, some feel inadequate and insecure in doing so. Nevertheless, other women appear very gifted or talented in teaching and are doing so, even in the presence of men in most churches. It is thus disheartening to see that in some churches women have never been seen teaching where men are present.

On the matter of hermeneutics, the question was asked whether women and men felt it was important for the church to have the women's point of view in interpreting the scriptures. The responses of the women (yes - 30, no - 1, I don't know - 1) and the men (yes - 25, no - 2, I don't know - 1) were remarkably similar. The women made comments such as: "Everybody has an experience of God that obviously means God has a relationship with women that must be heard when preaching is interpreted;" "You'll find that scripture text like women must keep quiet in the church, needs to be re-interpreted and to be contextualized as well. You'll find that some women are still slaves;" "Because women are also part of the Kingdom of God;" "But always men have the say against women;" "Yes and no. We do not need a strong feminist theology, but a healthy women's point of view;" "Male pastors often preach as if only women are in congregation and in need of change and improvement;" "Both men and women's point of view are good for people;" "There is no proof that God is only man. Because he created both male and female in God's image. God is neither male nor female;" "For as a woman I also have my understanding, not only as a woman but also as a person (Christian);" "Women are human beings like men. They are affected by everything that affects men. They are as responsible as are the men to lift up the spiritual status of the church."[14]

The men's comments on the value of women's hermeneutics, i.e., the woman's point of view in interpreting scriptures were: "Because the knowledge that she has is from God not from man;" "This aspect needs to be encouraged;" "The word of God does not originate with men only;" "Because the Bible is not only for man even woman only is for all believers. Now is important for us to listen to views of woman;" "Some of the woman had very good doctrine, take for example the radio programs;" "Because they become bias. Is like when they lead the service, they concentrate only on the scriptures that talks about women and it's unfair;" "If we allow people to consider contexts in interpreting even the women must do so;" "That is what is lacking in the Christian faith and what is wrong with the Christian view of God;" "This will enable the church to have a balanced view and interpretation of scriptures;" "No man and no women points of view but just interpret the scriptures;" "For the church to reach everyone it must allow a complimentary interpretation of the scriptures between men and women." The interviews of women and men substantiate the questionnaire findings in support of the need for women's hermeneutics. After all, was it not the Samaritan woman's point of view that was proclaimed to her village after she heard the "gospel" from Jesus? Udo (1997:23) calls the Samaritan woman the first evangelist during Jesus' earthly ministry.

Do women bring female strengths to the life and ministry of the church as they exercise leadership in the church? The tabulation for women (yes -28, no -3, I don't know -1) and men (yes - 24, no - 2, I don't know - 2) were similar. The vast majority responded in the affirmative. The women commented: "Any person can bring strength or weakness;" "Women are able to build and encourage even in a hopeless situation;" "They specialize in caring and exploring. You teach one of them you'll have taught a nation. They have started kindergartens, soup kitchens, they visit hospitals, prisons without any training;" "Today we have women like Brigalia Hlophe Bam who is the general secretary of the South African Council of Churches. She was a leader in her church, today in a council;" "Women are more caring and sensitive. Women are more building rather than destroying. Men are rough. They don't care;" "These women if they are given a task and being helped to do that task they become very effective in their ministry or leadership;" "I can say partly yes and partly no, depending on the strength of men in their responsibility in the church." The outstanding characteristics or strengths of women voiced by women are their ability to "build" and encourage, to care and "explore" (creative, innovative), and to be sensitive. Does the church need warmth and compassion, creativity and community-building?[15]

VIEWS AND EXPERIENCES IN THE BCSA

On the same issue, the men observed: "They stay with children, so they see things more compassionately;" "Women are indispensable, can't do without. It is not good for man to operate in leadership without a woman;" "They never give up. They are always there in times of trials;" "They pray for the church. That is one weapon for success;" "So that it must not be only few men who dominate;" "Women are still sidelined and have as a result also kept a low profile in the church. If fully utilize the church can grow rapidly." In summary, men view women's strengths as compassionate, energetic and committed ("they never give up"), courageous ("they are always there in times of trials"), high spirituality ("they pray for the church"), and evangelistic zeal ("if fully utilized the church can grow rapidly"). Quite a compliment!

On women's weaknesses, the men did not have anything substantial to contribute in the questionnaires. The women's comments were: "Just like anyone could bring a weakness;" "Because of their fears, and often voice them before really seeing the situation;" "But both men and women bring weaknesses to the church;" "This happens because women have been oppressed for a long time. This causes them to undermine themselves. They end up bringing many weaknesses in leadership." The comment that both women and men bring weaknesses to the church was expressed in different ways by several men. Women who "undermine themselves" are doing so out of "fears" and insecurities. This belief has been repeated time and again in remarks made by women and men. Lebaka-Ketshabile (1997a:3) contends that people have been made to feel shame, anger, guilt and fear in the name of God and the church. People easily judge and condemn themselves in the name of God. People need, therefore, a healthy spirituality, and this can be achieved by creating for them-

WOMEN AND LEADERSHIP

selves a positive view of God that will liberate them from the negative images. How one relates to God is directly influenced by the images one has of God. It is vital, then, that one's images of who God is are caring, loving, honest and liberative in all circumstances.

Finally, the questionnaire probed into the areas of intelligence, public speaking, commitment, spiritual strength, motivation, compassion, energy, or other natural abilities. Where do women stand? Are they inferior to men in these qualities? The women (yes - 8, no - 22, I don't know - 2) and men (yes - 9, no -18, I don't know - 1) showed mixed reactions, though both showed a majority feeling that women are *not* inferior in these leadership qualities. The women's expressions were: several said something like, "They are equal;" a few said, "They are equal or even more superior to men;" "Sometimes it happen because we have not yet psychologically healed;" "Not at all. At least their compassion is deeper. All others are equal;" "This has nothing to do with being a man or a woman;" "But some are inferior;" "They are more intelligent than men. They are more compassionate than men;" "But other women have confidence but not others;" "The problem is that most women do not have confidence. Men did not give women to practice all these;" "Now lately women have discovered their potential though some are not yet sure because other men have resorted to be Christians only at church and be lions at home to keep their wives neutral;" "I'm saying this because I'm one of the women who are not weakened by the intelligence of men. God has called me and is using me the way he uses men. I don't have a doubt about this. Even in the Convention we have strong women who can stand before men;" one woman who believed women are inferior said, "Women were always at the back seat, at home in the past days, women were not allowed to be educated for they believe that, she is going to be married, so why should she be taken to school;"[16] "Men can also be inferior in other abilities." The qualities of intelligence and compassion appear to be prominent. Women's self-confidence was questioned, thus hindering their ability to lead commensurate with their gifts and desires. An important point, it appears to me, is the degree to which men's dominance at home cripples women's abilities to take leadership roles at church. One is unsure of the psychological and emotional damage that has been done and is being done to women in their homes that ill equip female children, youth and adults to become leaders of confidence in the church.

The men's responses as to the inferiority of women in the aforementioned natural abilities were: "In my church young women are more capable than young man. But they are used to serve men even if men are not capable;" "Women are equal strong in intelligence, same with men;" "As I said that woman still have the older days minds" (which is why, naturally, this man stated in the questionnaire that women are inferior); "Women and men are the same in speaking public;" "In this life, there are women who are intelligent than men;" "Women have the same capacities, they are good in everything;" "There are many women presenters on T.V. today. There are many women in Parliament today;" "Women are just not being given opportunities." Again, as with the women respondents, the unequal privileges and opportunities in women's lives have caused many to be 'inferior' in abilities, though the respondents may not be saying that women are inferior in *natural* abilities. Cultural captivity takes many forms, and has certainly affected women differently. Yet for most their subservience since childhood has affected their minds as adults. What is surprising is the number of women who have overcome a mountain of prejudice and oppression and still are able to sustain mental strength and energetic, skilled service to the church and in society.

WOMEN AND LEADERSHIP

Both men and women laud the creative, dedicated manner in which women serve the churches. An example is the organization and activities of the Baptist Women's Department (BWD) of the BCSA. The organizational, entrepreneurial and spiritual strength and talents of women are demonstrated through the BWD. According to one woman interview respondent:

> The BWD is the strongest department in the Convention. It is the most active compared to other departments. National (once a year) and regional (every third month usually) rallies are active. The purpose is threefold: a) spiritual growth of women -- physical, social, relational growth of women;[17] b) reach out in evangelism -- equip women to evangelize; and c) develop financial strength to give to needy causes -- tents, food, personal hygiene supplies, etc.

Administrative skills and Christian maturity sustains the three-prong objectives of this women's organization. Women's natural abilities are tantamount to its success. Not least of which is the ability to weave a cohesive network for common goals. For Pato (1996:113), to be genuinely human is to participate positively, to belong, to contribute "in those activities that make self-fulfillment in life by all concerned possible."

The deacon quoted below had this to say about the abilities of women:

> In my church the deacon board has ten men and ten women. There are twenty of us. We started having women like myself serving on this board since 1996. I see no discrimination among us. Women with problems can more easily speak to women deacons to bring to the deacon board. Men do not dominate at meetings. The chairman is a lady.

VIEWS AND EXPERIENCES IN THE BCSA

In my acquaintances with BCSA churches throughout the country, the vast majority, if they have women deacons, men appear to outnumber the women and tend to dominate. Kagiso Baptist Church, where the respondent above is a member, is the only church of the BCSA (to my knowledge) that has so many women deacons and where women are preaching regularly before four hundred people in the Sunday morning services.[18] It engineers the most liberating praxis I have witnessed in Southern Africa or North America for that matter.

A woman from a Soweto church testified:

We are not competing with men. But I find that women are equal to men in the things we do, or can do things better than men. Many women are more eager sometimes to serve in leadership. I think in other churches women are not as free as in our church. This makes me feel good.

Women frequently complain about their place in the church. It is therefore very uplifting to hear someone share from her heart and say that she "feels good" about the freedom provided women in her church to serve according to their desires and abilities.

The following account indicates the importance of pastoral leadership in creating a spiritual climate in the church whereby men *and* women move beyond reluctant toleration to affirmation of women in leadership roles:

In my church, we have had the pastor allowing women to take leadership roles. We have had roles like deacons, treasurer, secretary, chairman or president of the church as such. We have never seen the pastor or church executive isolating women. No. Lately we have women taking very senior positions in the church because of the down pouring of the Holy Spirit. In Joel 2 we see how the Holy Spirit can pour His Spirit. Thank God for Meadowlands Baptist Church and other churches that have caught this down pouring of the Holy Spirit among old men and youth of the church and have allowed women to be used greatly of God.

The next story is one told by a young woman who apparently has ample ability and desire to serve in her church. She is sure she possesses spiritual gifts and natural abilities, only she has been treated badly by the men of her church. Her story tells us why:

I have not been given equal opportunities with men. I have been only considered when there is no man to take my position. When people talk of electing a committee they always have men in their minds. Women are always just elected to fill the space and have one woman in the committee.[19] I am a capable woman and I know that but I'm always elected to close the space. I am embarrassed because we end up being led by men who are not even capable.

This respondent is an example of someone who has spiritual strength and leadership abilities, who desires to serve the Lord, but finds it an uphill battle. She continues with the following memory of an incidence, which must deeply dampen her trust in men, her male-dominated church, even perhaps, her faith in God:

I was sexually abused by a brother in the church. He is a well-known man in the church. He is also active and loved by the pastor. After he did this to me I went to the church committee and I told them. They never believed me. They accused me of lying and they said girls or women are not good.[20] They are always looking for someone to accuse. I remember this was a committee of men talking to me and they all accused me of being a liar. I felt very hurt and I regretted to be a woman. Being a woman was like being a curse to me. That brother came to apologize to me but I refused to forgive him. He did that again and later it was discovered that he does it to most girls. I was happy to see him deciding to leave the church.

Women who have female strengths, God-given abilities, and devotion to serve the church and exercise leadership, when battered like this by a church rapist and arrogant men who refuse to have compassion on the cry of the heart surely must in some way be weakened in their spirit, weakened in their desire, weakened in their faith, weakened in their abilities. We do not know to what degree men in her church destroy the ambitions of those like her who seek spiritual fulfillment.

The man quoted below praised the bravery, strength and leadership potential of women:

Women today must be allowed more voice and more leadership. It depends on culture. Among Xhosas, women are not allowed as much freedom. But among we Tswanas, we allow more power for women. In many schools, however, older teachers can tell the students to only listen to men, that women should not be followed. I have seen many women who are brave today, who can stand up and be strong. Esther in the Bible was a bold woman, and women today can be like that. Women need to be encouraged, though, because many women are fearful or are intimidated of leadership because of the old system. They need to be encouraged to hold positions in the church.

It is clear from the interviews of women and men that, while a new window of opportunity exists for women in the church, the "old

WOMEN AND LEADERSHIP

system" of oppression and male control is still very much alive, stifling the natural abilities and leadership potential of women.

Here is another man's view:

> I think women are as capable as men. They only need to be given a chance to prove themselves. It frustrates me to see such women who are leaders in places where they work and to see that they are oppressed by men in the church. I say this because I've tried to talk to some of them about this issue and I discovered that they don't see anything wrong. . . . no one seems to notice that they are oppressed.[21] They just become happy when they are given certain women's day. This has something to do with their cultural background.

"They don't see anything wrong" with the stifling of women's gifts and hermeneutical skills in preaching and teaching, their energy and desire, their spiritual compassion and capacity for leadership.

This Xhosa man also has high views on women's potential:

> My understanding is that both men and women are equal before the Lord. Both can be qualified to hold any position and serve in any way. Women have the ability. There are many things lacking in the church that are not done, that if women are given the opportunities, these things can be done. Like counseling. Women ought not to feel they are hindered by lack of an 'office' to counsel. I believe that a person who is able to express herself to another woman is a woman. Men are not able to convey the gospel wholistically to another woman. Women can do that to other women much better than men.

VIEWS AND EXPERIENCES IN THE BCSA

His stress on the ability of a woman to convey the gospel "wholistically" to another woman is interesting. What does he have in mind? Does he mean, in part at least, that women bring 'female strengths' to Christian ministry, or compassion, understanding and emotional support, or that the woman's point of view in interpreting God's truth touches areas of women's needs men normally do not touch?

The following respondent paints a negative picture of women's desire to exercise leadership and their performance in church responsibilities:

> I think women are given opportunities in my church. These opportunities are not equal to that of men. My church is in the process of equipping them. This is just starting and women are still reluctant to take these chances. The new committee that we have in the church, we made it sure that we have women serving in it. They are also asked to elect one woman to preach once every month. I think this is a great moment in the church to realize capability of women. My problem is women have not really showed that they are willing and able to lead or maybe it is because it's still soon for them to be used. I think as the church and the pastor we are doing our best to support women empowerment and to also show other church members that women are capable. The problem is women at the moment have never really shown that they are capable. I am not against them but they are not yet serious. Even here in the church we elected a woman to be the secretary but she always makes big mistakes that causes the whole committee to be ineffective. Women are letting us down.

How much do we blame women's historical and cultural disadvantages and suppression for their 'failures' in leadership? For

WOMEN AND LEADERSHIP

their insecurity? Or is the account above merely a case of individual ineptitude and nothing more? Saayman (comments made to me on 26 July 1999) believes that women are often given very difficult or unpopular assignments, tasks men do not want and thereby "being set up" to fail, proving that women cannot get the job done like men.

We can conclude this section, as we did the similar section on the BUSA study, by stating categorically that the natural abilities of women, the abilities they bring to the church, are viewed by the clear majority of women and men respondents[22] as not in any way falling short of the natural abilities that men bring to the affairs and leadership of the church. In fact, both men and women often praise the superior talents of women. However positive *attitudes* may be, the *actuality* or *practice* in the churches is most often found wanting.

Views on women as pastors

The questionnaires and interviews in this final section seek to discover views on women as pastors. Since preaching the sermon on Sunday is a major responsibility for pastors, are women being given opportunities to preach in worship services in Baptist churches? Are women capable as men to be pastors? Are women capable of providing spiritual counseling to men? Are women in the churches against women becoming pastors?

I found that the majority of women (yes - 30, no - 2) and men (yes - 24, no - 3, I don't know - 1) said that their church does allow women to preach during the Sunday morning worship. One woman who answered "no" explained, "Not because they are women, if any woman can be able to preach the church will be very happy to give her a chance." Other women said: "But on certain times;" "They allowed us but most of the time they want us to be master of ceremony. If we come as a group of male and female pastors, they will ask one of the male to preach;" "Only on mother's day;" "Only sometimes;" "But unconsciously;" "Because most people who are leaders in my church are women;" "They believe that women can be called also. We do have a lady pastor from our church." Men commented this way: "Women are scheduled to preach the same way as men;" several said, "I have never seen one;" "But they respect pastors. They enjoy preaching on Sundays if the pastor is absent;" "We had one working as full-time preacher leading one preaching point;" "When the service is led by the BWD and when the pastor is not available;" "They are even involved in pulpit exchanges, preaching in other churches. They get invited to be speakers in major conferences like Easter and rallies." As we have seen with the BUSA women, when BCSA women preach in Sunday worship services it is infrequent and haphazard. Yet we see that they are allowed to preach more readily in some churches than in others.

On the question of women's capability equal to men in pastoral leadership, the women (yes - 29, no - 1, I don't know - 1) showed slightly more optimism than men (yes - 22, I don't know - 6). Both, then, were highly confident that women could be as good as men in the pastoral ministry. Women said: "If they can have a real and enough training;" "Both they have a call, and trained I believe they are both capable;" "Women are much strong as the men. And they can also play a big role in each and every area of the church;" "More than men. Women have long been pastoring their families;" "We have no experience of women pastors so we cannot compare as yet;" "Very much so;" "With the support of their husbands;" "Because we are all preaching the same gospel;" "I think it's early to tell

WOMEN AND LEADERSHIP

since the Baptist Convention has just started with the program of allowing women to study theology." Women are thus seen to be overwhelmingly confident in women's capability in the work of the pastor.[23] The woman who said women are stronger than men because they have long been "pastoring their families" makes a very insightful point. Many spiritually mature mothers or grandmothers undoubtedly have been the spiritual head of their households, which of course includes the extended family. This "pastoral" influence should not be trivialized. Their physical and spiritual stamina is admirable. Motherhood and household leadership becomes the natural "training ground" for church leadership for many who have been deprived of more formal training.

Men made these comments on women's pastoral capacity: "God has anointed and empowered them as well;" "I have never met a woman pastor, but if God called, don't undermine God's call;"[24] "They are not capable as men. Women need a help of a man of God for other parts of pastorate;" "But the women I've seen who are pastors and those who are studying to be pastors look down on themselves even during discussion in class. They respect views of man;" "I think they can. I have never seen one, but I know they are capable;" "I cannot say yes or no because it depends;" "Not really capable as men, but they can do the work of a pastor;"[25] "Even though there might be limitations in going out to do ministry alone." We note that two respondents said women would not be as capable as men. One man observed that women pastors and pastoral candidates "look down on themselves." Another said women would have "limitations" such as some forms of outreach ministries if she is alone. Yet the clear majority gave women high potential for doing the work of the pastor.

VIEWS AND EXPERIENCES IN THE BCSA

The respondents to the questionnaire declared almost unanimously that women are fully capable of providing spiritual counseling to men. This is similar to the BUSA respondents. Women (yes - 31, I don't know - 1) and men (yes - 26, no - 1, I don't know - 1) of BCSA affirmed that women can be gifted with the interpretation of the word of God and can share it with effectiveness in offering wise spiritual counsel to men as well as to women. The women's comments were: "It will depend if that man understood the woman pastor;" "Because by birth the women have a compassion;" "In our church women do counseling to all;" "That one will depend on individuals. Some men don't consider women as counselors;"[26] "If she is led to do this or she can refer him to other pastors to help;" "If she had the ability to do so;" "A man is a person. I do have my own friends who are males whom I do counsel. The only problem can be an attitude;" "Because the training is the same;" "Because in the eyes of the Lord there's no men, no women we are all equal;" "Depending on her spiritual growth." The men's comments were: "They are much better. There are things that a man cannot speak about to other men, which need a woman;" "Absolutely;" "I think both women and men pastors are good for spiritual counseling. They both meet problems;" "Women can even be more effective because of their nature and character;" "It will depend on a man who needs counseling that time;" "Partly." The woman who said that in counseling women have "compassion" and the man who said women can be more effective than men because of the "nature" and "character" may have been speaking of the same qualities. It would appear that some believe that women do bring female strengths to the counseling and pastoral roles. Both women and men indicated that man's attitude is vital in whether he will accept counseling from a woman, however skilled and compassionate she may be.[27]

WOMEN AND LEADERSHIP

As to the presence in churches of women who are against a woman becoming the pastor of the church, there is disparity in the views of women (yes - 7, no -19, I don't know - 6) and men (yes - 11, no - 7, I don't know - 10). Women who answered "no" were in the majority, while men who answered "yes" were in the majority. Could it be that there is a difference of perception but not of reality? Women's comments were: several said something like, "More especially the old ones;" "I never find out from the women;" "Not at all. Not so far as I know;" "They are happy even praying that God brings others for many churches are without pastors;" "The church have called one of our ladies who went to a theological training and accepted God's calling on pastorate. And we are with her now at our church;" "Women in our church would be excited to have a woman pastor;" "They are supporting the woman who has received a call fully." Men's comments were: several said, "More especially old women;" "But they are in minority;" "You get two different groups of women, of the older and today, that is why there is a difference;" "My wife was unanimously voted to go to BCC. But I have never tested their feeling about women becoming pastors;" "I have never heard of any complaint against that;" "Lack of education and resistance to change." "I have never tried to interview them about that point." What is clear from the responses of women and men is that they both believe that older women are the ones especially against women becoming pastors of churches. The men are very unsure of what women believe about women being against a woman serving as pastor (yes - 11 and no or I don't know - 17). We know that, unlike BUSA, the BCSA has been for many years openly affirming women in the ministry in their assemblies, Winter Schools of Theology, and at the Baptist Convention College. It is unknown to what degree the local churches are in support, but the data collected seem to indicate wide support in theory and less so in practice. We also have seen that women as well as men hinder women to serve in leadership.[28]

VIEWS AND EXPERIENCES IN THE BCSA

A woman interview respondent shared about her anger and frustration at the way she is treated by the pastor of her church. She is a theological student in training to be a pastor but is treated marginally in deference to a male theological student:

> We are not equal. It is like you are given a chance once in a while. Like serving in Holy Communion or preaching. Men get these opportunities more frequently. I don't like moving away from this church. I feel determined to prove myself. It hurts because I sometimes feel I am less important than a man. I am not being noticed that I can do something. I remember in 1996, I was not introduced in my church as a student pastor. A male student was asked to preach in the church, and the pastor casually introduced me as a student. It hurt to be treated in this way. With other members, men and women, they support me in church. When I am given a date to preach, they come to me afterwards and tell me how much they have been blessed. My pastor is more often an African man who knows that a woman's place is in the kitchen.[29] It doesn't make me feel good. I don't like it. I have never talked to him about it. If my pastor would change his attitude toward women, it would be better. My pastor's wife has been trained at theological college, but she preaches once a year!

Here is a case of the male pastor, not women or men of the church, who is repressing the abilities of this aspiring woman pastor (she is 30 years old). We have seen that a pastor, especially if he is wise and respected, can be the key figure in altering attitudes and behavior detrimental to women.

The following story defines the major role a male pastor plays in his view of women as well as his view of women as pastors. It also defines how he may or may not address the issue to his congregation:

WOMEN AND LEADERSHIP

> When I told my church board that I was registering to be a student at the theological college, I was never interviewed, never encouraged or supported in prayer or financial support. My church board never asked any questions on my announcement. Even today they do not ask how I am doing. It hurts a lot! One day they will realize a woman can be called of God. My church does not encourage me. It hurts a lot. They are not interested.

Note that the woman above stated "It hurts a lot" twice. This disinterest in her as a prospective pastor explains the lack of interest in using her as a preacher:

> Our pastor is very much supportive of women in leadership. But it is only men who are given the privilege of preaching in the church. I think women are there to preach. We are there. When we have "Women's Day" or "Children's Day," then a woman can preach. It's quite questionable why the pastor does not ask me a woman in training to preach. There are others.[30]

There is obvious emotional pain, as well as theological frustration seen in this woman of thirty years, who is a wife and mother. We have seen how the vast majority of women and men declare that women are as capable as men to be pastors, yet this woman is denied by her church to be fully accepted and affirmed as she suspects a male pastoral candidate would be under similar circumstances. Though Tetteh (1997:53) speaks in the context of the Akan culture in Ghana, her pristine theological grasp rings germane to Baptists of South Africa:

> People normally look to religion to fulfill two major needs: to answer life's questions and make the world meaningful for them. Christianity and Islam have not been able to answer women's questions in the area of discrimination, abuse and marginalization.

VIEWS AND EXPERIENCES IN THE BCSA

Another woman interview respondent said:

I believe that God didn't call men only to be pastor or leader. God call women and have purpose for them too. When God says we are his sons does not exclude women because he didn't say and daughters. We are all God's heirs both men and women to God. God is like parents who treat their children the same. The parents didn't give the opportunities than others but all children her something to do. God is doing that to us for that we may experience his goodness and supportive hand in our spiritual life.

Here is confirmation from this respondent that women are as capable as men to be pastors, implying that as pastors, women can perform all the duties of the pastor, including spiritual counseling to both women and men. Her rationale and conviction are simple, i.e., if God calls a woman to the pastoral ministry, he will equip her as he does a man who is called to the same pastoral ministry.

Another woman's view:

If a male pastor can interpret the Bible, women can do the same.[31] I know some females who have pastoral leadership abilities. Paul's idea of women cannot preach is an old concept. It does not apply for today. It's much nicer as a female to hear a female preacher. When you see her you get the encouragement and strength and self-esteem that can come from her. With the Word of God we shouldn't look at a male or female thing. The message is most important. If there are female prophets and deacons, why can't there be female pastors and evangelists. Some churches refuse to allow women to be pastors. So this attitude has affected the community. If we women can support a woman as pastor, the community can, in time, learn to accept this. Women can do without men support in a woman becoming a pastor. Women can be supportive 100% and

WOMEN AND LEADERSHIP

we can eventually win. Women can do without men. Men cannot do without women.

The above conviction on the absolute viability of women in the ministry of pastoral leadership is echoed by the following testimony of a woman 'called' by God to do his work:

God has called me to evangelism and to preach the Good News to the lost. I got saved in 1988. In 1990 I saw a certain man at the first crusade go forward to make a decision for Christ. On the Sunday service he came again and sat next to me and a certain sister. During the second crusade (a month later) I was sleeping during the day. I saw a vision. There was a man wearing a red and white tracksuit. He was sitting near me and another sister. Then I asked myself a question. During the night at the first evangelistic crusade this man was not the only one coming to the Lord. But now during the day in this vision he is the only one who comes to the church service. Why is he the only one who comes to the service? Then I heard a voice saying, 'This man is in need of the Lord. This man is not the only one. I want you to go out and preach the Word of God in the taxis, buses and public places.' I replied, 'How am I going to be able? I am a woman, and the other thing I'm not well informed in preaching and evangelism since I am a new convert.' Then the voice continued, 'I am God who called you. I will lead you in everything.' After that I just woke up. I was sweating. It was as if I was praying as I woke up. I was amazed because now I was meditating upon these things in the dream. How is it going to happen? I had another dream the same year. This time I was not quite sure if the dream was at night or during the day. I saw myself in a big tent and then I was on the stage. Behind me there were some male pastors. Then I was preaching. Thereafter I made an alter call. Most of the women came forward but men too were in the crowd who came forward. But most were women. I was preaching about the need to be filled with the fire. When they came forward after my prayer, I saw the fire surrounding them. Then I saw people were standing, but others were slain by that power. That was the end but when I wake up I was crying. I was crying as if the things in the dream were real and practical. The tears were a little of fear, but also a deep feeling that if God wills it, the dream can come to pass, but only by God's power.[32]

Today this thirty-four year old woman is a third year theological student at the Baptist Convention College, training to be a pastor or evangelist. Having been my student in missiology and theology courses, I know that she is convinced of her abilities to preach, to counsel, organize crusades and to pastor a local church if need be. She is highly motivated because she knows it was *God* who led her into the gospel ministry. Like the BUSA women who have been called by God, how can the BCSA churches, theologically, continue exclusion of women from the pastoral ranks? Are women's encounters with God invalid? Are their interpretations of scripture flawed?[33]

A male interview respondent stated that in his church women serve as deacons and they preach on occasion with no complaint from the older members. Another one states: "I also believe that women can be pastors. They only need to be encouraged and build self esteem in them." Here again we see that while women are viewed as *capable*, their 'self-esteem' is perceived to be a problem. We have noted elsewhere that if women's self-esteem is not nurtured in the home, then church and society, as beneficiaries, are weakened. We have also noted elsewhere that many black women have risen above their triple handicap of race, gender and poverty to roles in home, church and society that is nothing less than startling.

WOMEN AND LEADERSHIP

Oduyoye (1995:9) seeks for herself a quality of life that frees her, as an African woman, to respond to life in the fullness for which God intended. Oduyoye's own experience as a woman is not flattering of the Western churches in Africa. She claims that these churches do very little to challenge sexism and hence contradicts the church's boast that it fosters the worth (equal value) of all persons regardless of race, gender or socio-economic position. Christianity, instead, has shown itself to reinforce the cultural and historical conditioning of submission and compliance that leads to women's depersonalization. If Oduyoye is correct, then it is no wonder that black women's self-esteem is often problematical.

Another comment by a male respondent speaks to the challenge of being a pastor if a woman is single or married:

> If the woman pastor is single, some elderly people will say, 'What kind of pastor is this?' Ladies are afraid of ladies having positions in society. Ladies gossip, and are negative. But it will depend on the woman pastor. If she works with community and reaches out in practical ways to people and their needs, she will gain confidence and respect of community. She can be a role model for women in the community. If she is married, it will depend on her husband. Is her husband someone of respect? He must be around, not absent from his wife. He must be supportive of her pastoral work. If he is absent often from home, the woman will be endangered physically and her ministry with men can be limited. Respect of woman pastor to her husband will automatically bring respect from husband. This dynamic will affect views of community. Woman is leader and pastor of church, but in the home she must respect her husband and allow her husband mutual leadership in family affairs.

This man seems to be saying that women are capable to be pastors, but that there are particular challenges to overcome. One might ask, are there not particular challenges that men must overcome as well?

CONCLUDING REMARKS

Like the previous chapter, in evaluating the questionnaires and interviews, I have sought to make them descriptive of personal experiences and personal attitudes. I have also sought to make them revelational or exploratory in that I wanted the questionnaires and interviews to reveal sentiments, emotions, events and experiences, to explore areas of feeling and attitude that perhaps were unexpressed or unprocessed to any significant degree before. In this way the emphasis of the research technique was qualitative, not quantitative, though the objective, quantitative dimension of the questionnaire cannot be denied.

A Brief Evaluation

As seen in chapter two, some respondents to the questionnaire made scant subjective comments to the inquiries posed. Others made frequent and ample personal remarks or observations. I have often wished for an opportunity for follow-up questions to the brief remarks made. On the interviews, several were lengthy and immensely enriching. Others were more brief, sometimes enlightening and sometimes repetitious of what has been already said by others.

WOMEN AND LEADERSHIP

I found the interviews of the women and men to be frank and open as a whole. Others were guarded with their comments or feelings. The interviews supplied me with enormous qualitative information, often shedding new or deeper light into the questionnaire data. Women and men seemed cooperative, though perhaps the men sometimes were less comfortable or sure of their responses. Discussions went into directions unintended at many points. The excerpts of interviews shared in this chapter represent only a part of the entire data collected, but nevertheless a representative part of what had been collectively expressed by the women and men. One valued advantage to the interviews was the fact that they allowed me to observe tone of voice and facial expressions that aided in picking up pain, hope, fear or other nuances.

From the questionnaires, I have been surprised by the similar attitudes, with only a few exceptions, women and men of the BCSA have on the issues of: a) current church practices regarding women, b) perceptions of male attitudes toward women, c) natural abilities of women, and c) views on women as pastors. The interviews, while generally substantiating the findings of the questionnaires and the similarity of views between women and men, nevertheless altered the perceptions arising from the questionnaires at some significant points. Women were able to express their views and feelings in the interviews and revealed, not unlike the BUSA women, extreme dismay at the male-dominated church and their anguish over obvious discriminatory behavior. One can come to the conclusion that while one can *profess* favorably to women in church leadership, both women and men frequently *behave* differently. The difference between *theory* and *practice* explains the theoretical agreement with politically or theologically correct responses on the one hand but practical resistance on the other.

VIEWS AND EXPERIENCES IN THE BCSA

As with the BUSA women, I tried here to uncover women's *feelings* about their plight in the church. While many women appear satisfied with the way the church treats them, others are resoundingly unhappy if not embittered. But to what degree are women willing to express their unhappiness, or what avenues exist for the expression of their concerns in the local churches? To what degree, at the grassroots, are women's voices muted?

Villa-Vicencio argues that social analysis should be the foundation for a constructive theology. He claims we must know "what is going on" in society. That is, we must become aware of cultural values, socio-economic structures and power relations that foster exploitation, social conflict and suffering (1992:276)). In the context of women's suffering and exploitation in the church, these "values," "structures" and "relations" Villa-Vicencio talks about must be scrutinized from within the church and denominational matrix. The 'gestalt' deriving from the BCSA churches should be carefully assessed by what Oduyoye (1998:360) calls the four principals for African Women's hermeneutics:

1. Bible, Church and African tradition are interpreted contextually.

2. Community and motherhood agendas are the basis for interpretation.

3. Interpretation includes translation into African cultures.

4. There is no expectation of unanimity in interpretation.

WOMEN AND LEADERSHIP

The next chapter (chapter four) will conclude this study by summarizing the attitudes and experiences of the women and men of BUSA and BCSA, and then to see how they compare, generally, with Christian women in Zambia, in Hong Kong, in the United States and elsewhere in South Africa who are not members of BUSA and BCSA. Concluding observations will be made as well as comments related to the future of women in leadership in the Baptist Convention churches of South Africa. I will attempt to define what practical steps can be taken to promote a liberating praxis in the BCSA.

Musa W. Dube's (1997:150-151) poem employs traditional Tswana proverbs to portray women as pillars of strength. This intimate, heart-rending portrayal ends this chapter as it should, in praise of mothers:

MAMA

You
The Mother hen who spreads
Her wings over her chicks
I re-member, I re-call
The day blazing fire caught our pasture
Papa imprisoned in the gold caves
You
Spread your wings over your children
We emerged untouched, Mama grilled but
Alive!

You
The guard who holds the knife
By its cutting blade
I re-member, I re-call

VIEWS AND EXPERIENCES IN THE BCSA

The day a knifed thief burgled our doors
Papa an overdue fetus of diamond wombs
You
Grabbed the knife by its blade
We sought shelter, Mama deeply cut but
Alive!

You
Who nurses a nursing lion
Bare and single handed
I re-member, I re-call
The night a lion burst our fences
Papa a life time prisoner of gold mines
You
Grabbed the lion by its tail
While we ran for security, Mama scatted but
Alive!

You
Who grinds and cooks
But does not eat
I re-member, I re-call
The day we swept our granary clean
Papa fossiled with the Wit-waters-Rand rocks
You
Tied your groaning stomach
And found a job at the village shop
Mama, I re-member, I re-call
You.

WOMEN AND LEADERSHIP

NOTES ON CHAPTER THREE

1. Hastings (1993:111) asserts that in the early years of European missionary activity in Africa the first converts were frequently women. In part he attributes this to the feeling that they didn't matter, that it was politically and socially so insignificant. So it was viewed for male slaves. But it was not socially insignificant. Iwuchukwu (1997:46) seems to be more sure of herself when she declares that without women the evangelisation of Africa would have been ineffective.

2. Saayman's (1993:7-8) definition of 'mission' involves four dimensions: a) mission is to participate in the liberating activities of God in every sphere of human experience, b) mission is human liberation or humanisation in that it seeks to restore Jesus of Nazareth, the new human being, in every human and environmental relationship (the restoration of the earth), c) mission is contextual application everywhere it seeks to be the gospel, and d) mission carries us to a new level of awareness of the meaning of the Good News of Jesus of Nazareth. These four dimensions, claim Saayman, are the significance of the *missio Dei*. Mission as human liberation is apropos to the theme of this thesis. Women in the church must be freed not only from male dominance but also from their own insecurities and self-depreciation. See Cochrane (1991:23) for similar conclusions regarding 'the liberating spirit of the Gospel.'

3. Are most African women silent in the church, failing to agitate for change? Isabel Phiri (1997:44) thinks so. Even though they are in the majority their voice is quiet. Although the gift of God's Spirit is upon them to do the work of God, they are not allowed to exercise their gifts through the church except in the 'Spirit churches.' Phiri asks what African Christian churches could have been or could become if all women and men were freely permitted to use their divine gifts!

4. In the European context, Schmid's (1993:217-220) study concludes that while the majority of men still cling to past masculine beliefs, there are a growing number who accept the challenge to change to a 'new man' who is prepared to accommodate traditionally feminine responsibilities. However, ... the change tends to be largely superficial. To assist this 'emancipation' process, religious beliefs about man and patriarchal images of God, as found in Islam and Christianity, need to be

addressed and the role of women as facilitators should also be determined. I would argue that Schmid's findings apply to the challenges faced by South African churches.

5. See Daneel's (1992:226-231) descriptions of women's involvement in AICs, their leadership roles and limited emancipation in some movements.

6. Is this a veiled inference of sexual misconduct or proclivity? If so, it would perhaps be more accurate to accuse *men* of being "corrupt." Women have lived with the Victorian-missionary assumption that the original sin was sex and that Eve was solely responsible for the Fall. Women have suffered because they have been blamed for man's downfall.

7. The home environment may be critical to women's empowerment in the church. Lebaka-Ketshabile ("Various Voices Speak" 1997:5) conjectures: "Too often we fail to question the extent to which we promote our own and one another's oppression. One example is the issue of whether or not we African women prepare our daughters to be obedient, submissive and docile wives. If we do, are we not actually promoting women's oppression by passing it on to our daughters?" Of course, no one doubts that the fathers or men of the homes play a huge role in altering women's subservience and oppression in the home.

8. Lebaka-Ketshabile (1996:178) states: "I am convinced that even in those churches where women are allowed leadership positions there is feeling among the majority of men that these women should be seen and not heard. There is not much space for them to operate, or even to achieve their goals."

9. One also wonders to what effect the barrage of negative women's proverbs have on the minds of both women and men. According to Amoah (1997:209-211) the following Ghanaian proverbs are similar to those expressed and adhered to in many African societies. She claims that as a result in many societies wife battering is permissible as a means of controlling and shaping women to fit men's expectations. Amoah concludes, "It is no wonder also then that many women are kept from decision-making positions." Here are some negative proverbs: 'The hen knows when it is dawn but it leaves it to the cock to announce it,' 'The tongue is a very good thing if it is not the woman's,' 'Like a woman, but never trust her,' 'Women have long

WOMEN AND LEADERSHIP

hair but scanty (short) brain,' 'Women are as fragile as eggs,' 'A woman is like a blanket, she keeps you warm when around you but makes you feel uncomfortable at the same time,' 'Fear women and live long,' 'A beautiful woman does not belong to one man.'

10. The consequence of not being connected to one's own humanity, to one's *imago Dei*, stems from the decision to be who one is not. This leads to self-hatred and hatred of anything that reminds one of oneself or looks like oneself. This is the seedbed for women failing to support each other or to celebrate when another woman rises to a leadership role in the church. The practices and teachings of the church and culture promote women's self-hate. See Lebaka-Ketshabile (1997:7f).

11. On 27 February 1996 I interviewed an African-American missionary from the American Baptist Churches, USA, who was working among BCSA Churches in the Eastern Cape. Arising out of the context of her upbringing in America and her three years in South Africa, she shares with me her convictions. She says there will be changes in American black churches. Many women are leaving the National Baptist Convention to the Methodists where they can become pastors. Black women are saying to black men, 'You have been suppressed, okay, I know about that. But you can't keep on suppressing me too.' This is going to reach Africa, she contends. She observes that women here will not speak up against a man. Women hold leadership positions, but the social conditioning makes it difficult for women to speak up against a man. Women's courage and initiative will come. At present it is too traditional. She concludes that, in her experience with BCSA churches from King Williams Town to Alice and surrounding areas, without women there is no church. She reported that on 25 February 1996 twenty-five persons were baptised at Eternal Hope Baptist Church (Gqumahashe), and only two were males. She is convinced that if people will see that, under the pastoral leadership of women, the church can grow numerically and economically, attitudes toward women's leadership can change.

12. I have not ceased to be startled by the similarities in responses from both the women and the men. I have also seen how valuable the interviews have been in defining more accurately the 'heart feelings' of the respondents. The interviews have often altered the impressions one gets from the questionnaires alone.

13. Do African women and men experience Jesus Christ, God and the Holy Spirit

in the same way? Not exactly, according to Phiri (1997:35). African women read the scriptures and experience their biblical faith as lessons of liberation. African men use the same scripture to deny women their wholeness and freedom. Oduyoye (1995:175) accuses Christian theology and biblical interpretation in Africa of "sacralizing the marginalization of women's experiences."

14. In Cock's (1989:94) sociological study of Eastern Cape domestic workers, only sixteen percent felt that women are inferior to men in their personal abilities. Many in fact felt a sense of personal superiority to men, but a structural and cultural inferiority. They remark: 'We are the same, the problem is that we are women. Otherwise I have more power than my husband. Once he gets into difficulties at home he gives up;' 'We are equal but my husband couldn't manage things without me;' 'We are far better than men but we have to respect them so we don't lower their dignity;' 'Every woman knows we are stronger than men.' With such strength and capability, one can argue that the church would be dramatically revitalised with women preaching from their point of view, from the context of their unique struggles and spiritual victories.

15. Oduyoye's (1995:178) manner of speaking comes down like a sledgehammer: "Does the fact that men serve 'at table' in the church (spiritual) and women serve 'at table' in the home (material) mean that the church has succeeded in making motherhood incompatible with priesthood? Why are spiritual needs separated in this way from material needs? This docetic Christianity goes against any integrated worldviews, whether they are African or theological." Oduyoye is calling for equality and partnership in the leadership of Christ's church. In doing so, women can offer the church female qualities and strengths the church so desperately needs in its hunger and search for healing, wholeness and experience of *koinonia*. In an interview on 23 July 1999, Landman remarked that a liberative aim of women's oppression is healing. She observes that "we are moving out of a theology of liberation to a theology of healing." Story-telling becomes healing when alternative story-telling is utilized. See her very helpful insights in "Telling Sacred Stories: Eersterist and the Forced Removals of the 1960s" (unpublished paper), especially pages 3-5.

16. Have African theologies failed in addressing deeply and intelligently the oppressive, destructive patriarchal substructure of African culture? So believes

WOMEN AND LEADERSHIP

Maluleke (1997:57-58) who claims that violent, chauvinistic attitudes among African men should be arrested in order for the church to be liberated.

17. When is 'relational growth' a priority in men's organisations?

18. Masenya (1994:42) is firm in her conviction that women's lib-eration in the churches can be achieved with the cooperation of their subjugators and oppressors, male and female, but especially with the assistance of black men, perhaps because men are still the dominant powers in the churches.

19. Kritzinger (1988:341) believes with others that the triple handicap of black women, due to gender, class, and race, is a struggle for liberation against all three of these oppressions *simultaneously*. It is one struggle, for freedom cannot be a divided struggle. One is not free so long as one or more of these oppressions exist.

20. Women receive the least of the church income though they perform the lion's share of the church's work. The church is seen to be the place where the voiceless have a voice, where the oppressed find relief. Not so for most women. The church that proclaims freedom and hope in Christ is the same church that allows men to strangle women with sexism and blatant prejudice. See Kathindi (1991:254).

21. McEwan's (1991) book, Women Experiencing Church, is a chronicle of twenty-four women who share their thoughts and experiences of alienation, suppression, insensitivity and abuse in the Ro-man Catholic Church. Many of these women feel that their talents and contributions were ignored or marginalized. The dissatisfactions expressed are rooted in their sense of being invisible within their church, and of being dominated by priests and other men.

22. While it may be conceded that many men and women are different in attitudes, behaviour, and developmental crises, there are even wider differences within groups of men and within groups of women than between men and women. See Glaz (1991:96).

23. Yet we have seen elsewhere in BCSA churches the hindrances women can be to other women aspiring for church leadership and authority. This oppression has led the women students at the Moravian Seminary in Heideveld to jointly state that their preeminent concern is the unfavourable attitude many Moravian women har-

bour toward ordained women ministers. This negativism causes great pain for the women theological students. They wonder why men seem to be more open to change than women? Have women in the churches internalised their lowly status? Is the greatest ally of the oppressor truly the mind of the oppressed? Women demonstrate a severe lack of assertiveness and confidence, they do not reflect the image of God. See "Various Voices Speak" (1997:4). The dichotomy between the extreme confidence in women's pastoral abilities and women's oppression of women in leadership must be due to the gulf between opinion and praxis. Women must bring an enormous amount of emotional insecurity and historic, crippling baggage to the fore in being unable to accept women in power and responsibility heretofore designated as male enclaves.

24. I wonder if comments like this will really get backed up with concrete action, such as support for an aspiring woman leader or pastoral candidate?

25. This remark could imply that women, to be effective pastors, must perform their duties as men do them. Walters (1998:7) would object to this mentality. In the context of the Anglican Church, she asks whether women priests are simply expected to "slot into" the existing male model. She suggests it is a richer alternative for women priests to be allowed to affirm their humanity as women and thereby develop their own unique differences in the ministry of church leadership. This paradigm to priesthood, says Walters, would provide the Anglican Church greater authenticity and greater health.

26. Is this a doubt on women's ability or on some men's inability to tolerate a woman counselling them?

27. If African proverbs mirror African worldviews, then the following from Ethiopian, Lugbara and Yoruba hold to views of women that make their climb to respectability in church and society a tough one. From the Ethiopian tradition, Cotter (1997:3, 11, 96, 97) gives us these: 'A woman is never treated as a guest,' meaning, wherever she visits a woman works; 'A woman is like a spear shaft: if it breaks you replace it,' meaning, women risk divorce if they are not faithful to their husbands; 'I survived poverty but even a woman was superior to me,' meaning, there are times a man is only barely surviving; 'Where a woman rules streams run uphill,' meaning, women are not meant to rule. From the Lugbara tradition, Dalfovo

WOMEN AND LEADERSHIP

(1997:71, 72) gives us these two: 'One does not place a bow in the hands of a woman,' meaning, women and men have differentiated roles in the community; 'Fear is the dress of women,' meaning, for women to fear is typical of their nature. From the Yoruba tradition, Olayinka (1997:217-221) offers these proverbs: 'The husband is the head of the wife,' 'Women are deceptive,' and 'All women are witches.' Time-honoured negative worldviews such as these from these three traditions are bound to be expressed in time-honoured negative behaviour patterns, affecting church and society. (In review of this chapter on 26 July, 1999, Saayman states that the proverbs above reveal a tenacious cultural dimension reinforced by theological views broadly accepted in nineteenth century mission circles. He feels this insidious cultural dimension must be addressed in order to establish a better training programme. He then points to Penfield's contribution in the book Embracing the Baobab Tree, 1997, especially pages 172-174, as strengthening my argument here.)

28. Men need to be freed from the structures and debilitating attitudes that bind them. Both men and women should acknowledge and expose the fear and selfishness that is at the heart of patriarchy. The same coin has two sides, i.e., the twin need for female and male liberation. Both are essential for wholeness. See Kretzschmar (1995f:160).

29. Mark Mathabane's (1994:207) book, African Woman, is an account of real life in Alexandra. In the book, Florah confesses: "The chief purpose of ritual school, as it was explained to me during initiation, was to kill a young girl's self-will so she could be remoulded into a mature and complete woman: self-sacrificing, obedient, ca-pable of assuming the role of wife, and thus appealing to men as the perfect complement to their desires, wishes, and whims."

30. Since I know this pastoral candidate, I can say that she is a very keen student with a tremendous will to succeed. She will not succumb to the temptation to give up. Kretzschmar's (1995f:153) analysis is that it is 'insidious' when women internalise their suffering and suppression by assuming that they are to blame for their plight and misfortunes. Women are not so much sinful in their oppression but sinned against -- by men, by the church, by distorted biblical teachings.

31. And women can do it differently when necessary, from their point of view to address women's needs. West (1993:7) argues convincingly that we must relook

and renew our understanding of the Bible. Our context determines how God speaks to us. God speaks to us through the Bible. But because we are convinced of what the Bible says, we often cannot hear and heed the voice of God for today in our context. West contends we have tamed and domesticated the Bible. Are we willing to listen to the voice of God in our South African context? Then we must, with open hearts, eyes and ears, return to the Bible afresh.

32. See my book on religious dreams, which includes 'call' dreams to the Christian ministry (Hayashida 1993). Both women and men were 'called' in dreams.

33. If "human experience is the starting point and the ending point of the hermeneutical circle" as Ruether (1983:12) claims it is, then women's encounters with God in the crucible of their daily context informs their understanding of scripture. If the Bible speaks, it speaks to the experiences of women. West (1993:45-46) is helpful here: "Our reading does not require the text; the text remains the product of a patriarchal world. Appropriately, the oppressiveness in the text, in this case the oppression of women, remains both as a witness to that from which we have been saved and as a challenge to action on the side of God's righteousness and justice. But a reading *in front of the text* does reread the text, and this enables an engagement with the text, which is neither surrender to nor mastery of the text. We do not simply accept a past meaning as the only meaning, and we do not simply make the text say what we want it to say. Our rereading of the text along the axis of its central symbols, metaphors, and themes is, rather, an ongoing *dialogue* with the text." This study on Baptist women has brought clearly to light the necessity for a fresh dialogue with the Word of God. A wave of study groups of all kinds, for all ages, is needed in the local churches to begin the process of understanding and implementing what God is saying about roles of women and men in the churches.

CHAPTER FOUR

SUMMATION, COMPARISON, EVALUATION AND LIBERATING PRAXIS

A WOMAN'S HANDS

I sit in a pew
Waiting.
The Human
Becomes Divine.
The bread...
Perhaps kneaded by a woman's hands.
The wine....
Perhaps women worked in the vinery.

But when the Human
becomes Divine
a woman's hands are taboo!
"You shall not touch
the Divine!"

The Divine became human,
Penetrated a woman's womb.
(Patriarchy had no place!)
Like soft petals enfolding

a crystal dewdrop,
The seed nestled
in a female form.

"You shall not touch
the Divine!"
The battered body
taken off the cross...
Women's hands gently
perform burial rites.
The crimson blood
must surely stain those hands.
Women's hands --
caring hands.
"You shall not touch the Divine!"

Even as you knead the bread
And share the wine.
I sit in a pew
Waiting --
Hoping --
Sharing.

(Rebera 1996:12)

REVIEW OF PREVIOUS CHAPTERS

The *Introduction* was entitled "Purpose, Relevance and Method." A distinguishing mark of self-identity of the Baptist Convention of South Africa is its avowed support of women in all aspects

SUMMATION AND LIBERATING PRAXIS

of church leadership. Through descriptive and exploratory use of questionnaires and interviews, I proposed to discover the nature and extent of women's suppression in leadership roles in the BUSA and the BCSA. I proposed to evaluate the upliftment of women's roles in church leadership in the BCSA, to determine the essentialness of women's full participation in leadership for the relevancy and vitality of the new denomination.

Chapter One conveyed the views of women theologians in Africa and the Western world on women and leadership in the church. In the African context, women theologians gave biblical and theological justifications for women in church leadership, women and dignity, and women and the Christian ministry. They offered their perceptions on the challenges and obstacles to the ecclesiastical emancipation of women. I noted that while there are historical and cultural differences in women's experiences and challenges, Euro-American feminism, Afro-American feminism and African feminism share significant experiences of prejudice and discrimination in church and society. The challenge of redefining "servanthood" and the concomitant challenge of transforming the church were discussed.

The aim of *Chapter Two* was to describe the views and experiences of women, and a few men, of the Baptist Union of South Africa in regard to church leadership. Both theological and ecclesiastical categories were selected which deal with these views and experiences. They were:

1. Current church practices regarding women

2. Perceptions of male attitudes toward women

WOMEN AND LEADERSHIP

3. Natural abilities of women

4. Views on women as pastors

Questionnaires and interviews were used to collect these views and experiences. Though not limited to these four theological and ecclesiastical categories, the questionnaires and interviews certainly centered around them.

As was the aim of the previous chapter with BUSA, the aim of *Chapter Three* was to describe the views and experiences of women and men of the BCSA in regard to women in church leadership. Many more questionnaires and interviews were analyzed in this chapter since the principal focus of this study is on the black churches of BCSA. Both theological and ecclesiastical categories were selected which deal with these views and experiences. These categories were identical to those used for chapter four among the Baptist Union respondents. It has been seen that I have sought to allow the women and men to speak for themselves, to tell their stories for themselves.

THE AIMS OF THIS CHAPTER

The aims of this concluding chapter are fourfold. First, I will summarize the attitudes and experiences of the women and men of BUSA and BCSA regarding women in leadership in the churches. In doing so, I will provide comparative analysis on the responses of the respondents from the two groups. Second, I will make a comparison of the BCSA women respondents with South African women of non-BUSA and non-BCSA churches, with a woman of Zambia, a woman

SUMMATION AND LIBERATING PRAXIS

of Hong Kong, and with women of the United States. Third, I will evaluate the findings, i.e., the status of women in BCSA by way of theologization. Fourth, I will prescribe a strategy (action plans) in order to free BCSA churches for a liberating praxis in regard to church leadership.

Summation and Comparison of BUSA and BCSA Attitudes and Experiences

Chapters 2 and 3 clearly speak for themselves. By that I mean they convey, through the written questionnaires and oral interviews, the experiences, attitudes and perceptions of women and men of BUSA and BCSA. The comparisons made of the views and attitudes between women and men of BUSA (chapter two) and of BCSA (chapter three) reveal similar sentiments and observations, though some differences of views did occur, largely inconsequential. It is my observation that the BUSA and BCSA women were much more expressive and authoritative with their views and experiences, while the men were generally more unsure with their attitudes and more vague with their assumptions. Without a doubt, the narratives of the women should be given a high rating for their apparent honesty and courageous revelations. I therefore place more credence to the views of the women, and while it is impressive to see many men in "support" of women's leadership, one wonders if, again, we have a case of support in "theory" but impotence in "liberating action." Landman (1984:9) reminds us of Schussler-Fiorenza's view that men may say women are not inferior yet in the end treat them as inferior. That is, men may be sincere in their convictions on women in leadership but appear weak, hypocritical, or fearful of the liberation march of women.

WOMEN AND LEADERSHIP

    We have also seen clearly, again, that the women interviewed from BUSA and BCSA, though the former largely white and the latter totally black, share similar types of discrimination and struggle in the patriarchal church and its oppressive theology. In chapter one, I sought to describe the broad view of feminist theology (White, Afro-American and African) and the historical oppressions of the church with the peculiar hermeneutical habits promulgated by male "governors" of hierarchical power. It is unmistakable that the churches of both BUSA and BCSA lag far behind the ideals expressed by these women theologians who write and articulate their views in previously male academic and ecclesiastical domains. In spite of the fact that many women of BCSA laud the gains made in their denomination to free women for church leadership, pastoral ministry[1] and theological education, the questionnaires and stories with great candor depict a denomination that teeters on an *acceptance-rejection* syndrome for women in church leadership. More precisely, we seem to see a denomination that openly avows the acceptance of women in all realms of church leadership yet fails to embrace women convincingly and pervasively in many local churches. It has been my personal observation that BCSA women's full liberation against negative attitudes of women and men as well as negative practices against them are a myth in the majority of churches. In spite of this, it is also my observation that BCSA members and churches are much more adept at discussing women's issues and much more willing to move in the direction of a liberating praxis than the members and churches of BUSA. I believe our data from chapters two and three bear this out.

SUMMATION AND LIBERATING PRAXIS

A Comparison with Non-BUSA, Non-BCSA Women of South Africa, A Woman of Zambia, A Woman of Hong Kong, and Women of the United States

A Comparison with Non-BUSA, Non-BCSA Women of South Africa

I interviewed five women of South Africa who are not members of BUSA or BCSA. Two were Baptists of another group, two were assistant pastors of a Full Gospel Church, and one was a pastor of an African Methodist Episcopal Church. These interviews were held between 1998 and 1999.

A young Indian Baptist of eighteen years of age shared how one day she fasted and prayed and read her Bible. The quotation that gripped her that day was, "I will make you fishers of men." She felt called to be an evangelist or missionary or Christian counselor. She desires theological education. She feels no more hesitation or obstacles in her search for her future. She expresses confidence in the Lord's call in her life.

We have seen very similar testimonies among BUSA and BCSA women. God's clear, strong and persistent call to women to serve him unconditionally has propelled many women to sacrifice much. Will this young woman face the hardships encountered by the woman in the following story whose struggles reveal not only frustrations but courage to seek ways to bring about practical changes in her church? Without much doubt, she will.

The story is of an Indian Baptist of thirty-eight years of age who feels a strong conviction to use her social work and health science skills in the mission field. She has made trips to Mozambique

WOMEN AND LEADERSHIP

and Zambia. Each time, upon returning to her church, she gets the cold shoulder from her male pastor who considers her to be inferior as a woman. She feels women are equal to men in the ministry. She is convinced of this on biblical grounds. She states:

> The way to get women to take up their struggles is not to take up their struggles for them, but to find ways for women to take up their struggles for themselves. Women need to learn appropriate assertive skills, which helps them understand where they're coming from culturally, where they stand biblically, and what Christ would have them do in those situations. Unless they begin to do that, they will forever be undermined. No amount of affirmation or support would change things for women if the above is not done.
>
> I feel regretful because of the time lost, that I as a woman have been frustrated in doing God's work in the church. The loss of participation in church work and leadership is painful. Women make good contributions to the Lord's work among themselves, but find it difficult to be elected to significant leadership positions at the local church or denominational level.
>
> I think education and training must be implemented to help men and women to make changes. Men need attitudinal changes and practical skills training to help men know how to begin to make practical changes that will liberate women.
>
> Baptist pastors and women leaders in the church should explore biblically the role of women in the church. They should identify areas of training that will assist the church to create an environment conducive to women's participation in all levels of the church's ministries. This could bring up all kinds of issues that need to be addressed. The facilitators for these procedures should be people who would not proceed with a prejudicial view one way or another. Women should be involved in the actual design of the workshop.

SUMMATION AND LIBERATING PRAXIS

Many women need a cognitive restructuring of themselves, whereby they feel secure as women and have an optimistic view toward change.

We see again, as in BUSA and BCSA women, unmistakable conviction and strength of purpose to serve Christ. But this woman faces discrimination with male leaders of the church, in this case her pastor. Her advice on practical ways to implement changes in the church that will promote a liberating praxis is astute, pragmatic and courageous. For one who has had no theological training, she is an example of the kind of laypersons in the churches that God is leading to help transform his church -- pragmatic, insightful, courageous.

The narrative below is about a forty-eight year old Indian woman who is co-pastor of a Full Gospel Church with a man as the senior pastor. She has been in full-time ministry for ten years and is theologically trained. The following is an excerpt of her story:

> It took a long road for me to get where I am had it not been for prejudice. But now, mindsets are changing. Prejudice and discrimination is in subtle forms. I may contribute to helping women to serve God in the future. I let no man get in my way of serving God. Man has slowed me down, but they have not kept me from serving him. Man could not stop me. I did feel angry. A woman needs to work doubly hard to be accepted by men. I had my frustrations. Once, sitting in the church service, with my name being called, the pastor said, "Evangeline, women are to keep silent in the church." This made me red with anger. I was furious. I believe God will bring more women in pastoral ministry, but it is difficult for practical reasons.

WOMEN AND LEADERSHIP

Both males and females are made much the same and yet significantly and wonderfully different. 'Is a woman's place in the home?' This is a question that can be answered depending on whether she is married, whether she has children who need her care, and whether or not her husband is able to provide for the basic needs of the home in these changing times. One need not, through prejudice or discrimination, ignore the potentials that are excellent in women. Much talent has already been buried without achieving its due respect.

Familiarly, we see the conviction, courage and strength of this woman to carry forward her call to ministry in spite of obstacles along her path that brought her great anger. We notice her recognition, I think significantly, that she affirms women and womanhood, stating that women are like men in many ways "yet significantly and wonderfully different." The latter is a weighty statement because *it may suggest* that women can bring these "significant" and "wonderful" differences to church leadership at all levels. She is sensitive to women who are married, or with children, or the needs and kind of support of the husband. She affirms the unique role that women play, while affirming women in ministry if God so leads. Finally, and importantly, she bemoans the fact that "much talent has already been buried without achieving its due." Such sentiments were seen elsewhere in BUSA and BCSA women.

Another Indian woman co-pastor of the same Full Gospel church has a similar story of struggle. She is thirty-two years old. Her pastoral role is to direct a shelter for battered women and to provide crisis counseling for them. Her other significant task among these women is leadership training. She is one of twelve full-time pastors of the church (twenty if lay pastors are included). This multi-

SUMMATION AND LIBERATING PRAXIS

racial church has six thousand members. Four of the twelve full-time pastors are women. She has been in the ministry for fifteen years and has theological training. She narrates her story:

> In our Indian culture, women are put down. Women are considered as property for the husband. We desire to equip women, to discover their destiny and fulfill their gifts in the body of Christ. Jesus chose to restore the dignity of women.[2]

> I have experienced discrimination. It felt like I was a trailblazer. But now my identity in Christ is secure. The men who hindered me in ministry are the ones who set me free to serve God as a woman. It is the work of God. I recall how very rejected and discouraged I became during my struggles. I would question whether I was really called. The slander and critiques hurt me very much. A male pastor can get divorced and remarried and it is fine. I am divorced, but my husband divorced me. Mostly men criticize me. This has been painful. But it's a joy to hear women say, 'Ann, if you can make it, I can.' Men have tried us and we have proven our worth. I don't know that they like us but they respect us.

Again, with this Indian woman co-pastor of a large church, we notice common themes and obstacles women face in the church. Several BUSA and BCSA women encountered similar challenges with discrimination that threatened or limited their church leadership. We notice this co-pastor's determination and courageous faith, as well as her achievement in finding the grace of God in it all. We see how the very men who obstructed her ambitions to serve God were the very ones who later gave her strategic assistance. Finally, it is valuable to realize that her example of faith and victory (however partial) in overcoming resistance has been an inspiration to other women training for leadership: 'Ann, if you can make it, I can.'

WOMEN AND LEADERSHIP

The following account by a sixty year old woman pastor of the H.B. Senatle African Methodist Episcopal Church describes her obstacles to ordination:

> At first it was hard for me as an African woman. Firstly they discriminated against me because of age. I was fifty-four at the time. The fact that I was a woman applying for ordination made it hard to be ordained. I was very angry. In 1992 I was inquiring about pastoral work. I had gone through all the stages in preparation for ordination. But at the next to last stage the committee tried to stop me because of my 'age.'[3] I gave them a shock because I was the first woman to apply in this Conference for ordination. I was not admitted. I was very angry. I came back home bleeding from this discrimination. I was bitter. My pastor on the committee never uttered a word. The Assembly would have quickly admitted me as qualified to be ordained but this male committee kept me from being presented to the Assembly. It was my call that kept me going. I told these men, 'God has called me. I will not stop studying theology. No one can stop me.' These men saw my strength and stubbornness. I was again presented to the committee at the District Conference in 1995. It was smooth sailing this time. Since this time, two more women have followed me. Inferiority feelings can destroy women leaders. Women pastors need to be strong. They cannot be weak personalities.

The admonition for women to be strong in their striving for equality in leadership placement is often echoed. It is a summons for strength to heal and forgive when anger and bitterness seem overwhelming. It is a summons for strength to persist against relentless suppression. It is a summons for strength to exercise faith in a *gracious God*, for in women's darkest moments the temptation to view God as a male jokester and oppressor can become the ultimate fear.

SUMMATION AND LIBERATING PRAXIS

We notice in these accounts of non-BUSA and non-BCSA women of South Africa the emotional pain, even extreme anguish, at male obstinacy to female ambitions. This is a common theme. The story of churchwomen and the search for leadership is incomplete, to say the least, without an expression and acknowledgement of their cries. It therefore brings me satisfaction to have contributed in some small way to the telling of their stories in their own words.

A Comparison with a Woman of Zambia

A thirty-eight year old Zambian wife and mother, active in a Baptist church in Lusaka, shared her story of criticisms by women and men (interview taken 28 October 1998):

> Men do discourage women to do the work of the Lord. They cannot allow women to stand before men. This is a problem all over Zambia. But women are doing more work than men are. This is improving but it is still a big problem.

While she complains about the church rules men seem to place upon women, restricting her freedom, she later was quite explicit in giving her view that women should not on biblical grounds preach on Sunday mornings or become a pastor of a church. She said this view is held by most people in Zambia: "The women will not be in support of women preaching or to be a pastor." She was even graphic: "A woman given many leadership jobs in the church, she grows wings. She grows too big." She continues:

WOMEN AND LEADERSHIP

> I've got this problem which blocked me to do the work because of my little education. I cannot work as I want because I feel my little education and use of English causes me to fail to express myself well and confidently. But God is really using me. I am always in leadership. But I feel discouraged because of my lack of education and use of English. It makes me fear doing things I want to do in our denomination. If one cannot express oneself in English she is ridiculed as unable to contribute anything. This discourages me. This is my biggest problem. Now people are seeing me for who I am and are giving me more respect. But it is still very hurtful and painful for the criticisms to come my way. I do encourage women who are like me. They are gifted but are unable to lead because they fear the criticism. I understand them and their struggles. Women like these are not empowered because of the criticism. Those women with better education are taking pride in themselves and criticize those of us who are less educated. This weakens the power of women and the power of the church.

In Zambia, there are seventy-two languages and dialects. In Lusaka, where this woman lives, many of these dialects are represented. This mixture of dialects and cultures, as well as her leadership in the wider denominational sphere, makes the use of English a strategic mode of communication. Her frustrations arise from these realities. Her anguish at the male attitudes toward women and the criticisms from other women toward her over the years has been excruciating. Her cry has been heard.

A Comparison with a Woman of Hong Kong

A thirty-five year old Chinese woman theology student at Hong Kong Baptist Theological Seminary allowed me to interview

SUMMATION AND LIBERATING PRAXIS

her on 5 May 1998 in Johannesburg. She belongs to the Evangelical Free Church of Hong Kong. She shares her experiences:

> In the leadership levels, there should be no discrimination. But males get certain roles. Women's voices are not as easily heard. Most of my experience, and what I have observed, men are given preferential treatment. Women ministers who are not ordained cannot even obtain a license to perform the Lord's Supper or baptism. Men ministers who are not ordained but have a license can perform the Lord's Supper and baptism. If a man is present, he will take the leadership over women ministers. He is looked upon as the authoritative figure. Yet women are so gifted in so many ways. The church restricts women and subjugates them.
>
> There is also inequalities in salaries, allowances and benefits. For instance, allowances are only for men -- e.g., child allowance for the minister. Women ministers do not qualify.
>
> I feel frustrated with these inequalities. I know there is a circle drawn around me by the denomination. This circle makes me feel I must limit myself within this circle and I feel the pressure if I try to express myself or behave outside this circle. But I can sense now that people are beginning to respect me because of my devotion to God. I get criticism from women as well, not only men, if I step outside this circle. Not all women, but this is what I know from experience and speculation.
>
> This has occurred very frequently. My husband and I are partners in our cell group ministries. When people give credit or affirm our work, they will refer to my husband, even if my contribution is more. The individuality is ignored when a woman is married. I feel deprived of my individuality. I feel frustrated, even upset, at this loss of my personhood. Frequently, in public, the man is hon-

ored. Once, I was honored for my children's work, but I contributed more in my adult ministry, not in children's ministry, but I was remembered or recognized only for my work with children. I struggle with this. My feeling is hurt. I should overlook this, but I do feel the hurt. I struggle with this.

My pastor supports women as support people, not as font-line leaders. He sees me as being too aggressive. He once advised me, "You be careful you do not push yourself too much in front of people." I think I am being suppressed, but God is still using me. People come to me for advice and leadership. My pastor is sensitive about this. This hinders spiritual gifts and compassion I have deep inside me. I not always sure if it's a male-female issue or a power struggle issue. Perhaps it is mixed. This gender problem denies our humanity that God has given to us.

Most of the congregations like women leaders now. I think the main problem seems to come from the leadership of the church -- the pastor and deacons. The leadership of the church seems to be strategic to the congregation's attitude. This situation makes me feel very bad. I love my mother church, but I feel bad about this treatment of me and other women leaders. Several years ago my denomination turned down the suggestion of women to be ordained as ministers. This looks quite bad for us. In some of our churches, women are free to serve, even to become chairman of the deacons, but they cannot be ordained, and cannot be a full pastor.

The context of Hong Kong and the Chinese church in that culture may be different from the African milieu, but the themes of male control and dominance of the church are similar. The leadership inequalities between the roles of men and women in the church resonate with the African church. So do the pain, hurt and discouragement. BCSA women who struggle for emancipation in their churches can easily identify and empathize with their sister from Hong Kong.

SUMMATION AND LIBERATING PRAXIS

A Comparison with Women of the United States

The following accounts are interviews with women from the United States taken between 1997 and 1998.

A member of Redlands Bible Church, an independent church, this young woman of twenty-two testifies to the equality she has felt in her church, yet describing the male dominance in the higher leadership positions:

> I feel like I have been treated equally as men in my church. I served as an intern in the youth ministry of my church. I think the door is open for women to serve but the opportunities have not been taken. There are eight elders in my church, all men.[4] There are deacons and deaconesses, an equal number. But the elders are only men. Sometimes women are allowed to speak Sunday morning in place of the pastor. They are asked to speak to enrich the body. In adult Sunday School classes, the teachers switch from men to women as the topic changes.

The male pastor and eight male elders seem to imply an androcentric view of theology and the church. The fact that "sometimes women are allowed to speak Sunday morning" betrays the dominance of male speakers as well as the control of the male elders and the pastor in order for permission to be granted for a woman to speak ("allowed to speak").

The following young woman of twenty-one years of age had been very active in Christian leadership at college. She was a co-leader with a male student in a Christian missions project to Mexico. It required months of planning and preparation. She confides:

217

WOMEN AND LEADERSHIP

With Potter's Clay this last year at Westmont, I often felt that the pastors in Ensenada, Mexico, thought and treated Bryan as the leader and me as his assistant, even though we were co-leaders of Potter's Clay. This is the closest I have felt to relating to females in local churches who have been relegated to subservient roles or expectations. Now I can say that I've healed from it because it was an issue that was confronted and dealt with. Two pastors have apologized. But I still remember the pain. I felt small, overlooked, not as good, not as respected for the amount of work and effort I put into Potter's Clay. It hurt me deeply. All of my experiences at college lead to the conclusion that both females and males ought to be involved in Christian leadership. I think my experiences have helped me to feel empowered. It helps me to feel that I have the capabilities and certain skills to contribute in leadership. I now have the desire and confidence to leave college and pursue leadership in life.

We notice that while at college the respondent felt the equality of the sexes in terms of leadership, she was neither given that reception nor the honor by the Mexican male pastors. We see the hurt, the cry of the heart, and the healing, in part by the apologies extended. Through it all, she feels she has been strengthened for "leadership in life."

The following account by a thirty-seven year old woman uncovers a male dominated leadership in her church. All the deacons are male. She says the worship leadership is male-controlled. She believes that the compassionate qualities of women would allow them to be good leaders:

Many women have more compassion than men and would make better deacons. Many have more time to put into it. There is a

SUMMATION AND LIBERATING PRAXIS

group of four or five or six women who 'function' as deacons in ministry -- in visitation, counseling, etc.

I notice that women's attitudes need to change. Some older women who have spiritual gifts will not feel it right to become a deacon because it is perceived to be a man's role.

Can we surmise that these women would be critical of women aspiring to be deacons or to fill any role heretofore assigned to men? She continues:

Some men and women don't like a woman teaching if men are around. But in Sunday School a woman's point of view can be important.

Notice it is "men and women" who don't like a woman teaching in the presence of men. We have seen this in some of the Baptist churches of South Africa. She comments again on the issue of compassion:

Our pastoral staff does not have the deep love and compassion to the sick and bereaved, but if women were on the pastoral staff they would bring more compassion and real help to those needing counseling.

The seeming abundance of compassion on the part of women has been expressed by a number of women in the churches of South Africa, including BUSA and BCSA. We shall elaborate on the importance of this quality later in this chapter.

The following views are those of a sixty year old woman who serves as the church's choir director, a Sunday School teacher, and a prayer group coordinator. Asked about her view of women serving as deacons, she said "I don't see any problem with a woman serving as a deacon." Has she had any experiences of subjugation? She said, "I've had no confrontation of problems. I've had more encouragement than having been dealt a blow because I'm a woman." On the issue of women preaching in church, she remarked:

> I've never thought of that. I like to hear them talk, but I don't know about preaching. I know of one woman who's a dynamic pastor. I don't know if this is good or not. I'm not very sure.

Perhaps she is "not very sure" because of previous teachings, a history of negative attitudes fostered in the churches, or a lack of good models except this one woman who is a "dynamic pastor." This hesitancy and ambivalence appear to be fertile ground for teaching a liberating praxis for women. One wonders how many women of BCSA, or BUSA for that matter, are within this domain of uncertainty? We have indications from this research that there must be many.

On natural abilities she states:

> Leadership roles in many churches are women. Women have all the abilities to lead. If women were removed from leadership responsibilities of churches, the men are few to take over. I feel women can do as much or more than men. God gives us our talents, and it is up to us to be willing to use our talents.

Have we not heard these sentiments before among BCSA women?

The last U.S. respondent is a Korean-American intercultural studies professor at a seminary and member of a Korean Baptist

SUMMATION AND LIBERATING PRAXIS

Church. She is fifty-seven years old. When asked if she feels women are equal with men in spiritual gifts she replied:

> There is no difference. I Corinthians 12 is not reserved for men. If faith is relationship with God, women are better equipped in terms of relatedness. Men and women have their unique ways in evangelism. Men can be more direct, but women are more 'nutritional' oriented.

I asked her for her view of women as pastors. She said, "Why can't women be pastors like men?" Are women suppressed or oppressed in her church? She said, "It is not overt. Very subtle. Women are strong behind the scenes." I asked her if she believed the Southern Baptist Convention would some day change their negative views on women as pastors and theology professors. She replied, "Absolutely. I do believe in the power of God. What he worked through me he will work through the S.B.C. What God has ordained, no man-made institution can forever withhold."

On women pastors, I asked if she felt it to be as much a problem with women as with men. She answered:

> Women can be against one another more. Women pull themselves down where they used to be. Women hurt women more than men. I relate with men much better than women. Ninety-percent of men love the stimulation I give. Education is more peeling off the wrong layers we have put on, not an acquisition of cognitive learning.

Women "pulling down" and "hurting" other women is a common theme in church life among Baptists in South Africa. The observation that education is not so much an acquisition of new knowledge as it is "peeling off" the layers of inappropriate knowledge is a novel statement. It alludes to the need for the church to remove the burdensome baggage of the past that denies freedom for all the people of God to activate his call, to utilize their spiritual gifts and to serve the world through the people's church.

Conclusion

It is my conclusion that underneath the veneer of the American church "advancement" in women's roles and in attitudes and behavior, we easily detect similar types of oppression as we have seen in the BUSA and BCSA churches of South Africa. This brief foray into assessing the experiences and attitudes of women in non-BUSA, non-BCSA churches of South Africa, a woman of Zambia, a woman of Hong Kong, and a few women of the United States leads one to believe the unfortunate, i.e., that discrimination against women in the leadership positions of the church and negative stereotypes toward women in various parts of the world, in or out of Baptist circles, are common discriminations and common negative stereotypes. Can one surmise that the *debate* over women's issues in the United States may be "advanced" but the *praxis* of women's full liberation does not always match the rhetoric? If this is so, then a liberating praxis for women, and for the church in all parts of the global village, is an achievement still to be realized.

SUMMATION AND LIBERATING PRAXIS

An Evaluation of the Findings

The women of the Baptist Convention of South Africa are strategic to the health, vitality and growth of the churches. Their strength in numbers, their evangelistic zeal and their faith have been seen to be remarkable. The questionnaires and interviews of both men and women support this claim. The women of BUSA, the women of other churches of South Africa unaffiliated with BUSA or BCSA, a woman of Zambia, a woman of Hong Kong, and women of the United States share with BCSA women many stories of prejudice and marginalization in the church. Their cry is a cry of frustration, sadness, anger, even depression. It appears many women and men are content with the status quo of the churches, believing it to be the will of God, sanctioned by the scriptures and the church. We have made numerous evaluative remarks along the way. I would like to stress two at this juncture. So much of what we have learned in this study revolve around these two. My conversations with Christina Landman have helped me immensely here. They are: a) women do not need necessarily genderized roles, but roles based upon their gifts and abilities; and b) women leaders can change the concept of church and of power.

Women Do Not Need Necessarily Genderized Roles, But Roles Based Upon Their Gifts and Abilities

I suppose one could say that of the church: The *church* does not need necessarily genderized roles, but roles based upon the gifts and abilities of the people. It is not to say that mothers or those experienced in infant care would not do better serving in the church nursery. They more than likely would. It is not to say that men would not do better in certain types of church maintenance or projects where heavy lifting or machinery must be used. They would. But will the church ever agree that in terms of the ministries of the church and in terms of spiritual gifts and abilities both women and men of the church do not need genderized roles? Will the patriarchal church liberate not only women but, in doing so, the church itself?

In terms of church patriarchy, Chung (Report on the morning with Prof. Chung 1996:2) identifies three roles women tend to participate in:

1. The role of the **victim**, criticizing patriarchy (with a right to do so). Connected by suffering and mutual misery, there is solidarity among women, and work to improve themselves and the situation together. But when one woman does improve and in empowered, others may try to pull her down. She does not get the support she needs and used to have. She becomes a target.

2. The role of **accomplice**. This is the role of women with privilege who keep silent. Maybe they do not actively oppress, (saying "we did not do it; our men did") but they are content with the way things are because they get the crumbs from the men's tables. Think of the house, clothing, education. Complicit women are trained to be docile and passive -- not just passive to men, but passive to evil and injustice.

3. The role of **agent**, informed, aware, standing up, speaking out and breaking the silence.

The role of *agent*, informed, aware, standing up, speaking out and breaking the silence is the role that women must actively engage in. But not only women. Men too can be advocates of women's

SUMMATION AND LIBERATING PRAXIS

emancipation, most strategically pastors and male leaders of the church.

What Nurnberger (1994:139-149) has said about the challenge of the church to make an impact upon South Africa's economy is apropos for South Africa's churches:

> I suggest that our main potential strengths are reconstructing collective consciousness.... (We must) dethrone the gods. Explore the assumptions, values, norms and goals that guide people. Subject them to critique. Confront them. Offer a salutary alternative. Do not be intimidated by the accusation of religious imperialism. If it is the truth of God's redemptive concern, this truth is wholesome and necessary. Real challenges can best be achieved by organizing communal activities, which demand going beyond conventional values and norms.

In the case of the BCSA, the gods to be dethroned are there, and their power is conscious and unconscious. Nurnberger calls for "reconstructing collective consciousness." Born in 1987, the BCSA is a new denomination. I have argued that it is still shaping its identity, discovering its special role among Baptists in South Africa. The denomination's collective consciousness must be attacked by Chung's "agents" in order for change that leads to emancipation to take place.

Goba (1995:21-22) chooses to speak of a "restructuring of human relationships" that is at the core of building a new community. This new construction is rooted in the values of equal dignity, mutual respect, love, a complete surrender to tolerance, and freedom of expression. Goba in fact seems to be calling for a new humanity, a new community, a truly theological anthropology. He calls it a process of recreation whereby personhood and community are fundamentally altered. He urges churches to embark on a re-education process intended to reevaluate particular basic dogmas of the Christian faith, especially racism, sexism, exploitation and ethnic chauvinism. Goba's "re-education process" is comparable to Kim's idea gleaned from her interview (see 6.2.2.4) that "education is more peeling off the wrong layers we have put on, not an acquisition of cognitive learning."

Nurnberger's "reconstructing" (collective consciousness) and Goba's "restructuring" (human relationships), I would argue, are both akin to Jonas' (1996:80) concern about the ill effects of "collectivism" or "group-directedness." He is of the opinion that the intimate link between morality and collectivism or group-directedness in South Africa places profound pressure upon individuals to submit to group expectations. Jonas calls this the "moral code" stemming from group-directedness, ensuring everything that fosters appropriate interpersonal relationships (the elimination of friction in relationships), as well as attitudes such as complaisance, modesty, willingness to compromise, generosity, friendliness, adaptability, willing-ness to share resources, and respect for seniors. It is easy to see, then, how conservative views on women in society, in the church, or in families, will be difficult to change. Who would not be for these apparent positive and wholesome virtues? The sinister dimension of the above mind set is that these so-called virtues are shortsighted, or they are uplifted with strings attached. They are not unqualified. The qualifiers are damaging. They have been for women of the BCSA.[5] When aspiring women seek a non-sexist church, group-directedness lubricates the agitations.

Andre (no date:15) declares that the church is under obligation to promote justice, and those who desire the maintenance of an

SUMMATION AND LIBERATING PRAXIS

unjust church should relinquish their demands. In his little book entitled <u>Baptists and Politics,</u> Andre speaks of revolutionary violence, which must be deplored. But he adds that the *conditions that establish* revolutionary violence must be deplored as well. He continues with the following words, which I would like to apply to our discussion on the historical and systematic suppression of women in church leadership:

> The Gospel, with its message of hope, conflicts with the aspirations of those who wish to sue hopelessness as a means of furthering their own ends in the name of righteousness. It calls for moderation and opposes the lie that the end justifies the means. At the same time it calls for justice for the oppressed and will not allow people to be used as a means to an end. It is therefore bound to arouse the opposition of those who wish to retain a <u>status quo</u>, which frustrates legitimate aspirations and violates principles of justice.

The women of BCSA deserve to be assessed by a standard similar to the standard used for men. Are they equally created in God's image? If so, the implications are not difficult to discern. Women's church roles ought to be based upon spiritual gifts and God-given natural abilities, not upon patriarchal views on genderized roles.

It should not be a discussion only among women, but a discussion within the church, by the male and female people of God, about empowering *everyone* to the freedom of God's Spirit. It is not simply a problem of ordination. Nor is it simply deciding the limitations or areas of leadership and ministry women may engage in. It is more profound. It is about the whole understanding and attitude of "woman" and "womanhood."[6] In some churches where women are in leadership, even in ordained leadership, they still feel 'marginalized.' The larger picture must be addressed. The general attitudes toward women, and to the places of both women and men in the church, in society, and in the whole of creation, must be addressed (Chilver 1997:7-8). In this light we make more sense of Nurnberger's "reconstructing collective consciousness," Goba's "restructuring human relationships," and Jonas' warnings against "group-directedness." In this light we see the great challenge ahead for the BCSA.

Bosch (1991:151) appears to be speaking of this new community that has been reconstructed and transformed when he discusses Paul's view of the church. Bosch believes that since Paul saw the church as an end-time community, it naturally follows that the church has apocalyptic and ethical significance for the present situation. Scripture proclaims that Christ has accepted and affirmed everyone unconditionally. Hence it is absurd to consider Jews and Gentiles behaving with altogether different sets of ethical standards. They are equal in Christ and must therefore accept the other *unconditionally*. As articulated in Gal. 3:28, there is no longer Jew or Greek, slave or free, male or female. This is the new humanity. Set against this standard, all the churches of South Africa and in the world must cover their faces in shame and confession.

If the BCSA is to be liberated from genderized leadership roles, leadership roles must be founded upon a new stackpole. That stackpole should be the spiritual gifts and talents of all the people of God, male or female, Jew or Greek, slave or free. Perhaps if we free God from gender connotations we may facilitate freeing the institutional church from sexist role expectations.

SUMMATION AND LIBERATING PRAXIS

Women Leaders Can Change the Concept of Church and of Power

The stories not only of BCSA women but other women elsewhere portray a desire, even a hunger, to lead the community of faith, the church, to be a more "caring community," and a part of what that means is to find ways to celebrate life, to celebrate together, to experience healing and wholeness.[7]

This seems to be an important objective of *church feminists* around the world. They seek to transform the church from within. Undoubtedly many women within the BCSA and elsewhere are unaware of this potential and its major significance for the health and vitality of the church. Some African women theologians and laypersons, we have seen, are actively advocating the contributions women pastors and leaders can make in bringing compassion, celebration and healing to the church. This is not to say those religion feminists such as Mary Daly, or Jewish feminists for instance, do not have these concerns. But religion feminists speak from outside the church and want to study religion and the lives of women often for their sociopolitical consequences. Our emphasis in this study has been on women within the church and their passions for the church.

What sorts of changes can women leaders make? What practical difference can they make to the nature and function of the church? How will these changes affect the concept of the church?

We get a clue, I think, early in the missionary annals of South African Christianity. In 1799 mission consciousness among 'the heathen' was hardly known among the Dutch burghers. Matilda Smith converted her home into a school and Christian witness for the Khoi-Khoi. As a woman, she reached out to the Khoi-Khoi unseen before.[8]

WOMEN AND LEADERSHIP

At the time, the majority of the Dutch colonists felt there was little necessity for evangelization among the Khoi-Khoi and therefore were opposed to any sort of missionary activities, male or female (Millard 1996:27-28).

In our study of BCSA women, what Matilda Smith did among the Khoi-Khoi is comparable to what black churchwomen have been doing for so long in so many places. Let us dissect Millard's account above. Smith used her *home* and used it as a center for education and spiritual nurture. The home is central to a woman's consciousness. It is a place of warmth and intimacy. Perhaps finding obstacles in utilizing a proper church building, Smith's determination to demonstrate compassion for the Khoi-Khoi as God's children led her to launch an effort to bring education and Christian teachings to them. Sincere BCSA women have demonstrated those passions as well -- passion for teaching, learning and evangelism. Notice Smith's courage and determination to obey God and not man. She faced opposition from the male leaders of the church and community. She prevailed and altered the "mission consciousness" of the early church in South Africa. Smith demonstrated a pastoral heart, a people-friendliness. In providing a safe sanctuary for the Khoi-Khoi to gather, she offered an opportunity for warmth, perhaps some joy and celebration, to the time together. She undoubtedly had prayer, devotions and singing of hymns to go along with the Christian witness. What liturgical changes did she make along the way in her ministry in the home? Her home became the church, the liturgical center of worship. She had to be innovative. She was brave and committed. While I am only surmising about the exact nature of Smith's ministry, I believe I am not too far from the truth. So little is written in mission historiography about women's contributions (and significance) to mission Christianity.[9]

SUMMATION AND LIBERATING PRAXIS

What we may be saying is that women can redefine the meaning of leadership. For women of passion and compassion, leadership need not be about power. Leaders need not be there to enforce the rules or activities of the church. Leadership can be the means by which skills are used to nurture others more caringly, to represent others in such a way that the relational dimension of ministry becomes tantamount to the very notion and nature of ministry. Women need not repeat either men's role or their pitfalls. Women need not duplicate any leadership role of the church in exactly the same manner as men have behaved. We should not imply that all men are alike, that they all have identical leadership qualities. They don't. But we can see general characteristics or tendencies, we can see patterns of authoritarianism, power and control. Nor should we stereotype women leaders as well, that they have the same leadership qualities, or they cannot fall prey to power struggles themselves. We should not stereotype women nor create new stereotypes. Yet the potential and opportunity for constructive changes in leadership along the lines described above are there. Perhaps women can bring these changes about better than men. The church seems to need just such changes.

Matilda Smith used creativity. She had to improvise in converting her home into a worship, educational and evangelization center. Creativity and energy is what BUSA and BCSA women have frequently demonstrated in their service for God through their churches or independently of their churches. One white woman church leader of BUSA shared in an interview how she uses creativity in literature, in writing, in drama, in piecing together a program from scratch for the children's ministry or the women's bible study. She states:

WOMEN AND LEADERSHIP

> What I'm trying to do at the moment is recognize where my gifts are and work on those. I will always, I believe, have my heart with the local community. Call it pastoral ministry, call it what you like in order to make it politically correct. My heart will always be in local church ministry, involved with individuals and families. I'm particularly fond of children's ministries, and I've grown to love women's ministry and feel the importance of women's ministry. And then preaching is very much a part of that for me. But then I also feel the aspect of teaching.
>
> Academic teaching is more open to me as a woman in Baptist ministry than pastoral ministry. But even saying so I recognize that as a person I need team ministry, group support as a person. I'm not a trailblazer, I'm not a person to go out there and run the show although I have my sense of leadership qualities. So my situation at the moment suits me wonderfully. I work under a pastor and very much under his wife as well. She's as much a mentor to me as he is. I can bounce ideas off of them, and my marriage becomes part of that teamwork because I allow my husband to give input to me as well.

This woman is using her creativity and talents in serving the church with a pastoral heart and passion. She speaks of her "heart" being in ministry to "individuals and families," in "children's ministries," in "preaching" and "teaching" as opportunity may arise. She prefers a "team ministry" where "group support" is available. We thus see her rootedness to a *relational ministry* as the core value through which she serves God. Even her pastor, his wife, and her husband become her mentors, her confidants, her peers and colaborers. Her ministry does not seem to be about power and authority, but about a shared labor of love, a partnership, whereby the nature and concept of the church is somehow altered.

SUMMATION AND LIBERATING PRAXIS

Power in leadership must be an issue to reckon with for women. It is one thing to empower someone, but how do we help her to deal with that power? She can do a lot of damage with power, as she has seen in men. Women should not repeat the mistakes of men. They can, but they need not to. The above respondent demonstrates qualities of maturity that foster a keen sensitivity to "team ministry" and "group support," a more participatory and compassionate approach to service through the church. This approach to leadership can minimize the abrasiveness of administrative power tactics, church structure and organizations. It can restore a divine humanity to relationships and decision-making and increase morale and group solidarity.[10] This, women can help accomplish.

A Prescription for the Future

The attempt in this section is to focus on the women and churches of the BCSA. I will attempt to put the experiences of women and the prosperity of the church enroute to something better. What have we learned and how can we make use of what we have learned? That is our task. More descriptively: now that we have allowed the BCSA women (and others) to tell their stories (renaming)[11], now that we have analyzed (reclaiming) and theologized (rereading), we are ready for action plans. In a conversation with Christina Landman, she cautions that not all women's experiences are the same. They do not all fall into a "common pool." We have seen that cultural and sociological differences (between the white BUSA women and black BCSA women for instance) do distinguish the experiences of women into cultural patterns.[12] Cultural expressions of prejudice and discrimination in the church vary. So do the manner in

WOMEN AND LEADERSHIP

which men and women perceive, define or handle oppression in their respective cultural context. Yet as we have witnessed women rename their stories, reclaim their stories, and reread the bible and theologize about their stories in a new way, we see enough common features that what we prescribe here as action plans for the BCSA can be useful in other places among other cultural groups.

What will the BCSA look like in the twenty-first century? What do we want to see? For the sake of the health and dynamic well being of BCSA churches, what step or steps must be taken? I propose one grandiose scheme with two vital steps. I am convinced of its veracity.

Widespread Denominational Strategy for Biblical and Theological Re-Education

A total of sixty BCSA questionnaires were returned to me from thirty-two women and twenty-eight men. A total of twenty-five interviews were conducted involving eighteen women and seven men. All the respondents were black women and men with various types of leadership roles in the churches. Based on the information gathered, BCSA women must "rename," "reclaim" and "reread" before they are "ready" for specific action plans to liberate themselves and their churches. In surveying the documents stemming from the Convention's annual Winter Schools of Theology (which are generally up to one week in duration), women's issues were noticeably on the agenda on several occasions, and women were present and participative in each of the annual schools. Yet only sixty to seventy men *and* women attend each Winter School, frequently with the same core of regular participants. The overwhelming majority of BCSA

SUMMATION AND LIBERATING PRAXIS

members have not presented themselves for biblical and theological reflection (re-education) where sticky and challenging topics are bravely tabled for discussion.

The ultimate goal of "liberation" is *transformation*. If liberation or emancipation does not precipitate ecclesiastical transformation then liberation has failed to reach its potential. I am proposing a widespread denominational strategy for biblical and theological re-education that will affect or infect the whole people of God with the whole gospel of Christ. For instance, South Africa's liberation from apartheid does not mean the nation and its peoples are transformed economically, socially, politically and religiously. But transformation cannot take place without liberating achievements.[13] I do not believe women within the BCSA, for the most part, are truly liberated to serve Christ and his church on an equally shared basis with men. The patriarchal church at the local level, with a few exceptions, is functioning as ever. Hence if women are held captive, so is the church.

There are two specific steps to be taken if the BCSA would be courageous and prophetic enough to launch this widespread denominational strategy for biblical and theological re-education. They are expressed clearly in Landman's (1998a:140) assertion that, in order for African Women's Theologies to move forward, two steps should be taken:

> the experiences of religious women need to be exposed to the written tradition and retrieved from muteness . . . . liberative religious insights should be made available to women who do not have access to academic training, and may not even have access to the written word.[14]

WOMEN AND LEADERSHIP

Activate Women (and Men) to Expose the Experiences of Religious Women to the Written Tradition

An example of activating women to expose the experiences of religious women to the written tradition is Wendy Robins' Through the Eyes of a Woman: Bible Studies on the Experience of Women (1995). This book contains bible studies for small groups interested in Christian women's experiences. The book describes the experiences of biblical women and relates them to the experiences of religious women in today's societies. Robins concludes that the plights of many women have not improved over the centuries despite a long Christian heritage. The bible studies demonstrate, however, the liberative nature of the gospel of Christ for women living today.

The BCSA's annual Winter School of Theology compiles all the thematic papers, stories and testimonies of women and men and produces a book each year. Examples are Towards a Holistic, Afrocentric and Participatory Understanding of the Gospel of Jesus Christ (1995), Reading the Bible in Context: Reconstructing South Africa (1996), Being a Baptist in South Africa Today (1997), and Awakening the Sleeping Lion: The role of Baptists in Contemporary Africa (1998).

Other articles and books where women have been activated to expose the experiences of religious women to the written tradition are: Hearing and Knowing (Ooduyoye 1986), Women Hold Up Half the Sky (Ackermann, et al 1991), "Christology and an African Woman's Experience," Faces of Jesus in Africa (Nasimiyu-Wasike 1991), Women, the Bible and the Contemporary Church (Umtata Women's Theology Bible Study Series, no date), The Other Disciples of Jesus (Umtata Women's Theology Bible Study Series, no date), "The Will to Arise: Reflections in Luke 8:40--56," The Will to

SUMMATION AND LIBERATING PRAXIS

Arise: Women, Tradition, and the Church in Africa (Okure 1992), African Women in Religion and Culture (Phiri 1992), With Passion and Compassion: Third World Women Doing Theology (Fabella, Oduyoye 1994), "Reconstructing Theology: A Woman's Perspective," Journal of Black Theology (Lebaka-Ketshabile 1995), Daughters of Anowa (Oduyoye 1995), "The Church's Silence About Violence in the Home," Challenge (Musopole 1995/96), Groaning in Faith: African women in the Household of God (Kanyoro and Njoroge 1996), "Various Voices Speak", Bulletin for Contextual Theology in Southern Africa and Africa (1997), "Reading the Bible the Bosadi (womanhood) Way," Bulletin for Contextual Theology in Southern Africa and Africa (Masenya 1997), "Women in the Gospel of Luke: An African Woman's Perspective," Journal of Constructive Theology (Phiri 1997), and The Piety of South African Women (Landman 1999a).

This list of African women speaking through the medium of the written tradition, is making a major impact upon African theology which has for so long been the enclave of male writers. Women are now renaming, reclaiming, and re-reading their experiences in order to identify who they are and convey their hopes and dreams for themselves and for the church they love. Women are en route to discovering their future possibilities in the service of God through his church by dialoguing actively in the written media. They are participating at last, no longer muted. Yet their voices are few in comparison to the much longer and extensive tradition of male theologians who have been writing for some time. Of note, some male writers are actively taking up the cause of women: "The 'Smoke Screens' Called Black and African Theologies -- the Challenge of African Women Theology," Journal of Constructive Theology (Maluleke 1997) and "A South African Perspective on 'Transforming Mission,'" Mission in

WOMEN AND LEADERSHIP

<u>Bold Humility</u> (Saayman 1996). In the latter article Saayman believes that a "conspicuous omission" in David Bosch's <u>Transforming Mission</u> was a concerted, descriptive analysis of the contribution of women to mission and the "missionary dimension of the liberation of women" (51).

Aside from Louise Kretzschmar's writings, and the short articles or short stories by several laywomen, pastor's wives, and women theological students that are found in the Winter School of Theology books since 1995, the BCSA have not exposed the experiences of the overwhelming majority of women to the written tradition. The majority experiences and voices are *muted*. This study[15] is a contribution by a participant member of the BCSA, yet so much more needs to be done if the denomination is to find liberation for the silent majority and thereby transform the churches in the townships and rural areas where the preponderance of BCSA churches exist.

Van Schalkwyk (1996:58-59) claims that if the African Church is to become a servant church and play a significant role in development, "it must first of all transform its leadership patterns into ones of partnership and participation," which means the full involvement of the poor and the women of the church. She concludes, "Before a church can spread this message of transformation in word and deed, it should first transform itself and its own leadership structures." As I have noted earlier, transformation is the goal, liberation is the means. The debate must be tabled in the high places of academia and ecclesiastical hierarchies where books, articles, workshops and clergical forums thrive.

Chilver (1997:6-7) asks pertinent questions to which we shall attempt answers in the next section: "How can the Christian community be educated to a biblical view of 'woman' and of women's ministry in the church?" "What patterns and methods are most appropriate for the church in developing the full potential of women and their training for ministry in the church?" In addition, he advocates answers to the following challenges: "A biblical and theological understanding of women's identity, and of the Spirit's gifts and their distribution for leadership ministry in the church;" and "A biblical and theological response to various and specific cultural attitudes in Africa regarding the ministry and leadership of women in the church."

We turn now to step two.

Activate Strategic Church-Based Theological Education

A denominational plan can be activated that will not only encourage but help implement a liberating praxis by providing learning materials and learning models in re-educating BCSA members to a revolutionary experience of biblical and theological studies. As we have said before, both women and men must be freed from theological captivity that cripples the church.

For much of this church-based theological reflective-education, women need to meet together. Later seminars and workshops can involve men. There is so much healing for women that needs to take place. Story telling is a strategic means by which women's share groups or bible study groups can share their painful stories in a context that will be safe and secure from suspicion or ridicule. The BCSA can plan for workshops and training sessions by sending skilled women to the various regions of South Africa where

WOMEN AND LEADERSHIP

BCSA churches exist. There can be group leaders' training whereby local leaders can take over and sustain women's training sessions. African womanist "theologians" who are found at the grassroots in the BCSA can fill the role of advocates of healing and wholeness. BCSA women need to undergo the process of renaming, reclaiming, rereading in order to get ready for action plans in self-determination under the guidance of the Spirit of God. In women's health, strength and determination there is hope for Baptist women and the BCSA.

At the Official Opening of Faculty in 1997 sponsored by the Faculty of Theology and Religious Studies of UNISA, Father S. Mkhatshwa (a former priest at Soshanguve and presently Deputy Minister of Education) voiced some concern about theological education. He said the legacy of apartheid has been damaging in that there is now a serious lack of a culture of learning and academic discipline. Transformation in education is needed. He decried the big gap between theory and practice and the failure to take seriously contextualization. Western theology still dominates South African universities and theological colleges and seminaries. For instance he lamented, "It is a masculine theology. It does not deal with the questions and problems of women." While South Africa is highly religious, Mkhatshwa decried that "faith is uninformed, uncritical."

I am advocating a methodology of theological education (re-education) at the local churches of the BCSA that is de-westernized, contextual and relevant to the contemporary needs of the church. Hence careful preparations and model seminars must be experimented with. How does one publicize such events? How does one Africanize and make the process relevant and meaningful and not an exercise in futility? These are difficult questions and I shall not attempt in this study to cover that ground. Yet it is clear that highly trained and motivated women and men must be activated to master-

SUMMATION AND LIBERATING PRAXIS

mind this widespread strategic opportunity.[16]

In Ackermann's own study on women (1985:153), the majority of her fifteen respondents desired a church where there was true fellowship, warmth, freedom to exercise ministries based on spiritual gifts alone, and freedom from hierarchical structures. It was a hope for all of her respondents. They had no idea how to bring about this type of church.

Ackermann (154-155) then delineates her idea for a "liberating praxis":

> The first stage entails a clear analysis of the situation of women in their churches. In this stage the socio-cultural, historical, psychological and theological dimensions must all be taken into account. Oppressive structures are examined, that is those which are patriarchal or hierarchical; sexist language and exclusivistic theologies are subjected to criticism. This stage presupposes an awareness, a raised consciousness. One of the more effective ways to heighten women's consciousness is to initiate groups where they meet together: discussion groups, Bible study groups, groups which are directed at sharing experiences and extending care to one another. The empirical facts are gathered and their functions are examined critically with a view to seeking new options. In a nutshell, women's experience is placed under the microscope.
>
> Thereafter, as a second stage, a process of hermeneutical mediation takes place, through which the Bible, the source book of the Christian faith, is examined. Its prophetic core is sought in a critical manner, in the search for liberation. This is done in relation to the whole of human praxis, in an interdisciplinary manner so as to broaden the scope of the Christian praxis.

Lastly, a deliberate choice is made for liberating praxis, which translates itself into concrete actions. New models for ministry in which all participate according to their gifts are sought and the functions and structures of the church are formulated in a new way. At the same time, strategies are formed for action to help liberate those women and men who are caught in stereotyped roles.

These three stages are actually one and the same movement and should not be seen in isolation from one another. If separated they will become sterile theology, a socio-political exercise, or simply pragmatism. Seen as a unity, they hopefully offer a way for women to achieve liberating praxis in their churches and in so doing enable the church of Jesus Christ to be truly and fully church.[17]

I am in agreement with Ackermann's suggestions. Her three stages represent a generic model, though, and should not be seen as detailed enough or befitting every local church circumstance. Multiple variations can arise from this model. She does not even tell us how long each stage should last, or who exactly are involved or can be involved, or what size group these sessions ought to accommodate, or what kind of materials are to be used, or what languages. Her model is, nevertheless, a useful one for the BCSA to study and adapt. Local congregations can adapt it in myriad ways. Louise Kretzschmar, a member of the BCSA, writes convincingly of the need for "small action groups" to break the "conspiracy of silence" that degrades women and the church (1995d:90-104):

If women open themselves to transformation and form a variety of groups directed towards specific aims, we in Africa will be much further along the road towards truth, justice and wholeness in ten years' time than we are now. Such effort may indeed be costly, but it will be even more costly to ourselves, our families, churches and societies if we conform to the selfishness and fear of patriarchy. It

SUMMATION AND LIBERATING PRAXIS

is not slavery that Christ has called us, but to salvation, freedom and wholeness.

A decision by the National Executive Committee (NEC) of the BCSA can begin the process of implementation of a strategic plan for widespread church-based theological education. In the meantime, local churches need not wait. They are free to begin "the long walk to freedom."

CONCLUSION

In my research on dreams among Zambian Baptists (1993: 404-405; see also the recent publication <u>Dreams in the African Church: The Significance of Dreams and Visions Among Zambian Baptists</u>, 1999) I discovered that women received "call dreams," i.e., call "to the Christian ministry," even if this did not lead to the ordained pastoral ministry. It is my contention that women are called to the ministry to serve God, and the fact that the church does not officially recognize her call or give her ordination does not negate the divine activity nor the evangelistic zeal.

Not a few BCSA women are experiencing the call of God in their lives, through dreams or otherwise. While the nature of their call and the implications of it for church "ministry" can be debated, the *significance* of the call in their lives cannot be. God's Spirit is being felt by BCSA women in deep and extensive ways, and their faithfulness to him and the church bear witness to this fact.

WOMEN AND LEADERSHIP

The following three dreams, the first in 1994 and the second and third in 1998, helped this twenty-eight year old BCSA church member to be convinced that she must give up ownership of her life and serve God through his church:

Dream No. 1

In the year of 1994, I had a dream. Though I can't remember the date, but it was September. The dream goes as follows:

I was with my fellow Christians walking together. In front of me I saw a mountain. As we were walking, talking, I noticed that I left them behind. When I reached to the top of the mountain, I stopped trying to wait for them. But the man came to me on my dream. Though I couldn't manage to recognize him. One thing I noticed he was black in color. After all he showed me the house. And I said I am still waiting for my fellow Christians. Yet he told me that I must first get into the house. And the house had a big bright lamp. So he told me that when I get into the house I will also manage to lead those I left behind to the house.

Dream No. 2

This dream came also in June 1998. I was in the church. Mr. Ndlaleni who is the deacon of the church was preaching. I had time to recognize some members of the church. I was behind of everyone. But stood up in a high place covered with something like a blanket, and no one saw me in the congregation. The word came to me and commanded that I must read the scripture for everyone in the book of John 7, verse 8. Everyone in the church heard my voice but with a surprise not seeing me in person. So when I woke up I realized that I was dreaming.

SUMMATION AND LIBERATING PRAXIS

Dream No. 3

This also came in September 1998. The man was preaching but no one paid attention to his preaching. I noticed that my grandfather who died in 1986 was sitting next to me. My grandfather told me that I must stand up and preach the Good News of God. So I refused telling him that these people are older than me and that I am a female, they won't listen to me. He convinced me that I must stand up and I will see for myself. I stood and started to preach and people got saved. But at first I was afraid not knowing the words I will say.

Those dreams was my confirmation to my God's call.

We cannot debate the significance or meaningfulness of these "call" dreams for this young woman. She is studying in her second year at the BCSA's Baptist Convention College in Soweto. She hopes to be a pastor or evangelist. Will a Baptist church invite her to be the pastor of the church? No one knows. Will she be welcomed by a BCSA church to use her talents, training and spiritual gifts to serve God? What challenges or obstacles will she face? Who will come to her aid when the forces of resistance meet her head on?

According to Tienou (1997:53-54), the Christian life from its inception is a life in grace (Eph. 2:5-8). It is by grace and through grace that Christian ministry is offered (I Cor. 12:4-11, Eph. 4:7-12). If our service for Christ and our participation in Christ are both of grace, then no limiting factors should exist. Neither class, nor race, nor sex, nor preparation or lack of, it are impediments or qualifying conditions for being a follower of Christ or serving him and his church. Hence, if ministry in the church is comprehended in the sense of service, then all dimensions of church ministry are open to women and men. Tienou refrains from dealing with ordination here since, for him, ordination is an issue of power more than an issue of service. He concludes by saying:

> We may *de jure* say that women should be involved in all areas of ministry but we may *de facto* find ourselves restricting their participation.... My concern is that our deliberations... not remain theoretical. We must find ways of reforming practice. But in this area, does one dare to hope?

Does one dare to hope? Does one dare *not* to? For a liberating praxis in church life that leads to transformation we dare not lose hope.

WOMAN

You bring peace to earth
You bring reconciliation
Woman
You are magnificent
You are mother.

At the Inn there was no room
You were between life and death
You went to the stable
You brought forth your seed
You are woman.

SUMMATION AND LIBERATING PRAXIS

You have been despised
You have been hated
You know what it is to fear
To worry, to hunger and thirst
Woman
And still you know what it is to be triumphant.
Cry out for joy
For your seed has multiplied

Shout out with great joy
For you have grown strong
Woman
You will bring everything to pass.

(Radebe 1988:99)

WOMEN AND LEADERSHIP

NOTES ON CHAPTER FOUR

1. In a personal note to me (28 June 1999), Willem Saayman surmised that women may not be free or liberated if they are ordained to the pastoral ministry that is still under the umbrella of patriarchal expectations. He writes: "I think that the suffocating and oppressive nature which the ordained ministerial structures of the church have developed over the centuries must be debated very seriously and very urgently. The huge struggle needed in most churches to open the ranks of ordination to women, has, I think, often obscured the more important issue of how ordination should function -- so often as an oppressive institution, with lots of scheming, back-biting and power-plays. To put it very crudely: in our urgent struggle to make ordination accessible for women we often lost sight of the fact that the church in its very structures expect an ordained woman to prove that she can make it and take it in a MAN'S world -- not in a simply human world." I will address this issue later in this chapter when I take cues from the remarks of women in the questionnaires and interviews. I will build a case for the qualities women can bring to all types of church leadership (including pastoral leadership) that may mitigate against what Saayman describes as male "back-biting" and "power-plays."

2. We have earlier referred to a "hermeneutic of suspicion." This is in part to convey a caution regarding "orthodoxy." Church beliefs or personal beliefs about anything ought not to dominate our interpretation. Historical church doctrines ought not to dominate scripture; rather, scripture must persistently judge our doctrines. The bible should not be used manipulatively, conveniently, as a proof-text to "validate" church orthodoxy or personal beliefs. An example: to uphold the theory of the "submission" of women to men in the multiple categories of life is tantamount to upholding the captivity of scripture to personal or ecclesiastical assumptions.

3. One wonders to what extent the AME church of South Africa has outwardly affirmed women in ministry yet resist the ordination for women. In an interview with a male BCSA respondent, the opinion was voiced that BCSA women are used as "tools not as human beings." He expressed anger at this. The BCSA denominational leaders who outwardly promote the value and attributes of women at public forums are the very ones who "fail to practice it" (interview:1998).

SUMMATION AND LIBERATING PRAXIS

4. Are these eight elders men because of church law or because of "happenstance"? We cannot tell. Nurnberger (1994:140) declares that while we should not be ashamed to pronounce the gospel we should ensure that we proclaim the whole gospel, the empowering, liberating gospel of God's redemptive ambitions, his creative authority and comprehensive vision. We ought not to advocate a gospel which encourages narrow-mindedness, spiritual selfishness, conservatism or escapism.

5. We must face squarely two basic questions, Oduyoye (1992:11) insists, when examining the function of religion in Africa's cultures (Christian, Islam, or African traditional): In the structures of religious institutions, what responsibilities do women enjoy? For the sake of women's development, how does religion serve or obstruct?

6. The Circle of Concerned African Women Theologians adhere to a principle of "mutual-mothering" as well as seeking to accommodate the interests of those coming from the various African and religious communities. This "motherhood agenda," in church, sociological group or academy, of caring for life, making space for it and nurturing others also to honour, care and respect life, has meant that in doing theology this mothering sensitivity and disposition affect one's total theological reflection (Oduyoye 1998b:364).

7. It has been generally found that women are more empathic than men (Hoffman 1977:712-722) and more nurturant than men (Harlow 1971; Money and Ehrhardt 1972; Whiting and Whiting 1975). Women tend to value co-operation, beauty, harmony and love while men tend to value independence, competition, play and freedom (Feather and Feather 1984:604-620). Women seem to have the facility for parallel processing of analytical, logical and verbal aptitudes alongside more holistic, emotional and intuitive skills, while men's brain activities seem more lateralized in either right or left, but not both (Levy 1969:614-615; Buffery and Gray 1972:123-157; Seward and Seward 1980).

8. Smith's bold embrace of the Khoi-Khoi people reflects what Holness (1990:202) terms an "instinctive" urge to build "community": "It is my experience that women tend instinctively to include rather than to separate, to conserve and build up rather than to fragment and break down. Therefore it follows that a sense of community is one element of life -- and an essentially Christian one at that -- that incorporation of

the woman's perspective can offer to life and faith."

9. Remember Kim's 'nutritional' comment about women evangel-ists?

10. In an interview (7-3-98) with a pastor of a BCSA church, and now the elected General Secretary of the BCSA, women were praised for their administrative and decision-making qualities. The question is, will women do administration and decision-making differently from men? He answered yes: "When it comes to decision-making, women make good administrators. Women make decisions on the basis of 'community' in mind. Men often make decisions for self-interest. Hence, they don't meet their predetermined goals. They get bogged down in power struggles. Women can meet their target goals."

11. Pamela Young (1990:53-55) speaks of "women's experience" in five ways: a) women's *bodily* experience (what is encountered in life physically); b) women's *socialised* experience (what culture teaches about being female), c) women's *feminist* experience (personal responses to socialised experience), d) women's *historical* experience, and e) women's *individual* experiences. It was crucial that women began to acknowledge that they needed to articulate for themselves their individual, historical, feminist, socialised and bodily experiences rather than accept the male understanding and assessment of what it ought to be. They needed to ask themselves who women were, what were they like, and what they wanted for themselves. They realised they must possess the power of renaming, reclaiming and rereading the bible for themselves. They needed to call for equality with men and comprehend the meaning and implications of equality. Wherein were women different, and wherein were they similar to men? How do these similarities and differences affect social value and power in the structures and institutions of society?

12. One does not want to mis-speculate or create an unwarranted stereotype, but based upon what I have heard and seen in my questionnaires, interviews and associations with families of BCSA churches, black women in the townships face daunting hardships and challenges. I can only marginally contemplate at everything they encounter. But ill treatment often appears to be one of them. A Xhosa young man said that many women in BCSA churches "resist" empowerment and leadership in the church because of the ill treatment in their families at home. Frequently from a young age a girl can be ill treated verbally or physically. She loses emotional stability. Her experiences at home, even as mothers and adults, provide little opportu-

SUMMATION AND LIBERATING PRAXIS

nity or incentive for educational development or responsible social skills in institutional settings. This background gives a woman inadequate feelings about herself. It hinders the growth and vitality of the church in which she worships since she has been subdued, often humiliated. While such conditions may exist in white households, the prevalence of occurrence in black households may be the ingrained socio-cultural pattern.

13. De Gruchy (1984:76) noted that Bonhoeffer did not take a liking to conversion stories told by pietists, but one cannot doubt the reality of his conversion, his "inner revolution," in his early thirties. Bonhoeffer called it a "great liberation," which launched in him a new sense of passion and responsibility for the world in his remaining few years. He was freed not only from the bondage of privilege but also from a self-centered and powerful ego to an unusual concern for others in and through the service of the Christian church. Women in the BCSA need to be emancipated in order to exercise their spiritual gifts and their passion for service, and men need to be liberated from their bondage to blindness and arrogance. Needless to say, we should be equally concerned about the numerous women in the BCSA who are held captive by their blindness or traditional/conservative views regarding women and leadership and who systematically ridicule women aspiring to serve Christ according to their divine calling.

14. It has been the concern of Oduyoye and the Circle of Concerned African Women Theologians that all religious women of Africa need to do theology and allow their muted voices to be heard, not only the educated ones.

15. It is my strong conviction that men must be activated on a much larger scale in the BCSA. They are the pastors, elders, deacons, and family leaders. Baptist men must not only be vocal but *activistic* in the struggle for justice and righteousness in the church. When women and men are held captive, women *and* men must be activated to emancipate the sinful conditions. I fully agree, therefore, with Gabriel Mucavele (1994:158): "The oppression to which women have been subjected must be a concern of men. It is necessary that men be in a position to witness in solidarity with women in every locus: the home, social situations, and in the church itself."

16. We agree with the writer(s) of The Other Disciples of Jesus (no date:8) when she said what most of us know: in South Africa women are not encouraged to gain

theological training. The social function and level of women's groups within local congregations are such that women fail to attain the skills, learning, and tools to be equipped to make major contributions. The men make significant decisions and interact at a certain level, while women are busy with their "activities." Women therefore lack self-confidence to be full participants when provided with an opportunity to interact. My assessment is that, more often than not, this type of marginalization takes place in the rank and file BCSA churches.

17. See Cochrane, de Gruchy and Peterson (1991:95-96) on their comments on a "liberating praxis" for the churches.

LIST OF WORKS CONSULTED

ABBEY-MENSAH, Dinah 1997. Who Is This Woman? <u>Transforming Power: Women in the Household of God</u>, edited by Mercy Amba Oduyoye, Accra: Sam-woode, Ltd. (For the Circle of Concerned African Women Theologians), 158-160.

ACKERMANN, D., J. A. Draper and E. Moshinimi, eds. 1991. <u>Women Hold Up Half the Sky</u>. Pietermaritzburg: Cluster Publications.

ACKERMANN, D. M. 1984. The Role of Women in the Church -- Certain Practical Theological Perspectives, <u>Sexism and Feminism In Theological Perspective</u>, edited by W. S. Vorster, Pretoria: UNISA, 61-84.

ACKERMANN, Denise Mary 1985. <u>Woman and Ministries: A Feminist Perspective</u>, M.Th. dissertation, UNISA.

ACKERMANN, Denise 1991. Postscript: By a Feminist Practical Theologian, <u>In Word and Deed</u>, by J. R. Cochrane, J. W. De Gruchy, and R. Petersen, Pietermaritzburg: Cluster Publications, 106-111.

ACKERMANN, Denise 1992. Defining Our Humanity: Thoughts on a Feminist Anthropology, <u>Journal of Theology for Southern Africa</u> 79 (June): 13-23.

ACKERMANN, Denise 1996a. Engaging Freedom: A Contextual Feminist Theology of Praxis, <u>Journal of Theology for Southern Africa</u> (March): 32-49.

ACKERMANN, Denise M. 1996b. Participation and Inclusiveness Among Women, <u>Groaning in Faith: African Women in the Household of God</u>, edited by Musimbi R. A. Kanyoro and Nyambura J. Njoroge, Nairobi: Acton Publishers, 136-148.

WOMEN AND LEADERSHIP

ACKERMANN, Denise 1997. A Feminist Theology of Praxis for Today, <u>Bulletin for Contextual Theology in Southern Africa and Africa</u> 4:2 (July): 17-19.

ALBERTYN, Catherine 1995. National Machinery for Ensuring Gender Equality, <u>The Constitution of South Africa from a Gender Perspective</u>, edited by Sandra Liebenberg, Cape Town: The Community Law Centre with David Philip, 9-27.

AMANZE, James 1998. <u>African Christianity in Botswana: The Case of African Independent Churches</u>. Gweru: Mambo Press.

AMOAH, Elizabeth and Mercy Amba Oduyoye 1994. The Christ for African Women, <u>With Passion and Compassion: Third World Women Doing Theology</u>, edited by Virginia Fabella and Mercy Amba Oduyoye, Maryknoll: Orbis, 35-46.

AMOAH, Elizabeth 1997. Women as Portrayed in Some African Proverbs, <u>Embracing the Baobab Tree</u>, edited by Willem Saayman, Pretoria: UNISA, 203-213.

ANDERSON, Kathryn, Susan Armitage, Dana Jack, Judith Wittner 1990. Beginning Where We Are, <u>Feminist Research Methods</u>, edited by Joyce M. Nielsen, Boulder, San Francisco, London: Westview Press, 94-112.

ANDRÉ, Ellis s.a. <u>Baptists and Politics</u>. Roodepoort: Roodepoort Mission Press.

ANNEXURE I: MISSION STATEMENT 1995. <u>BCSA Handbook</u>.

BACCHIOCCHI, Samuele 1987. <u>Women in the Church: A Biblical Study on the Role of Women in the Church</u>. Beruin Springs: Biblical Perspectives.

BAL, Mieke 1991. <u>On Story-Telling: Essays in Narratology</u>. Sonoma: Polebridge Press.

LIST OF WORKS CONSULTED

BAM, Brigalia 1991. Seizing the Moment: Women and the New South Africa, Women Hold Up Half the Sky, edited by Denise Ackermann, Jonathan A. Draper and Emma Mashinini, Pietermaritzburg: Cluster Publications, 363-368.

BATE, Stuart 1994. Inculturation: The Local Church Emerges, Missionalia 22:2 (Aug.): 93-117.

BATTS, H. J. 1921. History of the Baptist Church in South Africa. Cape Town: T. Maskew Miller.

BEEK, Huibert van 1995. New Relationships in Mission, Euntes Studies 23 (September): 35-54.

BEN-AMOS, Paula Girshick 1994. The Promise of Greatness: Women and Power in an Edo Spirit Possession Cult, Religion in Africa, edited by Thomas D. Blakely, Walter E. A. Van Beek and Dennis L. Thomson, Portsmouth: Heinemann, 119-134.

BEVANS, Stephen B. 1992. Models of Contextual Theology. Maryknoll: Orbis.

BORQUIN, S., ed. and trans. and H. Filter, comp. 1986. Paulina Dlamini: Servant of Two Kings. Pietermaritzburg.

BOSCH, David J. 1991. Transforming Mission. Maryknoll: Orbis.

BOTHA, N. A. and Willem Saayman 1992. The Voluntarist Model of Mission, Missiology: Only Study Guide for MSA 100-3. Pretoria: UNISA, 107-143.

BOWIE, Fiona 1993. Introduction: Reclaiming Women's Presence, Women and Mission: Past and Present, edited by Fiona Bowie, Deborah Kirkwood and Shirley Ardener, Providence/Oxford: Berg Publishers, 1-19.

WOMEN AND LEADERSHIP

BRUCE, Debbie 1996. Impressions and Reflections, Reading the Bible in Context: Reconstructing South Africa, edited by Louise Kretzschmar and Ruben Richards, Johannesburg: BCSA, 195-207.

BRYARUHANGA-AKIIKI, A. B. T. 1994. Culture as a Source of Oppression of Woman in Africa, Culture, Religion and Lib-eration: Proceedings of the EATWOT Pan African Theological Conference, Harare, Zimbabwe, January 6-11, 1991, ed-ited by Simon Maimela, Pretoria: 32-47.

BRYCESON, Deborah, Linzi Manicom and Yusuf Kassam 1982. The Methodology of the Participatory Research Approach, Participatory Research: An Emerging Alternative Methodology in Social Science Research, edited by Y. Kassam and K. Mustafa. Canada, 24-32.

BUFFERY, A. and J. Gray 1972. Sex Differences in the Development of Spatial and Linguistic Skills, Gender Differences, edited by C. Ounted and D. Taylor, Edinburgh: Churchill Livingstone.

CARTER, Cassandra 1996. Interview in King Williams Town on 27/2/96 (missionary serving the BCSA churches in the Eastern Cape).

CHARTON, Nancy 1992. Women in the Church, South African Outlook 122 (Jan./Feb.): 2-5.

CHILVER, Alan M. 1997. Preface, Women's Ministry in the Church: An African Perspective, edited by Alan M. Chilver, Nairobi: Theological and Christian Education Commission of the Association of Evangelicals in Africa, 5-10.

CHIRAIRO, Lilian 1998. "The African Prophetess: Initiatives in Church Development," a paper presented at the conference in Pretoria entitled "African Christianity: Outreach and Encounter," (12-15 Oct.): 1-14.

CHITANDO, Ezra 1998. 'There Was at Joppa a Disciple': A Study of the Role of Women in a Rural Assembly in Zimbabwe, Journal of Constructive Theology, 4:1 (July): 73-88.

LIST OF WORKS CONSULTED

CLARK, Elizabeth A. 1983. Women in the Early Church. Wilmington: Michael Glazier, Inc.

COCHRANE, J. R., J. W. de Gruchy, R. Peterson 1991. In Word and in Deed: Towards a Practical Theology of Social Transformation. Pietermaritzburg: Cluster Publications.

COCHRANE, Renate 1991. Equal Discipleship of Women and Men: Reading the New Testament from a Feminist Perspective, Women Hold Up Half the Sky, edited by Denise Ackermann, Jonathan A. Draper and Emma Mashinini, Pietermaritzburg: Cluster Publications, 21-36.

COCK, Jacklin 1989. Maids and Madams. London: The Women's Press.

CORMICK, Diana Mary 1992. The Visual Portrayal of Mary Magdalene: A Case Study in Feminist Ethical Issues. M.Th. disertation, UNISA.

COTTER, George 1997. Ethiopian Wisdom (Series editor, John S. Mbiti, African Proverbs Series, Vol. 1). Pretoria: UNISA.

CUTHBERTSON, Greg and Louise Kretzschmar 1996. Gender and Mission Christianity: Recent Trends in South African Historiography and Theology, Missionalia 24:3 (Nov.): 277-301.

CUTHBERTSON, Greg 1997. Between God and Patriarchy: African Women, Gender and Christian Mission in Recent South African Historiography. (Paper delivered at UNISA during the 1997 Southern Africa Missiological Society annual conference), 1-21.

DALFOVO, Albert 1997. Lugbara Wisdom (Series editor, John S. Mbiti, African Proverbs Series, Vol. 3). Pretoria: UNISA.

DALY, Mary 1985. The Church and the Second Sex. Boston: Beacon Press.

WOMEN AND LEADERSHIP

DANEEL, M. L. 1992. The African Indigenous Model of Mission, <u>Missiology: Only Study Guide for MSA 100-3</u>, edited by Willem Saayman, Pretoria: UNISA.

D'AZEVEDO, Warren L. 1994. Gola Womanhood and the Limits of Masculine Omnipotence, <u>Religion in Africa</u>, edited by Thomas D. Blakely, Walter E. A. Van Beek and Dennis L. Thomson, Portsmouth: Heinemann, 343-362.

DE GRUCHY, John W. 1984. <u>Bonhoeffer and South Africa</u>. Grand Rapids: Eerdmans.

DENIS, Philippe, ed. 1995. <u>The Making of an Indigenous Clergy in Southern Africa</u>. Pietermaritzburg: Cluster Publications.

DENNIS, Trevor 1994. <u>Sarah Laughed: Women's Voices in the Old Testament</u>. London: SPCK.

DLAMINI, Beauty Nomtandazo 1995. Three Pastors Under the Same Roof: The Story of a Woman Minister, <u>The Making of an Indigenous Clergy in Southern Africa</u>, edited by Philippe Denis, Pietermaritzburg: Cluster Publications, 178-180.

DUBE, Musa W. 1997. Mama, <u>Transforming Power: Women in the Household of God</u>, edited by Mercy Amba Oduyoye, Accra: Sam-Woode, Ltd. (for the Circle of Concerned African Women Theologians), 150-151.

DU TOIT, C. W. 1996. Empowerment of the Poor: Changing Our Minds on Affluence and Poverty, <u>Empowering the Poor</u>, edited by C. W. Du Toit, Pretoria: UNISA, 10-36.

EDET, Rosemary and Bette Ekeya 1994. Church Women of Africa: A Theological Community, <u>With Passion and Compassion: Third World Women Doing Theology</u>, edited by Virginia Fabella and Mercy Amba Oduyoye, Maryknoll: Orbis, 3-13.

EISLER, Riane 1987. <u>The Chalice and the Blade</u>. San Francisco: Harper & Row.

LIST OF WORKS CONSULTED

EKO, Ebele 1997. A Harvest of Hate, <u>Transforming Power: Wo-men in the Household of God</u>, edited by Mercy Amba Oduyoye, Accra: Sam-Woode, Ltd. (For the Circle of Concerned African Women Theologians), 156-157.

EVANS, Rev. E. G. 1933. <u>The Romance of the Early Years of the Baptist Church of South Africa</u>. Cape Town.

EVANS, Mary 1983. <u>Woman in the Bible</u>. Exeter: Paternoster.

FABELLA, Virginia and Mercy Amba Oduyoye, eds. 1994. <u>With Passion and Compassion: Third World Women Doing Theology</u>. Maryknoll: Orbis.

FEATHER, N. and L. Feather 1984. Masculinity, Femininity, Psychological Androgyny, and the Structure of Values, <u>Journal of Personality and Social Psychology</u>, 47:604-620.

FEELING AT HOME IN THE CHURCH (A pastoral letter of the Southern African Catholic Bishop's Conference, November 1995) 1996. <u>Challenge</u> 34 (Feb/March): 12-13.

FINCA, Bongani Blessing 1998. A Man's View of the Decade of the Churches in Solidarity with Women, <u>Women in God's Image</u> 5 (Dec.): 8-10.

FORRESTER, Duncan 1989. <u>Beliefs, Values and Policies: Conviction Politics in a Secular Age</u>. Oxford: Clarendon.

FRANCISCO, Carol 1996. Christian Women on the Red Road, <u>A Journey into Crisis</u>, edited by J. A. L. Saunders, Charlotte: A Nilses Publication, 107-118.

FROISE, Marjorie, ed. 1996. <u>South African Christian Handbook</u>. Welkom: Christian Info.

GAITSKELL, Deborah 1990. Devout Domesticity? A Century of African Women's Christianity in South Africa, <u>Women and Gender in Southern Africa to 1945</u>, edited by Cheryl Walker, Cape Town: David Philip, 251-272.

WOMEN AND LEADERSHIP

Germans in Kaffraria s.a. Pinetown: J. F. Schwar and B. E. Pape.

GETUI, Mary N. 1996. Women's Priesthood in Relation to Nature, Groaning in Faith: African Women in the Household of God, edited by Musimbi R. A. Kanyoro and Nyambura J. Njoroge, Nairobi: Acton Publishers, 31-39.

GLAZ, Maxine 1991. Gender Issues in Pastoral Theology, Journal of Pastoral Theology 1 (Summer): 93-115.

GOBA, Bonganjalo 1995. The Role of Religion in Promoting Democratic Values in the Post-Apartheid Era: A Personal Reflection, Journal of Constructive Theology (1:1): 11-24.

GOEDHALS, Mandy M. 1994. The Expansion of Christianity in the Nineteenth Century, A History of Christianity in South Africa (Vol. 1) edited by J. W. Hofmeyer and Gerald J. Pilley, Pretoria: HAUM Tertiary, 123-144.

GOEMANS, Loek 1997. Unnamed song, Women in God's Image 4 (Nov.): 7.

GOOD NEWS FOR THE POOR IN VISUAL ART, REFLECTION AND PRAYER (Reprinted from the Jubilee prayer book of Church World Service, For the Healing of the Nations) 1997. Journal of Constructive Theology 3:1 (July): 87-91.

GOVINDEN, D. Betty 1996. In Search of Our Own Wells, Groaning in Faith: African Women in the Household of God, edited by Musumbi R. A. Kanyoro and Nyambura J. Njoroge, Nairobi: Acton Publishers, 16-22.

GOVINDEN, D. Betty 1997a. Dominion to Rule -- the Abuse of Women in Christian Homes, Bulletin for Contextual Theology for Southern Africa and Africa 4:2 (July): 26-31.

GOVINDEN, Betty 1997b. Re-Imaging God, Transforming Power: Women in the Household of God, edited by Mercy Amba Oduyoye, Accra: Sam-Woode, Ltd. (For the Circle of Concerned African Women Theologians), 148-150.

LIST OF WORKS CONSULTED

GRANT, Jacquelyn 1994. 'Come to My Help Lord For I'm in Trouble': Womanist Jesus and the Mutual Struggle for Liberation, Journal of Black Theology 8:1 (May): 21-34.

HADDAD, Beverly 1996. En-gendering a Theology of Development: Raising Some Preliminary Issues, Archbishop Tutu: Prophetic Witness in South Africa, edited by Leonard Hulley, Louise Kretzschmar and Luke Lungile Pato, Cape Town: Human & Rousseau, 199-210.

HADDAD, Beverly 1997. En-Gendering Theology: South African Voices, Bulletin for Contextual Theology in Southern Africa and Africa 4:2 (July): 1-3.

HARLOW, H. 1971. Learning to Love. San Francisco: Album.

HARRIS, Brian 1994. Findings of the Commission of Inquiry into Women in Leadership in the Baptist Union of Southern Africa. Unpublished paper.

HARRIS, James Ian 1996. Baptist Identity in Ecumenical Perspective: A Critical Exposition of the 1987 Statement on Baptist Principles of the Baptist Union of South Africa. Ph.D. thesis, University of Cape Town.

HASELBARTH, Hans 1976. Christian Ethics in the African Context. Nairobi: Uzima Press.

HASTINGS, Adrian 1993. Were Women a Special Case? Women and Mission: Past and Present, edited by Fiona Bowie, Deborah Kirkwood and Shirley Ardener, Providence/Oxford: Berg Publishers, 109-125.

HAUBERT, Katherine 1997. The Nature of Woman and the Order of Creation, Women's Ministry in the Church: An African Perspective, edited by Alan M. Chilver, Nairobi: Theological and Christian Education of the Association of Evangelicals in Africa, 21-34.

HAYASHIDA, Nelson O. 1993. The Significance of Dreams and Visions Among Members of the Baptist Convention Churches of Zambia with Special Reference to the Manyika Baptist Association and to Selected Urban Areas. Ph.D. thesis, University of Edinburgh.

HAYASHIDA, Nelson O. 1999. Dreams in the African Church: The Significance of Dreams and Visions Among Zambian Baptists. Amsterdam: Editions Rodopi B.V.

HAYTER, Mary 1987. The New Eve in Christ: The Use and Abuse of the Bible in the Debate About Women in the Church. Grand Rapids: Eerdmans.

"HEARING THE AIC-VOICE", Conference sponsored by Research Institute for Theology and Religion, UNISA, at Unisa Sunnyside Campus, Pretoria, 2-3 Sept. 1998.

HIRD, Cathy 1997. Open Doors to Liberation: Two Stories of Ordinary Women Bringing Change to their Communities, Journal of Constructive Theology 3:2 (Dec.): 66-74.

HOFFMAN, M. 1997. Sex Differences in Empathy and Related Behaviors, Psychological Bulletin, 84: 712-722.

HOFFMEISTER, Des 1990. The Relationship Between the Baptist Convention and the Baptist Union, The Barkly West National Awareness Workshop, edited by Des Hoffmeister and Brian J. Gurney, Johannesburg: The Awareness Campaign Committee of the BCSA, 46-52.

HOFFMEISTER, Des 1998. General Secretary's Report to the National Assembly of the Baptist Convention held at the 17th Shaft Conference and Training Center from 8-12 December 1998, The Baptist Convention of South Africa Handbook, 21-26.

HOFFMEISTER, Des and Brian J. Gurney 1990. Foreword: "...an empowered future..." The Barkly West National Awareness Workshop, edited by Des Hoffmeister and Brian J. Gurney, Bromfontein: BCSA, 5-6.

LIST OF WORKS CONSULTED

HOFFMEISTER, D. and L. Kretzschmar, eds. 1995. Toward a Holistic, Afrocentric and Participatory Understanding of the Gospel of Jesus Christ. Johannesburg. BCSA.

HOFFMEISTER, D. and L. Kretzschmar, eds. 1996. Reading the Bible in Context: Reconstructing South Africa. Johannesburg: BCSA.

HOFFMEISTER, D. and L. Kretzschmar, eds. 1997. Being a Baptist in South Africa Today. Johannesburg: BCSA.

HOFFMEISTER, D. and L. Kretschmar, eds. 1998. Awakening the Sleeping Giant: The Role of Baptists in Contemporary Africa. Johannesburg: BCSA.

HOLNESS, L. J. 1990. Contextualizing Faith from the Perspective of a South African Woman, M.Th. dissertation, UNISA.

HOLLAND, Joe and Peter Henriot 1991. Social Analysis: Linking Faith and Justice. Maryknoll: Dove Communication and Orbis.

HOPKINS, Dwight. N. 1989. Black Theology USA and South Africa. Maryknoll: Orbis.

HUDSON-REED, Sydney 1972. South African Research: Baptist Beginnings in South Africa 1820-1877. Pietermaritzburg: S.A. Historical Society Archives.

HUDSON-REED, Sydney 1977. Together for a Century: The History of the Baptist Union of South Africa 1877-1977. Pietermaritzburg: S.A. Baptist Historical Society.

HUDSON-REED, Sydney 1983. By Taking Heed...The History of Baptists in Southern Africa 1820-1977. Roodepoort: Baptist Publishing House.

HUDSON-REED, Sydney 1992. Channels for 100 Years of Missionary Endeavor. Cape Town: S.A. Baptist Historical Society.

WOMEN AND LEADERSHIP

Hugo Gutsche s.a. Published by the S.A. Baptist Historical Society.

HULLEY, L. et al, eds. 1996. Archbishop Tutu: Prophetic Witness in South Africa. Cape Town: Human and Rousseau.

ISICHEI, Elizabeth 1993. Does Christianity Empower Women? The Case of the Anaguta of Central Nigeria, Women and Mission: Past and Present, edited by Fiona Bowie, Deborah Kirkwood and Shirley Ardener, Providence/Oxford: Berg Publishers, 209-228.

ISICHEI, Elizabeth 1995. A History of Christianity in Africa. London: SPCK.

IWUCHUKWU, Becky 1997. Women and Religion in Africa, Where God Reigns: Reflections on Women in God's World, edited by Elizabeth Amoah, Accra: Sam-Woode, Ltd. (for the Circle of Concerned African Women Theologians), 39-48.

JACOBS, Alvean 1998. Two Women and Their Responses in a Controversial Issue: Martha and Mary (Luke 10:38-42), Sermon Outlines, edited by Francois Swanepoel, Pretoria: C.B. Powell Bible Centre, 28-30.

JAKOBSEN, Wilma 1997. (In) Various Voices Speak, Bulletin for Contextual Theology in Southern Africa and Africa 4:2 (July): 4-9.

JAMES, A. H. Jeffree 1997. Christians in Socio-Political Activism: A Protestant and Baptist Union Perspective, The South African Baptist Journal of Theology (Vol. 6): 123-131.

JOHNSON-HILL, Lydia 1995. Foundation Stones and Building Blocks: 'Constructing' a Centre for Constructive Theology, Journal of Constructive Theology 1:1 (Dec.): 4-10.

JOHNSTON, Robert K. 1978. An Evangelical Impasse: Women in the Church and Home, The Reformed Journal (June): 11-14.

LIST OF WORKS CONSULTED

JONAS, P. J. 1996. Collectivism and Mission in a South African Context, Missionalia 24:1 (April): 78-90.

JONSSON, John N. 1977. The Theological Outlook, Together for a Century: The History of the Baptist Union of South Africa 1877-1977, edited by Sydney Hudson-Reed, Pietermaritzburg: S.A. Baptist Historical Society, 29-57.

JORDAAN, Roxanne 1987. The Emergence of Black Feminist Theology in South Africa, Journal of Black Theology in South Africa 1:2 (November): 42-46. (The author has since changed her name to Roxanne Cleaven-Jordaan)

JULES-ROSETTE, Bennetta 1985. Cultural Ambivalence and Ceremonial Leadership: The Role of Women in Africa's New Religions, The Church and Women in the Third World, edited by John C. B. and Ellen Low Webster, Philadelphia: The Westminster Press.

KAISER, Elke 1997. The Silence of Job's Wife, Women in God's Image 4 (Nov.): 8-10.

KANYORO, Musimbi R. A. 1996a. God's Call to Ministry, Groaning in Faith: African Women in the Household of God, edited by Musimbi R. A. Kanyoro and Nyambura J. Njoroge, Nairobi: Acton Publishers, 149-160.

KANYORO, Musimbi 1996b. African Women's Quest for Justice: A Review of African Women's Theology, Journal of Constructive Theology 2:2 (Dec.): 5-18.

KANYORO, Musimbi R. A. and N. J. Njoroge, eds. 1996. Groaning in Faith: African Women in the Household of Faith. Nairobi: Acton Publishers.

KATHINDI, Nangula 1991. Women's Struggle in the Church: A Namibian Voice, Women Hold Up Half the Sky, edited by Denise Ackermann, Jonathan A. Draper and Emma Mashinini, Pietermaritzburg: Cluster Publications, 254-266.

WOMEN AND LEADERSHIP

KESHEGIAN, Flora A. 1996. Suffering, Dictionary of Feminist Theologies, edited by Letty M. Russell and J. Shannon Clarkson, Louisville: Westminster John Knox Press, 278-280.

KETEYI, Xolile 1998. Inculturation as a Strategy for Liberation. Pietermaritzburg: Cluster Publications

KETSHABILE, Libuseng 1997. Turning Disempowerment into Empowerment: A Black South African Woman's Experience in Theological Education, Journal of Constructive Theology 3:1 (July): 3-14.

KIDD, Rosemary 1996. Women in Ministry, Reading the Bible in Context: Reconstructing South Africa, edited by Louise Kretzschmar and Ruben Richards, Johannesburg: BCSA, 163-167.

KING, U. 1996. Women, Spirituality, and Interfaith Dialogue, Spirituality in Religions, edited by C. W. Du Toit, Pretoria: Research Institute for Theology and Religion (UNISA), 13-26.

KONGELA, Thandi Rose 1996. Impressions and Reflections, Reading the Bible in Context: Reconstructing South Africa, edited by Louise Kretzschmar and Ruben Richards, Johannesburg: BCSA, 102-105.

KRETZSCHMAR, Louise 1990a. A Theology of Dominance -- An Alternative History of the South African Baptist Union, The Barkly West National Awareness Workshop, edited by D. Hoffmeister and B. J. Gurney, Braamfontein: BCSA, 24-32.

KRETSCHMAR, Louise 1990b. Hermeneutics, Culture and the Apostle Paul's View of Women, Women's Studies 2:1, edited by Dolina Dowling, 37-51.

KRETZSCHMAR, Louise 1991. The Relevance of Feminist Theology Within the South African Context, Women Hold Up Half the Sky, edited by Denise Ackermann, Jonathan A. Draper and Emma Mashinini, Pietermaritzburg: Cluster Publications, 106-121.

LIST OF WORKS CONSULTED

KRETZSCHMAR, Louise 1992. The Privatization of the Christian Faith Amongst South African Baptists: With Particular Reference to its Nature, Extent, Causes and Consequences. Ph.D. thesis, University of Cape Town.

KRETZSCHMAR, Louise 1995a. Introduction, Towards a Holistic, Afro-centric and Participatory Understanding of the Gospel of Jesus Christ, edited by D. Hoffmeister and L. Kretzschmar, Johannesburg: BCSA, 1-3.

KRETZSCHMAR, Louise 1995b. What is a Holistic Spirituality and Why is it Important for the Church Today? Towards a Holistic, Afro-centric and Participatory Understanding of the Gospel of Jesus Christ, edited by D. Hoffmeister and L. Kretzschmar, Johannesburg: BCSA, 31-44.

KRETZSCHMAR, Louise 1995c. Theological Education Committee (TEC), The Baptist Convention of South Africa Handbook, 45.

KRETZSCHMAR, Louise 1995d. Women and Culture: Ecclesial and Cultural Transformation, Many Cultures, One Nation, edited by Charles Villa-Vicencio and Carl Niehaus, Cape Town: Human & Rousseau, 90-104.

KRETZSCHMAR, Louise 1995e. History, Authority and Ministry: Implication of lives of Seventeenth Century English Baptist Women for Contemporary Women in South Africa, Journal of Theology for Southern Africa (Dec.): 17-31.

KRETZSCHMAR, Louise 1995f. Gender and Oppression: A South African Feminist Underview, Missionalia 23:2 (Aug.): 147-161.

KRETZSCHMAR, Louise 1997. An Overview of Baptist Principles in Historical Context, Being a Baptist in South Africa Today, edited by Louise Kretzschmar, Paul Msiza and John Nthane, Johannesburg: Baptist Convention College, 16-57.

KRETZSCHMAR, Louise and Msiza, Paul 1997. Christians and Socio-Political Activism: Two Perspectives from Within the Baptist Convention of South Africa, The South African Baptist Journal of Theology (vol. 6), 132-135.

KRETZSCHMAR, Louise 1998a. The Ethos and History of the Baptist Convention of South Africa's Winter Schools of Theology, Awakening the Sleeping Lion: The Role of Baptists in Contemporary Africa, edited by L. Kretzschmar, P. Msiza and J. Nthane, Johannesburg: Baptist Convention College, 2-15.

KRETZSCHMAR, Louise 1998b. Privatization of the Christian Faith: Mission, Social Ethics and the South African Baptists. Accra: Legon Theological Studies Series.

KRITZINGER, J. N. J. 1988. Black Theology -- Challenge to Mission. D.Th. thesis, UNISA.

KRITZINGER, J. N. J. 1995. Studying Religious Communities as Agents of Change: An Agenda for Missiology, Missionalia (Nov.) 366-396.

KROEGER, Richard and Catherine Clark Kroeger 1978. Sexual Identity in Corinth: Paul Faces a Crisis, The Reformed Journal (Dec.): 11-15.

KUZWAYO, Ellen 1985 Call Me Woman. London: The Women's Press.

KUZWAYO, Ellen 1990. Ellen Kuzwayo, In Their Own Voices: African Women Writers Talk, edited by Adeola James, London: James Currey.

LANDMAN, Christina 1984. A Profile of Feminist Theology, Sexism and Feminism In Theological Perspective, edited by W. S. Vorster, Pretoria: UNISA, 1-30.

LANDMAN, Christina 1992. Europe's Role in a South African Methodology: A Sideline and Female Perspective. Frankfurt and Main: Peter Lang.

LANDMAN, Christina 1994. The Piety of Afrikaans Woman. Pretoria: UNISA.

LIST OF WORKS CONSULTED

LANDMAN, Christina 1995a. Ten Years of Feminist Theology in South Africa, Journal of Feminist Studies in Religion 11:1 (Spring): 143-148.

LANDMAN, Christina 1995b. The Death of Women's Theology, ATISCA Bulletin 4: 13-24.

LANDMAN, Christina 1996. Christian Women in South African Historiography -- An Overview, Digging Up Our Foremothers, edited by Christina Landman, Pretoria: UNISA, 3-26.

LANDMAN, Christina 1997a. Educating Ourselves -- A Challenge for Women's Theology in South Africa, Bulletin for Contextual Theology in Southern Africa and Africa 4:2 (July): 13-14.

LANDMAN, Christina 1997b, Religious Women and Transformation, Journal of Constructive Theology 3:2 (Dec.): 13-22.

LANDMAN, Christina 1998a. African Women's Theology, Initiation Into Theology: The Rich Variety of Theology and Hermeneutics, edited by Simon Maimela and Adrio König, Pretoria: J. L. Van Schaik.

LANDMAN, Christina 1998b. A Story of Christian Piety in South Africa, Missionalia 26:3 (Nov.), 358-377.

LANDMAN, Christina 1998c. Athaliah and the Use of Power (2 Kings 11), Sermon Outlines, edited by Francois Swanepoel, Pretoria: C.B. Powell Bible Centre, 31-33.

LANDMAN, Christina 1999a. The Piety of South African Women. Pretoria: C.B. Powell Bible Centre.

LANDMAN, Christina 1999b. Interview on 23 July.

WOMEN AND LEADERSHIP

LANDMAN, Christina 1999c. Telling Sacred Stories: Eersterust and the Forced Removals of the 1960s. Unpublished paper of the Research Institute for Theology and Religion, UNISA.

LEAVEY, Bonnie Lee 1998. Give Me, A Widow, the Strength to Execute My Plan: Ruth, Tamar and Rachab, <u>Sermon Outlines</u>, edited by Francois Swanepoel, Pretoria: C.B. Powell Bible Centre, 34-37.

LEBAKA-KETSHABILE, Libuseng 1995. Reconstructing Theology: A Woman's Perspective, <u>Journal of Black Theology</u> 9:2 (Nov.): 43-52.

LEBAKA-KETSHABILE, Libuseng 1996. Challenges Facing Women in South Africa, <u>Archbishop Tutu: Prophetic Witness in South Africa</u>, edited by Leonard Hulley, Louise Kretzschmar and Luke Lungile Pato, Cape Town: Human & Rousseau, 171-181.

LEBAKA-KETSHABILE, Libuseng 1997. <u>Liberating Action: A Perspective on Contextual Spirituality</u>. Pretoria: C. B. Powell Bible Centre.

LEBONA, Clossy 1993. A Passover for Women in Makeleketla, <u>Challenge</u> 13 (Mar.): 23-25.

LETSOALO, Essy 1986. The Changing Role of Women in Employment, <u>Hammering Swords into Ploughshares</u>, edited by Buti Tlagale and Itumeleng Mosala, Grand Rapids: Eerdmans, 225-231.

LEVY, J. 1969. Possible Bases For the Evolution of Lateral Specialization in the Human Brain, <u>Nature</u>, 224(219): 614-615.

LIEFELD, Walter L. 1986. Women, Submission and Ministry in I Corinthians, <u>Women, Authority and the Bible</u>, edited by Alvera Mickelsen, Downers Grove: IVP, 134-154.

LIVING LETTERS: A REPORT OF VISITS TO THE CHURCHES DURING THE ECUMENICAL DECADE -- CHURCHES IN SOLIDARITY WITH WOMEN 1997. Geneva: WCC Publications.

LIST OF WORKS CONSULTED

LONGENECKER, Richard N. 1986. Authority, Hierarchy and Leadership Patterns in the Bible, Women, Authority and the Bible, edited by Alvera Mickelsen, Downers Grove: IVP, 66-85.

LUERA-WHITMORE, Mark Willard 1980. The Role of Story/Storytelling in Christian Spiritual Formation, D. Min. thesis, The School of Theology at Claremont.

MAKHANYA, Gideon 1990. History of the Baptist Convention of Southern Africa, The Barkly West National Awareness Workshop, edited by Des Hoffmeister and Brian J. Gurney, Johannesburg: The Awareness Campaign Committee of the BCSA, 33-41.

MALULEKE, Tinyiko Sam 1996. Recent Developments in the Christian Theologies of Africa: Towards the Twenty-First Century, Journal of Constructive Theology 2:2 (Dec.): 33-60.

MALULEKE, Tinyiko 1977. The Agonising of an African Male Theologian, Challenge (Dec.): 19.

MALULEKE, Tinyiko Sam 1997. The 'Smoke Screens' Called Black and African Theologies -- The Challenge of African Women Theology, Journal of Constructive Theology 3:2 (Dec.): 39-63.

MANTHLWA, Stephen 1995. Black Baptist History in South Africa, Towards a Holistic, Afro-centric and Participatory Understanding of the Gospel of Jesus Christ, edited by Des Hoffmeister and Louise Kretzschmar, Johannesburg: BCSA, 101-103.

MASENYA, Joyce 1994. Freedom in Bondage: Black Feminist Hermeneutics, Journal of Black Theology in South Africa 8:1 (May): 35-48.

MASENYA, Madipoane J. 1995. African Womanist Hermeneutics: A Suppressed Voice from South Africa Speaks, Journal of Feminist Studies in Religion 11:1 (Spring): 149-155.

WOMEN AND LEADERSHIP

MASENYA, Madipoane Joyce 1996. Proverbs 31:10-31 in a South African Context: A Bosadi (womanhood) Perspective. D.Lit. et Phil. thesis, UNISA.

MASENYA, Madipoane 1997. Reading the Bible the Bosadi (Womanhood) Way, Bulletin for Contextual Theology in Southern Africa and Africa 4:2 (July): 15-16.

MASENYA, Madipoane and Christina Landman 1997. Their Story is Ours: Biblical Women and Us. Pretoria: CB Powell Bible Centre.

MASHAO, E. N. 1989. The Role of Women in the Spiritual Upbuilding of the Church, in Theologica Viatorum 7 (Dec.): 129-135.

MASHIANE, Rebecca 1996. Impressions and Reflections, Reading the Bible in Context: Reconstructing South Africa, edited by Louise Kretzschmar and Ruben Richards, Johannesburg: BCSA, 106-113.

MASHININI, Emma 1991. Women Between Church and Society, Women Hold Up Half the Sky. Edited by Denise Ackermann, Jonathan A. Draper and Emma Mashinini, Pietermaritzburg: Cluster Publications.

MATHABANE, Mark 1994. African Woman. New York: HarperCollins.

MC CORD, Margaret 1995. The Calling of Katie Makanya. Cape Town.

McEWAN, Dorothea, ed. 1991. Women Experiencing Church. Herefordshire: Gracewing Books.

MC GRATH, Sister Albertus Magnus 1972. What a Modern Catholic Believes About Women. Chicago: Thomas More Press.

MEMELA, Zodwa 1994. Racism and Its Impact on Black Women: A South African Perspective, Journal of Black Theology 8:1 (May): 12-20.

LIST OF WORKS CONSULTED

MEO, Elisapeci 1997. Women's Journey Toward Empowerment Through Theological Education: A Personal Testimony, Journal of Constructive Theology 3:1 (July): 15-34.

MEYER-WILMES, H. 1995. Rebellion on the Borders: Feminist Theology Between Theory and Praxis. Kampen: Kok Pharos.

MGHWIRA, Anna 1994. Women's Ordination: A Liberative Motif, Culture, Religion and Liberation: Proceedings of the EATWOT Pan African Theological Conference, Harare, Zimbabwe, January 6-11, 1991, edited by Simon Maimela, Pretoria: 152-158.

MHLOPE, Jessie 1996. Impressions and Reflections, Reading the Bible in Context: Reconstructing South Africa, edited by Louise Kretzschmaar and Ruben Richards, Johannesburg: BCSA, 195-207.

MHLOPE, Jessie 1997. The Relationship Between A Church and a Pastor's Wife, Being a Baptist in South Africa Today, edited by L. Kretzschmar, P. Msiza, J. Nthane, 178-181.

MILLARD, Joan 1996. Mrs. Matilda Smith -- A Link Between Three Cultures, Studia Historiae Ecclesiasticae 22:1 (June): 22-34.

MNCUBE, Sister Bernard 1991. Sexism in the Church and in the African Context, Women Hold Up Half the Sky, edited by Denise Ackermann, Jonathan A. Draper and Emma Mashinini, Pietermaritzburg: Cluster Publications, 355-362.

MNDENDE, Nokuzola 1997. Feminist/Womanist Theology in South Africa -- A Voice from Within African Traditional Religion, Bulletin for Contextual Theology in Southern Africa and Africa 4:2 (July): 23-25.

MOFOKENG, Takatso 1990. Black Theology in South Africa: Achievements, Problems and Prospects, Christianity in South Africa, edited by Martin Prozesky, Bergvlei: Southern Book Publishers, 37-54.

WOMEN AND LEADERSHIP

MOFOKENG, Kenosi 1993. Doing Theology Together, Challenge 13 (Mar.): 6-7.

MOHLAMONYANE, Rabatho Elias 1995. Women, Men and the Ministry: Should Women Preach and Lead? Towards a Holistic, Afro-centric and Participatory Understanding of the Gospel of Jesus Christ, edited by Des Hoffmeister and L. Kretzschmar, Johannesburg: BCSA, 104-106.

MOHLAMONYANE, Elias 1997. Baptist Churches, Development and Mission, Being a Baptist in South Africa Today, edited by L. Kretzschmar, P. Msiza and J. Nthane, Johannesburg: Baptist Convention College, 79-97.

MOKITIMI, Makali I. 1997. The Voice of the People: Proverbs of the Basotho (Series editor, John S. Mbiti, African Proverbs Series, Vol. 4). Pretoria: UNISA.

MOLLENKOTT, Virginia Ramey 1987. The Divine Feminine: The Biblical Imagery of God as Female. New York: Crossroad.

MONEY, J. and A. Ehrhardt 1972. Man and Woman, Boy and Girl. Baltimore: Johns Hopkins.

MOSALA, Itumeleng J. 1989. Biblical Hermeneutics and Black Theology in South Africa. Grand Rapids: Eerdmans.

MPUMLWANA, Thoko 1991. My Perspective on Women and Their Role in Church and Society, Women Hold Up Half the Sky, edited by Denise Ackermann, Jonathan A. Draper and Emma Mashinini, Pietermaritzburg: Cluster Publications, 369-385.

MSIZA, Paul 1997. Baptist Church Government, Being a Baptist in South Africa Today, edited by L. Kretzschmar, P. Msiza and J. Nthane, Johannesburg: Baptist Convention College, 58-64.

MUCAVELE, Gabriela Samuel 1994. Women's Experience: Women's Struggle for Pastorhood in a Male-Dominated Structure, Culture, Religion and Liberation: Proceedings of the EATWOT Pan African Theological Conference, Ha-

LIST OF WORKS CONSULTED

rare, Zimbabwe, Jan. 1994, 155-158.

MUGABE, Henry J. 1995. Salvation from an African Perspective, Towards a Holistic, Afro-centric and Participatory Understanding of the Gospel of Jesus Christ, edited by Des Hoffmeister and Louise Kretzschmar, Johannesburg: BCSA, 11-20.

MUGABE, Henry 1995. Towards an Afro-centric Gospel, Towards a Holistic, Afro-centric and Participatory Understanding of the Gospel of Jesus Christ, edited by D. Hoffmeister and L. Kretzschmar, Johannesburg: BCSA, 7-10.

MUHANDO, Penina 1990. Penina Muhando, In Their Own Voices: African Women Writers Talk, edited by Adeola James, London: James Currey.

MUSOPOLE, Anne Nachisale 1992. Sexuality and Religion in a Matriarchal Society, The Will to Arise: Women, Tradition, and the Church in Africa, edited by Mercy Ambo Oduyoye and Musimbi R. A. Kanyoro, Maryknoll: Orbis, 195-205.

MUSOPOLE, Anne Nachisale 1995/1996. The Church's Silence About Violence in the Home, Challenge 33 (Dec.): 4-5.

NAKAWOMBE, Jessica Keturah 1996. Women in the Kingdom of God, Groaning in Faith: African Women in the Household of God, edited by Musimbi R. A. Kanyoro and Nyambura J. Njoroge, Nairobi: Acton Publishers, 40-52.

NASIMIYU-WASIKE, Anne 1991. Christology and an African Woman's Experience, Faces of Jesus in Africa, edited by Robert J. Schreiter, Maryknoll: Orbis, 70-81.

NDAZULWANA, Nobantu 1997. Ubufazi, Journal of Constructive Theology 3:1 (July): 34.

NEWBIGIN, Leslie 1989. The Gospel in a Pluralist Society. Grand Rapids: Eerdmans.

WOMEN AND LEADERSHIP

NGADA, N. H. 1998. Notes from "Hearing the AIC-Voice," Conference sponsored by the Research Institute for Theology and Religion, UNISA, at Sunnyside Campus, Pretoria, 2-3 Sept.

NGONGO, N. 1998. Notes from "Hearing the AIC-Voice," Conference sponsored by the Research Institute for Theology and Religion, UNISA, at Sunnyside Campus, Pretoria, 2-3 Sept.

NIELSON, Joyce M., ed. 1990. Feminist Research Methods. Boulder, San Francisco, London: Westview Press.

NJAU, Rebekah 1990. Rebekah Njau, In Their Own Voices: African Women Writers Talk, edited by Adeola James, London: James Currey.

NJOROGE, Nyambura J. 1996. Groaning and Languishing in Labour Pains, Groaning in Faith: African Women in the Household of God, edited by Musimbi R. A. Kanyoro and Nyambura J. Njoroge, Nairobi: Acton Publishers, 3-15.

NKUMBI, Owen 1997. Thusong Skills Training Center, in Convention News 3:2 (Oct.): 6.

NOLAN, Albert 1993. Independent and African, Challenge 13 (March): 2-4.

NOLAN, Albert 1996. Are You a Sexist Too? Challenge 38 (Oct./Nov.): 10.

NTHANE, Grace 1996. Impressions and Reactions, Reading the Bible in Context: Reconstructing South Africa, edited by Louise Kretzschmar and Ruben Richards, Johannesburg: BCSA, 195-207.

NTIBANA, Thuli 1996. Impressions and Reflections, Reading the Bible in Context: Reconstructing South Africa, edited by Louise Kretzschmar and Ruben Richards, Johannesburg: BCSA, 195-207.

NÜRNBERGER, Klaus 1994. The Task of the Church Concerning the Economy of a Post-Apartheid South Africa, Missionalia 22:2 (Aug.): 118-146.

LIST OF WORKS CONSULTED

NYAGA, Ada 1996. Women's Dignity and Worth in God's Kingdom, Groaning in Faith: African Women in the Household of God, edited by Musimbi R. A. Kanyoro and Nyambura J. Njoroge, Nairobi: Acton Publishers, 74-83.

OBAGA, Margaret 1998. Is the Church a Tomb or a Womb? A Decade of Solidarity with the Bible: Decade Festival -- Vision Beyond 1998, edited by Musimbi Kanyoro and Nyambura Njoroge, Geneva: WCC Publications, 98-102.

ODAGA, Asenath 1990. Asenath Odaga, In Their Own Voices: African Women Writers Talk, edited by Adeola James, London: James Currey.

ODEN, Amy, ed. 1994. In Her Words: Women's Writings in the History of Christian Thought. Nashville: Abingdon.

ODUYOYE, Mercy Amba 1986. Hearing and Knowing. Maryknoll: Orbis.

ODUYOYE, Mercy Amba 1992. Women and Ritual in Africa, The Will to Arise: Women, Tradition, and the Church in Africa, edited by Mercy Amba Oduyoye and Musimbi R. A. Kanyoro, Maryknoll: Orbis, 9-24.

ODUYOYE, Mercy Amba 1995. Daughters of Anowa. Maryknoll: Orbis.

ODUYOYE, Mercy Amba 1997. Proceedings of the Pan African Conference of the Circle of Concerned African Women Theologians, Nairobi, August 25-30, 1996, Transforming Power: Women in the Household of Faith, edited by Mercy Amba Oduyoye, Accra: Sam-Woode, Ltd. (For the Circle of Concerned African Women Theologians), 1-6.

ODUYOYE, Mercy Amba 1998a. Women-Centredness and Religion: The African Woman's Dilemma, There Were Also Women Looking on From Afar, edited by Nyambura J. Njoroge and Irja Askola, Geneva: World Alliance of Reformed Churches, 109-122.

WOMEN AND LEADERSHIP

ODUYOYE, Mercy Amba 1998b. African Women's Hermeneutics, <u>Initiation Into Theology: The Rich Variety of Theology and Hermeneutics</u>, edited by Simon Maimela and Adrio Konig, Pretoria: J. L. Schaik, 359-371.

OKURE, Teresa 1992. The Will to Arise: Reflections on Luke 8:40-56, <u>The Will to Arise: Women, Tradition, and the Church in Africa</u>, edited by Mercy Amba Oduyoye and Musimbi R. A. Kanyoro, Maryknoll: Orbis, 221-230.

OLAYINKE, Bolaji Olukemi 1997. Proverbs: Issues of Yoruba Femininity from a Feminist Hermeneutical Perspective, <u>Embracing the Baobab Tree</u>, edited by Willem Saayman, Pretoria: UNISA, 214-224.

OOSTHUIZEN, G. C. 1995. Indigenous Christianity and the Future of the Church in South Africa, <u>Journal of Constructive Theology</u> 1:1 (Dec.): 25-41.

OPOKU, Kofi Asare 1997. <u>Hearing and Keeping: Akan Proverbs</u> (Series editor, John S. Mbiti, African Proverbs Series, Vol. 2). Pretoria: UNISA.

OSEI, Mensah 1996. Women in transition: a socio-religious study of the changing role of rural Hlubi women, <u>Digging Up Our Foremothers</u>, edited by Christina Landman, Pretoria: UNISA, 92-113.

OSIEK, Carolyn 1997. Changing Images of God and Christ, <u>Journal of Contextual Theology</u> 3:2 (Dec.): 3-12.

OWANIKIN, R. Modupe 1992. The Priesthood of Church Women in the Nigerian Context, <u>The Will to Arise: Women, Tradition, and the Church in Africa</u>, edited by Mercy Ambo Oduyoye and Musimbi R. A. Kanyoro, Maryknoll: Orbis, 206-219.

PACKER, J. J. 1986. Understanding the Differences, <u>Women, Authority and the Bible</u>, Downers Grove: IVP, 295-299.

PARNELL, C. W. 1977. The Detailed History, <u>Together for a Century: The History of the Baptist Union of South Africa 1877-1977</u>, edited by S. Hudson-Reed, Pietersmaritzburg: SA Historical Society, 59-150.

LIST OF WORKS CONSULTED

PARNELL, C. W. 1980. Being a Baptist. Roodepoort: Baptist Publishing House.

PARNELL, C. W. 1991. Baptist Vision in Southern Africa. Roodepoort: Baptist Publishing House.

PATELIS, Athena R. and Randell L. Sorenson 1997. The 'Silence' of Women in Integration: Exploratory Qualitative Research, Journal of Psychology and Theology (25:2): 188-198.

PATO, L. L. 1996. Being Fully Human: A Traditional African Culture and Spirituality Perspective, Spirituality in Religions, edited by C. W. Du Toit, Pretoria: Research Institute for Theology and Religion (UNISA), 109-121.

PHIRI, Isabel Apawo 1992. African Women in Religion and Culture. Ph.D. thesis, University of Cape Town.

PHIRI, Isabel Apawo 1995. The Initiation of Chewa Women of Malawi: A Presbyterian Woman's Perspective, Religion in Malawi 5 (Nov.): 13-21.

PHIRI, Isabel Apawo 1997. Women in the Gospel of Luke: An African Woman's Perspective, Journal of Constructive Theology 3:1 (July): 35-48.

PLAATJIE, Gloria Kehilwe 1997. Various Voices Speak, Bulletin for Contextual Theology in Southern Africa and Africa 4:2 (July): 4-9.

POTGIETER, Sharon 1996. Church Praxis and Women Who Remain Within the Church, Growing in Faith: African Women in the Household of God, edited by Musimbi R. A. Kanyoro and Nyambura J. Njoroge, Nairobi: Acton Publishers, 16-22.

PROCTER-SMITH, Marjorie 1985. Images of Women in the Lectionary, Women -- Invisible in Church and Theology, edited by Elisabeth Schüssler Fiorenza and Mary Collins, Edinburgh: T & T Clark, 51-62.

WOMEN AND LEADERSHIP

RADEBE, Ndlaleni 1998. Woman, <u>Women in South Africa: From the Heart -- an Anthology</u>, Johannesburg: Seriti sa Sechaba Publishers, 99.

RAKOCZY, Susan 1995. The Spirit As the Heart of Mission, <u>Missionalia</u> 23:1 (April): 30-44.

RAKOCZY, Susan 1997a. How Can We Talk About the Ordination of Women in the Catholic Church? <u>Women In God's Image</u> 3 (June): 8-9.

RAKOCZY, Susan 1997b. (In) Various Voices Speak, <u>Bulletin for Contextual Theology in Southern Africa and Africa</u> 4:2 (July): 4-9.

RAMODIBE, Dorothy 1994. Women and Men Building Together the Church in Africa, <u>With Passion and Compassion: Third World Women Doing Theology</u>, edited by Virginia Fabella and Mercy Amba Oduyoye, Maryknoll: Orbis, 14-21.

RAMPHELE, Mamphele 1991. Foreword, <u>Women Hold Up Half the Sky</u>, edited by Denise Ackermann, Jonathan A. Draper and Emma Mashinini, Pietermaritzburg: Cluster Publications, vii-ix.

REBERA, Ranjini 1996. A Woman's Hands, <u>Women In God's Image</u> 2 (Nov.): 12.

REPORT OF AN AD HOC COMMITTEE REGARDING THE MINISTERIAL RECOGNITION AND ORDINATIONOF WOMEN 1988. <u>BUSA Handbook.</u>

REPORT OF THE AD HOC COMMITTEE IN RESPECT OF THE ROLE OF WOMEN IN MINISTRY 1989. <u>BUSA Handbook.</u>

REPORT ON THE MORNING WITH PROF. CHUNG 1996. <u>Women In God's Image</u> 1 (May): 1-2.

RITTER, Kathleen Y. And Craig W. O'Neill 1996. <u>Righteous Religion</u>. New York: The Haworth Pastoral Press.

LIST OF WORKS CONSULTED

ROBERT, Dana L. 1993. Mount Holyyoke Women and the Dutch Reformed Missionary Movement, 1874-1904, <u>Missionalia</u> 21:2 (Aug.): 103-123.

ROBERT, Dana L. 1996. American Women and the Dutch Reformed Missionary Movement, 1874-1904, <u>Mission in Bold Humility</u>, edited by Willem Saayman and Klippies Kritzinger, Maryknoll: Orbis, 94-112.

ROBINS, Wendy S., ed. 1995. <u>Through the Eyes of a Woman: Bible Studies on the Experience of Women</u>. Geneva: WCC Publications.

RUETHER, Rosemary Radford 1983. <u>Sexism and God-Talk: Toward a Feminist Theology</u>. Boston: Beacon.

RUSSELL, Letty M. 1993. <u>Church in the Round</u>. Louisville: Westminster/John Knox Press.

SAAYMAN, Willem 1993. <u>Christian Mission in South Africa</u>. Pretoria: UNISA.

SAAYMAN, Willem 1996. A South African Perspective on 'Transforming Mission', <u>Mission in Bold Humility</u>, edited by Willem Saayman and Klippies Kritzinger, Maryknoll: Orbis, 40-52.

SAAYMAN, Willem 1999. Comments made to me on 5 April in reaction to contents of chapter three.

SAAYMAN, Willem 1999. Comments made to me on 28 June in reaction to contents of chapter four.

SAAYMAN, Willem 1999. Comments made to me on 26 July in reviewing a draft of chapter five.

SAMUEL, Vinay and Chris Sugden 1998. A Spoiled Creation, <u>The Lion Handbook of Christian Belief</u>. Herts, England: Lion Publishing, 256-274.

WOMEN AND LEADERSHIP

SCHMID, Peter F. 1993. A New Image of Man? Toward Male Emancipation, Theology Digest 40:3 (Fall): 217-220.

SCHOLER, Jeannette F. 1986. Turning Reality into Dreams, Women, Authority and the Bible, Downers Grove: IVP, 300-304.

SCHÜSSLER-FIORENZA, Elizabeth 1982. In Memory of Her: A Feminist Reconstruction of Christian Origins. New York: Crossroads.

SCHÜSSLER-FIORENZA, Elisabeth 1985. Breaking the Silence -- Becoming Visible, Women -- Invisible in Theology and Church, edited by Elisabeth Schüssler Fiorenza and Mary Collins, Edinburgh: T & T Clark, 3-16.

SCHÜSSLER-FIORENZA, Elizabeth 1992. But SHE Said. Boston: Beacon.

SENAVOE, Juliana 1997. The Nature and Fatherhood of God: Headship, Subordination and Submission, Women's Ministry in the Church: An African Perspective, edited by Alan M. Chilver, Nairobi: Theological and Christian Education of the Association of Evangelicals in Africa, 11-19.

SEWARD, J. and G. Seward 1980. Sex Diffferences: Mental and Tempermental. Lexington: Lexington Books.

SIBEKO, Malika and Beverly Haddad 1996. Reading the Bible "With" Women in Poor and Marginalised Communities of South Africa, Bulletin for Contextual Theology 3:1 (February): 14-18.

SOUGA, Terese 1994. The Christ-Event from the Viewpoint of African Women, With Passion and Compassion: Third World Women Doing Theology, edited by Virginia Fabella and Mercy Amba Oduyoye, Maryknoll: Orbis, 22-29.

STATEMENT ISSUED JOINTLY BY THE BAPTIST CONVENTION OF SOUTH AFRICA AND THE LOTT CAREY BAPTIST FOREIGN MISSION CONVENTION FOLLOWING THEIR INTERNATIONAL MISSION CONFERENCE HELD FROM 1 to 4 MAY 1997, IN CAPE TOWN 1997. The Baptist Convention of South Africa Handbook 1997, 33-36.

LIST OF WORKS CONSULTED

TAM, Gloria San Fun 1997. Feminist Theological Movement, (Research assignment for Hong Kong Baptist Theological Seminary), 1-31.

TAMEZ, Elsa 1993. Hermeneutical Guidelines for Understanding Galatians 3:28 and I Corinthians 14:34, Voices from the Third World 16:1 (June): 48-60.

TERRIEN, Samuel 1985. Till the Heart Sings: A Biblical Theology of Manhood and Womanhood. Philadelphia: Fortress.

TETTEH, Rachel Etrue 1997. Regulating Women's Sexuality: Rituals and Taboos Associated with Chastity and Marriage, Where God Reigns: Reflections on Women in God's World, edited by Elizabeth Amoah, Accra: Sam-Woode, Ltd. (for the Circle of Concerned African Women Theologians), 51-62.

THE BAPTIST CONVENTION OF SOUTH AFRICA HANDBOOK 1995.

THE BAPTIST CONVENTION OF SOUTH AFRICA HANDBOOK 1996.

THE BAPTIST CONVENTION OF SOUTH AFRICA HANDBOOK 1997.

THE BAPTIST CONVENTION OF SOUTH AFRICA HANDBOOK 1998.

THE BARKLY WEST DECLARATION 1990. The Barkly West National Awareness Workshop, edited by Des Hoffmeister and Brian J. Gurney, Johannesburg: The Awareness Campaign Committee of the BCSA, 72-73.

THE OTHER DISCIPLES OF JESUS. s.a. (Book 3 in the series The Empowerment of Women in Church and Society, Umtata Women's Theology Bible Study Series). Pretoria: CB Powell Bible Centre.

THERON, Pieter F. 1995. Theological Training for Social Transformation in Africa, Missionalia 23:1 (April): 45-56.

THE SOUTH AFRICAN BAPTIST HANDBOOK 1940-1941.

WOMEN AND LEADERSHIP

THE SOUTH AFRICAN BAPTIST HANDBOOK 1995-1996.

THE SOUTH AFRICAN BAPTIST HISTORICAL SOCIETY 1996-1997.

THE SOUTH AFRICAN BAPTIST HANDBOOK 1998.

THOMAS, Linda 1996. Womanist Theology, Epistemology, and a New Anthropological Paradigm, Journal of Constructive Theology 2:2 (Dec.): 19-32.

THOMAS, Linda 1997. Womanist Theology and the New South Africa, Bulletin for Contextual Theology in Southern Africa and Africa 4:2 (July): 10-12.

THORPE, Shirley 1996. Women and Power in African Traditional Religions: Nongqawuse and the Mujaji, Digging Up Our Foremothers, edited by Christina Landman, Pretoria: UNISA, 77-91.

TIENOU, Tite 1997. Legitimate Areas of Women's Ministry in the Church: 'Full-time' versus 'Part-time' Ministry, Women's Ministry in the Church: An African Perspective, edited by Alan M. Chilver, Nairobi: Theological and Christian Education Commission of the Association of Evangelicals in Africa, 51-54.

TISANI, Nomathamsanqa 1989. Christ the Liberator: The Attitude of the Church to the Oppression of Women, Journal of Theology for Southern Africa 66 (March): 79-83.

TUCKEY, Caroline 1996. Children, Sexism and the Church, Archbishop Tutu: Prophetic Witness in South Africa, edited by Leonard Hulley, Louise Kretzschmar and Luke Lungile Pato, Cape Town: Human & Rousseau, 156-170.

UDO, Akon E. 1997. Women in God's World: Some Biblical Affirmation, Where God Reigns: Reflections on Women in God's World, edited by Elizabeth Amoah, Accra: Sam-Woode, Ltd. (for the Circle of Concerned African Women Theologians), 20-25.

LIST OF WORKS CONSULTED

UMTATA WOMEN'S THEOLOGY BIBLE STUDY SERIES s.a. <u>Women, the Bible and the Contemporary Church</u>.

UMTATA WOMEN'S THEOLOGY BIBLE STUDY SERIES s.a. <u>The Other Disciples of Jesus</u>.

VAN SCHALKWYK, Annalet 1996. The Church, Community Development and Liberation: A search for answers to basic questions, <u>Missionalia</u> 24:1(April): 40-62.

VAN SCHALKWYK, Annalet 1997. Women's Research from the Periphery, <u>Missionalia</u> 25:4 (Dec.): 607-632.

VARIOUS VOICES SPEAK 1997. Bulletin for Contextual Theology in Southern Africa and Africa. 4:2 (July): 4-9.

VENTER, David 1995. Mending the Multi-Coloured Coat of a Rainbow Nation: Cultural accommodation in ethnically-mixed urban congregations, <u>Missionalia</u> 23:3 (Nov.): 312-338.

VILLA-VICENCIO, Charles 1992. <u>A Theology of Reconstruction: Nation-Building and Human Rights</u>. Cape Town: David Philip.

VINK, Jan 1993. <u>The Impact of Liberation Theology on the Baptist Union of Southern Africa</u> (Ph.D. thesis, University of Witwatersrand).

WALTERS, Gillian 1998. ...do I dare step inside this place that has been responsible for so much oppression to women?, <u>Women in God's Image</u> 5 (Dec.): 6-7.

WAMUE, Grace N. 1997a. Restrictions on Women's Participation in the Ministry of the Church, <u>Women's Ministry in the Church: An African Perspective</u>, edited by Alan M. Chilver, Nairobi: Theological and Christian Education Commission of the Association of Evangelicals in Africa, 65-70.

WOMEN AND LEADERSHIP

WAMUE, Grace N. 1997b. The Ministry of Women in the Church: Some Reflections, <u>Women's Ministry in the Church: An African Perspective</u>, edited by Alan M. Chilver, Nairobi: Theological and Christian Education of the Association of Evangelicals in Africa, 55-62.

WEST, Gerald 1990. Can a Literary Reading Be a Liberative Reading? <u>Scriptura</u> 35 (Sept.): 10-25.

WEST, Gerald O. 1991. <u>Biblical Hermeneutics of Liberation</u>. Maryknoll: Orbis.

WEST, Gerald 1993. <u>Contextual Bible Study</u>. Pietermaritzburg: Cluster Publications.

WHITING, B. and J. Whiting 1975. <u>Children of Six Cultures: A Psychocultural Analysis</u>. Cambridge: Harvard University Press.

WILLIAMS, David T. 1997. The Image of God: A Basis for Christian Social Action, <u>The South African Baptist Journal of Theology</u> 6: 32-40.

WITTENBERG, Gertrude 1991. The Song of a Poor Woman: The 'Magnificat' (Luke 1:46-55), <u>Women Hold Up Half the Sky</u>, edited by Denise Ackermann, Jonathan A. Draper, and Emma Mashinini, Pietermaritzburg: Cluster Publications, 3-20.

WOLTERSTORFF, Nicholas 1986. Hearing the Cry, <u>Women, Authority and the Bible</u>, Downers Grove: IVP, 286-294.

WOMEN AT PRAYER 1971. Cape Town: Methodist Publishing House.

WOMEN, THE BIBLE AND THE CONTEMPORARY CHURCH. s.a. (Book 1 in the series The Empowerment of Women in Church and Society, Umtata Women's Theology Bible Study Series). Pretoria: CB Powell Bible Centre.

WORKSHOP NOTES 1990. <u>The Barkly West National Awareness Workshop</u>, edited by Des Hoffmeister and Brian J. Gurney, Johannesburg: The Awareness Campaign Committee of the BCSA, 67.

LIST OF WORKS CONSULTED

WYATT, Mark A. 1995. Board Adopts Statement on Women as Senior Pastors, The California Southern Baptist 54:11 (June): 4.

WYATT, Mark A. 1998. Texas Church Calls Woman Pastor from California, The California Southern Baptist 57:12 (June 12): 5.

YINDA, Helen M. N. 1997. A Biblical and Theological Understanding of the Gifts of the Spirit of God and Feminine Leadership in the Church, Women's Ministry in the Church: An African Perspective, edited by Alan M. Chilver, Nairobi: Theological and Christian Education Commission of the Association of Evangelicals in Africa, 45-50.

YOUNG, Pamela Dickey 1990. Feminist Theology/Christian Theology: In Search of Method. Minneapolis: Fortress.

ZEIGLER, Leslie 1992. Christianity or Feminism, Speaking the Christian God, edited by Alvin F. Kimel, Jr. Grand Rapids: Eerdmans, 313-334.

ZOKOUE, Isaac 1997. Foreward, Women's Ministry in the Church: An African Perspective, edited by Alan M. Chilver, Nairobi: Theological and Christian Education Commission of the Association of Evangelicals in Africa, 1-2.

ZONDI, Phumzile 1998. The Significance of Christ in My Life as an African Woman, Women in God's Image 5 (Dec.): 4-5.

ABOUT THE AUTHOR

Nelson Hayashida's Japanese-American heritage originated in Hawaii and was nurtured further in Southern California. After high school, he moved to Texas, where he studied at Wayland Baptist University (B.A.) and Baylor University (M.A.). He returned to California to attend Golden Gate Seminary (M.Div.), and later completed a D.Min. at Southern Seminary in Kentucky, a Ph.D. at the University of Edinburgh in Scotland, and a D.Th. at the University of South Africa.

Nelson Hayashida's professional experiences include pastoral roles in Texas and California, four years as Baptist Campus Minister at the University of Hawaii-Manoa, seventeen years of missionary work in theological institutions in Zambia and South Africa, and three years as Associate Professor of Cross-Cultural Studies and Missiology at Eastern University in Pennsylvania. In addition, he has served as guest professor at Golden Gate Seminary, Southern Seminary, Eastern Baptist Seminary, and Kawthoolei Karen Baptist Bible School and College (Thailand), and is an adjunct faculty member at the American Baptist Seminary of the West in Berkeley.

A member of a number of professional societies, Nelson Hayashida has authored numerous articles and three books: *Stormy Road for this Pilgrim*, *Lasers of the Mind/Voices of the Soul*, and *Dreams in African Christianity: The Significance of Dreams and Visions Among Zambian Baptists*. He and his wife Sandra currently reside in Hawaii.

www.ingramcontent.com/pod-product-compliance
Ingram Content Group UK Ltd.
Pitfield, Milton Keynes, MK11 3LW, UK
UKHW022238230426
12048UKWH00018BA/1329